The Problems

Rese

Experiments and The
the Supernormal

Hereward Carrington

Alpha Editions

This edition published in 2024

ISBN 9789362518095

Design and Setting By
Alpha Editions
www.alphaedis.com
Email - info@alphaedis.com

As per information held with us this book is in Public Domain.
This book is a reproduction of an important historical work.
Alpha Editions uses the best technology to reproduce historical work
in the same manner it was first published to preserve its original nature.
Any marks or number seen are left intentionally to preserve.

Contents

PREFACE

In the following pages I have dealt chiefly with the *mental* or psychological phenomena of psychical research, and have not touched upon the "physical" manifestations to any extent. The book is mostly theoretical and constructive in tone; and, because of its speculative character, it may, perhaps, prove of value to future psychical investigators. It represents the author's conclusions after several years' experimentation; and, in a field so new as this, scientific hypotheses and speculations are assuredly helpful— indicating the road we must travel, and the possible interpretation of certain facts, which have been accumulated in the past, as the result of years of laborious research. I believe that practically *all* the phenomena of spiritualism are true; that is, that they have occurred in a genuine manner from time to time in the past; that they are supernormal in character, and are genuine phenomenal occurrences. But as to the further question: "What is the nature of the intelligence lying behind and controlling these phenomena?"—*that*, I think, is as yet unsolved, and is likely to remain so for some time to come. I do not believe that the simple spiritistic explanation—especially as at present held—is the correct one, nor one that explains all the facts; for I believe that the phenomena are more complicated than this. Nor are the ordinary psychological explanations at present in vogue adequate to cover them. The explanation is yet to seek; and the solution will only be found when a sufficient number of facts have been accumulated and the various explanatory theories have been tested,— to see which of them is really adequate. My hope is that the present book may help to accomplish this result by supplying a little in both directions!

The present edition of this book is to some extent an abridgement of the first edition, which appeared some seven years ago. I have, for instance, omitted a number of "cases" which were originally included, and also my "sittings" with Mrs. Piper—which material will be published at a later date in another volume. I have also omitted the original First Chapter,—since much of this material was subsequently included in my *Modern Psychical Phenomena*. On the other hand, I have included a new chapter on Recent Experiments in Psychic Photography,—composed partly of original and hitherto unpublished material, and partly of the experiments undertaken, some years ago, by Dr. Baraduc,—in "photographing the soul." The account of his experiments was originally published in my book, *Death: its Causes and Phenomena*, but they are now included here as being more in line with other experiments recently undertaken in this field. I have also added a brief chapter on the Scientific Investigation of Psychic Phenomena by means of Laboratory Instruments.

A word, finally, as to the necessarily slow progress which has been and is being made in the study of "psychics." As this objection is often raised, I cannot do better, perhaps, than to quote an admirable passage from Prof. William James (*Memories and Studies*, pp. 175-76), where he says:—

"For twenty-five years I have been in touch with the literature of psychical research, and have had acquaintance with numerous 'researchers.' I have also spent a good many hours (though far fewer than I should have spent) in witnessing (or trying to witness) phenomena. Yet I am theoretically no 'further' than I was at the beginning; and I confess that at times I have been tempted to believe that the Creator has eternally intended this department of nature to remain *baffling*,—to prompt our curiosities and hopes and suspicions all in equal measure, so that, although ghosts and clairvoyances, and raps and messages from spirits, are always seeming to exist and can never be fully explained away, they also can never be susceptible of full corroboration.... It is hard to believe, however, that the Creator has really put any big array of phenomena into the world merely to defy and mock our scientific tendencies; so my deeper belief is that we psychical researchers have been too precipitate in our hopes, and that we must expect to mark progress not by quarter-centuries, but by half-centuries or whole centuries."

In the present book, I have endeavoured to show why this must necessarily be so; also to indicate the manner in which the subject may be studied in order to arrive at definite knowledge at an earlier date than might otherwise be possible.

H. C.

CHAPTER I

IS PSYCHICAL RESEARCH A SCIENCE?

Is Psychical Research a Science?

It seems to me that the answer to this question must be somewhat as follows: If the phenomena be true, Yes; if not, No!

If *one* single prophecy, clairvoyant vision, telepathic impulse, or mediumistic message be true—if veritable supernormal information be thereby conveyed—then psychical research is a science, and illimitable avenues are opened up for further research and speculation.

More especially is this true in the case of mediumistic messages. If these prove to be delusory—the result of subliminal activity and so forth—if there be no spiritual world, then "psychics" may be said to be "founded upon the sand." It can hardly be called a "science." Only when the *fact* of communication is proved, will the real study of the subject begin. Much of the work, up to the present, has been undertaken with a view to establishing the reality of the facts. But this is a question of evidence, not scientific research. When the facts themselves are established, then the real study—the work of the future—will begin. It will probably be the task of future generations to attack the problem from this standpoint.

Let me illustrate what I mean by a somewhat striking example. Take the facts presented in the case of Mrs. Piper. Hitherto the question has resolved itself into that of the *evidence* for survival. Have or have not the various personalities who have communicated through her entranced organism proved their personal identity? That is the problem; and, as we know, opinions differ! But, granting the reality of the facts, granting that "spirits" really do communicate, as alleged—then the study of the question, from the "scientific" point of view, will only have begun. *How* do they communicate? Why are these communications so rare? Why such trouble with proper names? How do the "spirits" manipulate the nervous organism, and particularly the brain, of the medium? Upon what cells or centres do they operate? and how? Does the psychic constitution of the communicator affect the results—and if so, how? What is the condition of the communicator's mind while communicating? Is the medium's spirit entirely removed from the body during the process of communication? and if so, where is it, and what is it doing? How does the medium's mind affect the content of the communications—and to what extent? These, and a thousand other questions of a like nature, immediately present themselves, and call for solution, as soon as the reality of the facts be granted—as soon as spirit communication be accepted as a fact. This will constitute the work of the future—the detailed study of the facts—not merely regarding them from the point of view of evidence. Real, scientific psychical research will then begin. The subject will then, for the first time, become a legitimate branch of human study.

Yet, even now, it may not be altogether unprofitable to adduce a few reflections which have been suggested by a study of the facts, up to the present time. If theories and speculations of this nature have in themselves no value, they often stimulate others to experiment or to reflect upon the same line—sometimes with strikingly important and interesting results. It is chiefly with this object in mind that I offer the following suggestions—the result of some years of thought and research in this particular field.

(1) Before it is possible for any one to appreciate the importance and significance of psychical research, it is necessary for him to become "inoculated," as it were, with materialism! To one who admits, *a priori*, the reality of a spiritual world, and sees no difficulties in the way of accepting it, there is, of course, no need to convince him further. But once admit the position held by modern science (particularly biological science) that life is a function of the organism, and that thought is a function of the brain, and the phenomena assume a very different importance. To state the case in precise terms, I could not do better than to quote the words of Professor John Lewis March, when he says "Mind is not found to exist apart from matter" (*A Theory of Mind*, p. 11). And it must be admitted that—apart from the facts of psychical research—there is no evidence that it does so exist. So far as we can prove, life and consciousness become obliterated at the moment of bodily death. And the only way to prove the contrary is to produce evidence that consciousness does so persist; and this is only possible by the methods adopted in spiritism and psychical research. In no other way can the facts be established; by no other method can the persistence of human consciousness be scientifically proved.

(2) It may be contended that consciousness, as such, may persist, but that individuality does not survive bodily death: the human is merged into the All. But such a view of the case seems to be directly opposed to evidence no less than to moral feeling. For, in the first place, persistence without memory and individuality would not be worth having at all; and secondly, this idea is, it seems to me, directly opposed to evolution, which tends more and more to accentuate individuality, and separate and perfect it.

(3) On the other hand, it might possibly be that our persistence depends upon our *ability* to persist. The theory of mind developed by modern researches in psycho-pathology is that the mind of man—instead of being a

single "unit," as was formerly supposed—is composed of a number of threads or strands, so to speak, held together by our attention and our will. Once these are relaxed, the mind "unravels" and goes to pieces. A single, strongly-woven, and well-bound rope might stand a sudden wrench and shock, while a less perfectly-made one would tear and snap under the strain. Similarly, it might be urged, if the mind be sufficiently balanced, strengthened, and controlled, it might withstand the shock of death; otherwise it would not. Whether or not we persist would thus depend upon our ability to control and hold ourselves together, as it were; upon our strength of will; upon the degree of development of the central personality. When this is lacking, "psychical disintegration" takes place, and we fail to survive the last great Ordeal.

While this theory may possibly be true, it seems to me that it is very probably untrue, for the reason that this is not a question of moral worth which we are considering, but of scientific law—of the Conservation of Energy, of the ability of life and consciousness of any sort—good or bad— to exist apart from brain-functioning. That is the question! Once grant that mind of any kind can persist by and of itself, independent of a physical organization, and you have so far broken down the barriers of materialism that there should not be the slightest objection to granting the persistence of consciousness of any sort—with the probability that it *would* so persist. Cosmic Law could hardly act otherwise.

(4) I know well enough that psychic investigation is, at present at least, in a chaotic and uncertain condition, and that little beyond uncertainty and discouragement has been attained in the past. As Mr. F. C. Constable remarked:

"Many of us who have devoted our lives to psychical research can but have moments of profound depression. We *feel* our labours cannot be in vain, but we are faced by such a complexity of fraud, deliberate and unconscious, mal-observation, denial of scientific restrictions, and ignorance of what is trustworthy in evidence and deduction, that at times our search for truth seems as futile as the search of past alchemists for the philosopher's stone."

And even more forcibly Count Aksakof states the objections which have occurred to him:

"As years went by, the weak points of spiritualism became more evident and more numerous. The insignificance of the communications, the poverty of their intellectual content, and finally the fraud, etc.—in short, a host of doubts, objections, and aberrations of every kind—greatly increased the difficulties of the problem. Such impressions were well calculated to discourage one, if, on the other hand, we had not at our disposal a series of indisputable facts." (*Animism and Spiritism.*)

While this is doubtless true, it is nevertheless a fact that psychical research is, as yet, in its infancy; and it is in a sense unfair to judge the results by the few years of progress which have been possible in the past. For while other sciences—physics, chemistry, anatomy—are more than two thousand years old, psychical research is but forty years old—some of the original founders of the S.P.R. being still alive and actively engaged in the work! It is, then, somewhat premature to pronounce upon the ultimate outcome of the investigation, and we must wait for at least a hundred years or so before it will be possible to see whether or not the subject has proved its claims and justified itself in the eyes of the world. And this view of the case is further supported by the fact that, in so exact a science as cytology, but little definite can be said. Thus, Professor E. B. Wilson, on p. 434 of his work *The Cell*, says: "The study of the cell has, on the whole, seemed to widen rather than to narrow the enormous gap that separates even the lowest forms of life from the inorganic world." It will thus be seen that the uncertain and unsatisfactory condition of psychics is shared also by other branches of scientific investigation, and it is as yet too soon to say whether or not the ultimate verdict will swing in this direction or in that. We can only hope, and continue to experiment!

5. Psychical research, therefore, may continue to progress, in spite of the innate difficulties and the obstacles with which the subject is surrounded. It is our duty to see that it does! For it is certain that the subject will receive serious set-backs, from time to time, in the shape of unjust misrepresentations or bitter attacks from the outsiders, determined to "prove a case," even if the cause of truth be abandoned in order to do so. Take, e.g., the recent volume of Dr. Tanner and Dr. G. Stanley Hall (*Studies in Spiritism*). They received certain "lying communications," in spite of Professor William James' warning that "the personalities are very suggestible" and that "every one is liable to get back from the trance very much what he puts into it." Even Deleuze could have told Drs. Tanner and Hall this fact—having ascertained it nearly a hundred years before (1813); for he wrote in his *Critical History of Animal Magnetism* (pp. 134-5), in reply to those who would question the somnambulist upon points of practical advantage:

"You will gain nothing; you will even lose the advantages which you might derive from his lucidity. It is very possible that you could make him speak upon all the subjects of your indiscreet curiosity; but in that case, as I have already warned you, you will make him leave his own sphere and introduce him into yours. He will no longer have any other resources than yourself. He will utter you very eloquent discourses, but they will no more be dictated by the internal inspirations. They will be the product of his recollections or of his imagination; perhaps you will also rouse his vanity, and then all is lost; he will not re-enter the circle from which he has wandered.... The two states cannot be confounded.... These somnambulists are evidently influenced by the persons who surround them, by the circumstances in which they are placed."

And Dr. A. E. Fletcher, in *The Other World and This*, says:

"Trance mediums, more than any others, are the victims of the embodied and the disembodied. If the medium is subject to the influence of a spirit, how much more likely is he to be affected by the character of those around him! Strong minds in the body may take control of his brain, instead of spirit intelligences. Such persons must be of a highly sensitive order, and cannot come under the same line of human criticism and judgment as might be applied to those in everyday life."

Even Maudsley, in his *Pathology of Mind* (p. 77), says:

"The main feature which the abnormal states (trance, etc.) present in common are: first, that coincident with a partial mental activity there is more or less inhibition, which may be complete, of all other mental action; secondly, that the individual in such condition of limited mental activity *is susceptible only to impressions which are in relation with his character and are consequently assimilated by it....*"[1]

These passages illustrate, at least, the delicate and often-times suggestible nature of the trance; and how inconclusive, to say the least, are such experiments as those of Drs. Tanner and Hall!

6. On the other hand, it may be asked: If the messages we receive at séances really *do* come from the departed, why should they be so fleeting and so uncertain as they are? And why should not many more messages be received from the hundreds and thousands who die yearly, and who are doubtless longing to communicate?

Answers to these questions are manifold. In the first place, it may be pointed out that the ability to communicate may be rare indeed, and not a universal possibility, as is generally supposed. As Dr. Hodgson expressed it (*Proceedings*, xiii., p. 362): "It may be a completely erroneous assumption that all persons, young or old, good or evil, vigorous or sickly, and whatever their lives or deaths may have been, are at all comparable with one another in their capacity to convey clear statements from the other world to this." Further, it must not be supposed that all "messages" received by mediums (even granting their complete honesty) really issue from the "Great Beyond." Many mediums simply tell their sitters the ideas, impressions, and "messages" which come into their minds, and which they believe to come from external sources, i.e., "spirits," but which, as a matter of fact, issue from their own subconsciousness. These scraps of information resemble "bubbles" breaking upon the surface of water—the finished product of latent incubation, and doubtless have every appearance and every feeling of external origin. Even if genuine spirit-messages are at times received, it is highly probable that the bulk of the messages are the product of the medium's subliminal, which catches up and amplifies the original external impetus received from without. Professor William James believed, e.g., the following: that "genuine messages have been given through Mrs. Piper's organism, but he also contended that every time an intelligence appeared, calling itself Hodgson, and beginning: 'Hello! Here I am again in the witness-box! How are you, old chap?' etc., this was not Hodgson at all, but Mrs. Piper's subliminal, and that genuine supernormal information only came in 'touches' or 'impulses,' as it were, as though the spirit could touch or come into contact with the medium's mind at a number of points, making a number of 'dips down,' ... as it were, imparting information at each dip which the medium's mind thereupon seized upon, elaborated, and gave out in its own dramatic form and setting." If this be true of Mrs. Piper (whose messages are shot at you from a cannon's mouth, as it were), how much truer must it be of other types of mediums, in which the communications are certainly far less direct and impressive? Mrs. Piper might be styled the "possession" type of medium—as opposed to the "subliminal" type—commonly seen; and, as before said, if the messages be so indirect in the case of Mrs. Piper, how much more fragmentary and indirect must they be in the case of all other mediums—less developed and less direct than she? It is hardly to be wondered at that the information given is of the vaguest, the most hazy and indistinct character, and that recognition and proof of identity is almost an impossibility.

7. As to the theory that comparatively few (of those who die) make good communicators, I may be permitted to suggest, perhaps, a tentative explanation of the rarity of good communicators (and communications), based upon this principle. Certain it is that special adaptability and idiosyncrasy are necessary to the one on this side—this constituting, in fact, a "medium," as we understand it. It seems highly probable that a medium is born and not made, that the gift is hereditary, and that it depends but little, if at all, upon physical, mental, or moral characteristics, but rather upon a peculiar and innate make-up which is independent of all of these. A person is a good psychic or medium just as another is a good painter or sculptor or pianist. It can be cultivated by training, but the "germ" must be latent within the individual, in order that its development may be possible at all.

Granting all this, it seems to me very natural to suppose that some similar characteristic might be essential to the one on the "other side," in order that *he* might be a good communicator. Only a few might possess this special gift—without which communication would be impossible—no matter how gifted or clever the individual might be, in other respects, or how much he longed to communicate. Further, it might be that this deceased person could only get *en rapport* with our world when some one on this side was also and simultaneously endeavouring to reach him. Neither alone could effect the communication, could bridge the chasm.

Let me make the theory clearer by means of an analogy. One theory of consciousness contends that it depends for its existence altogether upon the touching or inter-connection of certain nervous fibres, without which consciousness would be impossible, and is, in fact, abolished—as in sleep. When these "dendrites" touch, communication is established; when this contact is broken, it is non-existent.

To apply the analogy. When a medium goes into a trance, she throws out (symbolically) psychic "arms," or pseudopodia, much as an octopus might feel about him with his tentacled arms. On the other side, a communicator would also stretch out these mental arms, feeling about for something to grasp and cling to, something capable of receiving and transmitting the messages he desired to send. Only when these two groping arms find each other "in the dark," as it were, would communication become possible. If only *one* thus sought, nothing would result. The rare combination of good sender and good recipient must be found before this communication is possible at all, and even then, they must both be striving to communicate at the same moment before any results follow. It is because of the rarity of this combination and this coincidence that mediumistic messages are so scarce. In addition to the earnest desire and longing on the other side, there must be a medium on this, capable of receiving the messages. And when this medium is lacking (as is usually the case) no communications are received. This fully explains to us, it seems to me, why it is that messages of this nature are so rarely received: the necessary conditions on this side are lacking.

8. Such a theory would also enable us to understand one fact, very puzzling to most investigators in this field. It is that one's friends and relatives are almost invariably present immediately the medium goes into the trance! Sometimes there is a wait, it is true, and they have to be "sent for." But as a rule they are "on tap" at once—and, no matter where we may be, they are there *instanter*—ready to communicate!

Of course such facts naturally lead one to suppose, *a priori*, that these personages are not present at all, in reality, but merely the medium's subliminal, personifying these various personages—no spirit being concerned, directly or indirectly, with their production. This, I say, is the natural view of the facts.

But on the theory above outlined the genuine nature of these messages may readily be assumed. Suppose our friends and relatives are more or less *en rapport* with us all the time (like "guardian angels"). Time and space need not be considered factors in the problem—since all spirits say that they do not exist in "their" world. Then, all we should have to do, in order to effect communication, would be to supply the necessary conditions on this side— when the chasm would at once be bridged, and communication established.

(I wish it to be distinctly understood, however, that I consider the vast bulk of such messages the product of the medium's subliminal, and not at all coming from the source from which they claim to proceed. I am only arguing on general grounds for the *possibility*.)

9. It will be seen that I have spoken throughout the above argument of the *trance* as a necessary condition for communication, or at least assumed that it is invariably present. Why should the trance state have this effect? What is the nature of the trance, and what peculiarity within it renders these results possible?

The sceptic might begin by questioning the fact itself; but I think it now so well established that argument on this score is unnecessary. Further, the deeper the trance, *ceteris paribus*, the better the phenomena. There is no denying that fact. While certain striking results are often obtained while the medium is in light trance, they are not nearly so striking as those which are obtained when the medium is in the deeper stage. And this applies, I believe, to mediums producing both mental and physical phenomena. The question therefore remains: What happens in this trance state to render such results possible? *Why* should the peculiar condition involved be instrumental in producing such striking results?

It must be admitted at once that the innermost nature of this trance state is unknown. Certainly no purely physiological explanation suffices to explain the "medium-trance," even were it sufficient to account for similar conditions better known. No matter what the condition of the medium's nerve centres may be, this would not account for the supernormal information given during the trance state. No matter how much nervous or mental "instability" or "disintegration" were postulated, it would not at all explain or elucidate the primary question: *How is the supernormal information acquired?*

It seems to me that the answer to this question can only be found by assuming some such theory of the facts as the following:

When a person falls asleep, he loses consciousness when *en rapport* with *himself*.[2] When he is placed in the "mesmeric" trance, he remains *en rapport* with the operator, and the deeper the trance, the more complete and effective this *rapport* is. Explain it as you will, the facts remain. The writings of the early mesmerists are filled with records of cases of this *rapport*, in which "community of sensation" was present, and various supernormal phenomena, such as clairvoyance, etc., were manifested. No such phenomena are recorded in hypnotic séances, as a rule, which makes me suspect most strongly that mesmerism and hypnotism are not identical, in spite of the general belief that they are fundamentally one—all mesmeric phenomena being due to "suggestion." Of this, however, later. For the moment, I wish only to draw attention to the fact that, during these deep trance states, *rapport* was noted, and supernormal information frequently given.

Now, it seems plausible to suppose that, by way of analogy, the medium trance would represent a trance state induced by hypnotism *from the "other side."* We know that telepathic hypnotism is a fact—the numerous cases recorded by Myers and Janet being good proof of this. Further, we know that dreams may be induced experimentally, by means of telepathic suggestion. (See Ermacora's paper, *Proceedings*, xi. 235-308.) Might we not assume, then, that the medium-trance represents a certain condition induced by influence from deceased minds—which would fully account for the supernormal information given (for the medium would be *en rapport* with these minds), and for the fact that the medium is not usually susceptible to suggestion, pain-tests, &c., on *this* side. The deeper the trance, the more the medium is in touch with the other world, the less with this; and *vice versa*. The medium-trance is, therefore, probably a hypnotic or mesmeric trance, induced telepathically by operators out of the body.

10. When the trance has been induced, however, how does the "spirit" succeed in imparting information to the medium's brain and organism? Inasmuch as the phenomena are usually of the motor type—speech or writing—the motor centres in the brain must somehow be employed; *how* they are employed, and whether other centres in addition to these are used is a question calling for solution—but one which will take probably years of patient research to solve.

As we know, Dr. Hodgson was of the opinion that the ordinary centres were not used in the production of the automatic writing, for he said (*Proceedings*, xiii. pp. 398-9): "What the precise relation is between this consciousness and the movements of the hand I do not know. I do not know whether or not the motor centres of the brain ordinarily concerned in the movements of hand and arm are in operation or not. I incline to think not—certainly not in the ordinary way...." The statement of the "controls" is that they use the "empty corners" of Mrs. Piper's brain—which probably means that certain unused areas are pressed into service, as far as possible, in the production of the phenomena. Still, this is not very definite information! Another theory offered by the communicators is that they get into contact with the "light," think their thoughts, and these thoughts are then registered or expressed in motor phenomena—speech or writing. What the "light" may be, we have not the slightest means of knowing, but it is a very significant fact that a "light" of this nature is nearly always associated with spiritual phenomena. We hear of the "interior illumination" of the saints and martyrs, and of those who have experienced an influx of "cosmic consciousness"; of the "halo" which surrounds the heads of holy persons; of the "internal light" experienced by many who have had a special conversion or illumination; of the "aura" surrounding the bodies of certain individuals—always perceptible to clairvoyants, and lately (it is asserted) to any one who observes the subject through specially prepared chemical screens;[3] of the "light" diffusing itself over the region of the forehead, which certain mesmeric subjects have inwardly perceived,[4] and of the "aura" which may be produced experimentally by means of high-tension electric currents. We must not forget, also, that Christ Himself is called "the light of the world," and that He once made the very significant remark: "If thine eye be single, *thy whole body shall be full of light.*" Lastly, it is somewhat significant, it seems to me, that Andrew Jackson Davis used to see the nervous system of the person he was studying, while in the "superior condition," as *light*—as though it were illuminated by some interior glow, or was more or less phosphorescent. (And we know that phosphorus is certainly connected with the activities of the nervous system—even though it be not so intimately as before supposed.) This string of coincidences is at least remarkable; and it will be observed that the "light" is usually associated with nervous centres and nervous activity—for the head, e.g., is certainly the part most highly illumined, as a rule; while it is certainly the seat of the most active self-consciousness.

11. These facts throw an interesting side-light, also, upon another oft-observed phenomenon in psychical research. I refer to the fact that apparitions ("ghosts") are nearly always seen to be clear and distinct as to the head and upper portions of the body, while they taper off to vapour and "filmy nothingness" in the lower limbs, so that often the feet are not visible at all. While this may be due in part to the fact that the observer's attention is not directed to the lower limbs, but more or less centred upon the head and face, it appears to me that there may be another interpretation of the facts, more in accordance with the phenomena above mentioned, which is this:

During life we are conscious of our body in varying degrees—of the head most of all, then of the arms and upper portions of the body; and finally, of the lower limbs and feet, we are, a large part of the time, hardly conscious at all. Now, if the light accompanies nervous activity, and is present in proportion to it, it is obvious that those portions of the organism would have most "light" which were most active mentally—i.e., the brain and those portions of the nervous system controlling the hands, face, and upper portions of the body—while those portions which had become entirely automatic and unconscious in their activity would have least light—being physiological to the point almost of being mechanical. If this "light" corresponded in any way to visibility, therefore, it would only be natural to suppose that the face and upper portions of the phantasmal figure should be more or less distinctly visible, to one at all sensitive to such impressions, while the lower portions of the figure would fade into practical invisibility,—owing to lack of "light." This explanation would certainly be in accord with the facts, as we know them, regarding phantasmal figures.

12. We are still far from the answer to our question, however: How does spirit act upon matter, and in what way does the spirit manipulate the nervous mechanism of the medium, during the process of communication? Let us now consider this question further.

Andrew Jackson Davis, in his *Great Harmonia*, vol. i. pp. 55-65, discussed this problem, and stated that "spirit acts upon the bodily organism anatomically, physiologically, mechanically, chemically, electrically, magnetically, and spiritually." The trouble with such a statement is that it explains nothing (even as elaborated by him), and that it is far easier to believe, e.g., that one part of the body acts chemically and mechanically, etc., upon another part than to suppose that "spirit" has anything to do with the affair whatever. To postulate its activity would be merely to multiply causes without necessity.

Just here, it might be interesting to inquire what the modern conception is as to the relation of mind and brain—of soul and body; and particularly the question of the "seat" of the soul—that central point which was, until late years, always considered necessary as a fulcrum or point of contact upon which the soul might act.

The older psychologists and philosophers always took such a "seat" for granted—Descartes, as we know, imagining that the pineal gland occupied that important function. But as the science of psychology progressed, this notion was more and more given up, until the prevailing opinion of late years seems to be that the *whole* of the cortex is equally the seat of consciousness, and that its *total* functioning is responsible for the psychical activities which we know under the head of personality or individuality or ego.

It is interesting to note, however, that Dr. Frederick Peterson, of Columbia University, New York, has lately put forward the theory that there is, or may be, a seat of consciousness, after all! In a striking article in the *Journal of Abnormal Psychology* (vol. iii. No. 5), he says:—

"I will say at once that the 'seat' of that power which produces the manifestations of consciousness is in the basal ganglia (probably the *corpora striata*), and that consciousness is a peculiar summation of energy at that point, capable of being directed, like the rays of a searchlight, into this or that portion of the brain."

Dr. Peterson then goes on to give some facts which seem to him to support this view. Among these are the phenomena of sleep (the reasons being too long to detail here); the fact that, although every individual brain is stored full of experiences, only a small area is illuminated by consciousness at any one moment; and the phenomena of epilepsy— concerning which Dr. Peterson speaks in the following terms:

"The one disorder which has led me to think much of this subject is epilepsy, in which disease, loss of consciousness is the most extraordinary and often the only symptom. I allude chiefly to such remarkable conditions as the *tic de salaam* and the other forms of *petit mal*, in which the patient drops suddenly to the floor with loss of consciousness, and quite as suddenly rises again in full possession of his faculties. I have watched such cases for hours, and always with increasing marvel. The loss of consciousness is complete, and often lasts but a fraction of a second. How account for such phenomenon! If consciousness were a diffused attribute of the whole brain, what spasm of blood-vessels or other physical process familiar to us could act and be adjusted with such speed? If, however, the 'seat' of consciousness be limited to some very small portion of the brain, some physical process such as is suggested could easily account for the instantaneous loss and regaining of consciousness."

Other facts in support of this theory are given, and the statement of Dr. C. L. Dana that, in poisoning by illuminating gas, the chief symptom is loss of consciousness, and the only lesion discovered is softening of the *corpora striata*; then the following:

"Assuming now that it were proved that the power which creates consciousness has some definite seat, and that it is a summation of energies physiologically varying in sleep and waking, which may be directed to any part of our store of experiences for purposes of illumination, what portion of the brain is so constructed as to be in apparently intimate connection with every other? The *corpora striata!*... There is no portion of the brain we know so little of.... Here we have a portion of the brain which must be of enormous significance, otherwise it would not be always present, from the fish up to man."

It will be seen that Dr. Peterson is here opposed to the doctrine maintained by both Lotze[5] and MacDougall,[6] who both maintained that: "There are a number of separate points in the brain which form so many 'seats' of the soul. Each of these would be of equal value with the rest; at each of them the soul would be present with equal completeness." But whether there be one or several "seats" of consciousness, it is obvious that there must be contact of *some* sort, at one or several points (granting the correctness of the theory that spirit acts upon matter at all), and the question is: *How* may this action be supposed to take place?

In discussing this question in a former book[7] I said:

"It is more than probable, it seems to me, that there exists some sort of etheric medium between mind and even organic nervous tissue, upon which the mind must act first of all. Thus, we should have the chain of connection: mind, vital or etheric medium, nervous tissue, muscle, bone. So mind acts upon matter; and it will be seen that there is an increasing density of structure, and that just in proportion to this density is mind incapable of affecting matter directly. We must, it seems to me, always postulate some sort of etheric medium through which mind acts, in order to affect and move matter—organic or inorganic. And without this vital intermediary there can be no action, and consequently no manifestation."

Now, it would appear rational to suppose that some action of this sort takes place when mind acts upon, or influences, matter. Air is invisible, and practically imperceptible to our senses—*when stationary*. But set into motion, a current of air will close a door with a bang—will have the effect of definitely moving a heavy mass of inanimate matter, in the manner indicated. It may be that in somewhat the same way mind affects brain. Mind may reside in a sort of etheric vehicle, and be more or less stable or stationary, save at the times when volition or intense, active conscious operations are in progress—when, in short, *effort* is exerted. At such times, it is surely conceivable that what was static becomes dynamic; something is set into motion which in turn brings into activity some more "physical" energy, and so on, until sufficient material momentum has been gained to affect that most unstable and mobile substance, nervous tissue. It is certainly quite conceivable that certain nervous centres in the brain (*which* centres, we cannot say) might be set into actual operation by some such process; or at least that the impulse or energy supplied in this manner might be sufficient to release the nervous energy stored in the cell, much as the trigger of a rifle would, when pressed, release the energy contained within the cartridge. Such "hair trigger" action has been postulated by both William James and Bergson, and is certainly in line with modern speculations in this direction. There are also certain analogies to be drawn from physical science to guide us here.

In electricity, e.g., what are known as "relays" are constantly employed, and beautifully illustrate the principle here outlined. In working over long lines, or where there are a number of instruments in one circuit, the currents are often not strong enough to work the recording instruments directly. In such a case there is interposed a "relay" or "repeater." This instrument consists of an electro-magnet round which the line current flows, and whose delicately-poised armature, when attracted, makes contact for a local circuit, in which a local battery and the receiving Morse instrument (sounder, writer, etc.) are included. The principle of the relay is, then, that a current too weak to do the work itself may get a strong local current to do its work for it.

It may be the same in the case of mental action. Volition or thought may be too weak, *per se*, to influence nervous processes; but, when exceptionally active or potent, they may set into activity specific nerve energies which manifest in the manner known to us as motor and physical phenomena. Here is, it seems to me, a rational explanation of the facts, and one which is in accord, not only with ordinary psychological phenomena, but with those more puzzling and obscure manifestations witnessed from time to time in psychic research.

13. It may be objected that such a conception of the facts supposes that will (and conscious thought) are physical energies—for however *slight* we make this energy, it is still energy none the less. The air which closed the door would not move it *of itself*—unless some pressure were exerted upon it from without. Could "life" act otherwise?

One reply to this objection is that the distinguishing characteristic of life is this very power of original, spontaneous movement. It is life, and life alone, which possesses this power. Were this doctrine true, it would of course upset the present theory of the Conservation of Energy, for it would admit the constant infusion into the world of energy from without. Despite the theoretical difficulty thus presented, it seems probable that life is, in a certain sense, a physical energy, or at least its manifestation is. It is possible that the two states are similar to the difference between potential and kinetic energy; and we must remember that *energy is always noticed or experienced by us, as energy, in its expenditure, never in its accumulation.*[8]

If life be a physical force, if vitality be a specific energy, then, it seems to me, many things fall into line—many phenomena, hitherto inexplicable, become at once intelligible.

Let me illustrate this conclusion by mentioning a few such facts:

Take, for instance, the phenomena manifested in the presence of Eusapia Palladino. I shall not now stop to discuss the reality of these manifestations, because I consider them just as certain as any other facts in life, and not at all open to discussion. Now, in these phenomena there is an intelligence *of some sort* at work producing them; that is certain. But as to the *nature* of this intelligence—*what* it is—that is altogether another matter, and a much more difficult question to answer. Whether this be a low order of deceiving and "lying spirits," as Professor Barrett and others are apparently inclined to believe, or whether it be a fraction of the medium's own mind (Flournoy, Morselli), or whether it be the spirit it claims to be, or whether it belongs to some other even more doubtful order of intelligence, such as postulated by the Theosophists and certain Mystics and Occultists, *that* is a question which we cannot at present answer, and for which we may have to wait for several hundred years before one can be satisfactorily given.

But, granting the reality of the phenomena, they themselves demand solution, solely from the point of view of physics and physiology, and quite aside from the nature of the intelligence with which they are at times associated. The facts themselves still need elucidation.

Some years ago a gentleman of my acquaintance started out with the intention of constructing a telephone by means of which it would be possible to speak directly to the spirit world! He had in mind great delicacy of apparatus, a system of "relays," by means of which it would be possible to augment an initial stimulus, however slight, a magnifying apparatus which would greatly increase the volume of sound, on the lines of the ampliphone and the microphone, etc. I do not believe that very definite results were ever achieved, and he is still at work upon the problem. Needless to say, this idea of his was ridiculed in all quarters; but I myself do not see any valid reason why some such device should not succeed—provided, of course, that a spiritual world exists at all. If such a world exists, if the intelligences which reside therein can at times produce physical phenomena, then it is certainly conceivable that some energy may be set into operation which may produce the desired results—some energy which we, too, can utilize and which the spiritual entity can also manipulate; in other words, *an energy common to the two worlds*. Were such a common medium or mediator found, communication would certainly be established, and it only remains for us to discover the common energy. Personally, I believe that this intermediary is most probably *vitality*—the life-force, without the presence of which such manifestations would be impossible. A living, human being is necessary, upon whose presence these phenomena depend, and without whom they could not occur. It is thus obvious that there is a definite connection between these phenomena and *life*, which can hardly be due to chance; it must stand in some intimate and causal relation.[9]

14. Many students of psychical phenomena believe that, in the case of Eusapia Palladino, e.g., this connection is clearly discernible, and that it is upon the externalization of her vital force that many of these phenomena depend. Even the materializations are thought to be due to this same cause—due to the moulding, in space, of this plastic intermediary projected beyond the limits of her bodily organism. Certain it is that such a projection does at times take place, and it seems rational to suppose that "raps" may be due to the explosive expulsion of this neural energy after it has reached a certain "tension." One quite striking incident which has been narrated to me by a physician of my acquaintance tends rather to confirm this view. It is that, when he was trying on various occasions to move a table, *à la* Palladino, he failed to do so, but whenever he lifted his hands away from the table, "sparkling" took place between his hands and the table-top, closely resembling the electric spark which jumps from point to point when the tension has reached a certain limit.

Another interesting fact, related to me by the same physician, serves to throw a light upon the connection of vital and physical energies. The doctor in question was treating a patient, who was apparently "obsessed," by means of electricity. The galvanometer needle showed what slight variations in the current there were during the course of the treatment. In the middle of the process, while the patient was conversing with the doctor, she was suddenly "obsessed." *Coincidental* with this obsession, the galvanometer showed a tremendous and permanent fluctuation, indicating that the resistance of the body to the current had suddenly and greatly changed!

Whatever view we may take of the facts, here is, at least, a striking incident, which the current theories of the varying causes of bodily resistance (in these psycho-galvanic reflexes) hardly serve to explain. Can it be that the subject's "etheric body" was in some way disturbed by an invading intelligence, and that this disturbance was manifested in the fluctuations recorded? Is there a nervous fluid, after all, as the magnetizers and mesmerists contend so strongly, but which has been relegated to oblivion since the advent of suggestion and hypnotism? Personally, I believe that there *is*, and I shall indicate very briefly some of my reasons for thinking so.

In the *first* place, the modern hypnotist can very rarely succeed in cultivating clairvoyance in his subject, whereas the records of mesmerism teem with cases which were developed under the old *régime*. Surely the dissimilarity in the effect points to a dissimilarity of cause. It has always appeared to me highly probable that mesmerism and hypnotism are dependent upon entirely different causes, and were not at all the same in the last analysis.

In the *second* place, the exhaustion which "healers" sometimes experience when treating patients of a certain temperament can hardly be due altogether to suggestion. I have been informed by "magnetic" and "spiritual" healers that this feeling of exhaustion is very great when a self-centred, selfish person is being treated, and correspondingly less whenever a generous, large-souled individual is receiving the treatment. "Osteopaths" have told me the same thing. Those possessing an active mind and brain, and who are analytical and unsympathetic by nature, are far harder to treat, and leave a far greater exhaustion, than those who are not so. This bears a very striking resemblance to the "good" and "bad" sitters in the Piper case, and also the Palladino case; in fact, it is true of everyday life, to a certain extent. The more active the mind, the greater the *grasp* over life and self which we possess, the less susceptible are we to external or internal influences. Let us call to mind in this connection the remark of Dr. Snow in his treatise on *Anaesthetics*, that "the more intelligent the patient, the more anaesthetic is required to put him under."

Thirdly, the phenomena presented by Eusapia Palladino completely prove the reality of such a "fluid" to my mind, without any other proof being necessary.

Fourthly, the impression said to be left in or upon objects or houses, and the phenomena of "psychometry" seem to indicate the same thing.

Fifthly, the recent reinforcement of the evidence in favour of the human "aura" strongly supports the same view.

Sixthly, the French experiments in "exteriorization of sensibility," "thought-photography," "radiographs," etc., point to the same conclusion.

Seventhly, the successful experiments conducted by Professor Alrutz and others with his instrument—which is thought to register "will power"—is a long step towards recognizing the existence of a nervous, vital energy, which can at times be externalized and made to pass into and "charge" an inanimate object.

Finally, the facts of materialization and kindred phenomena, which find so ready and complete an explanation on this theory.

For these and other reasons, therefore, it seems fairly certain that there is a nervous "fluid" which can at times be externalized beyond the normal bodily limits, which is operative in mesmeric "passes," and which plays so large and hitherto unsuspected a part in the production of many physical and psychical phenomena.

15. As we know, it is this "fluid" which is drawn upon, so it is said, by materializing mediums for the production of their phantoms, and the following interesting experience seems to confirm this view. I quote *verbatim*:

"It was an autumn afternoon, about six o'clock. I had returned from a stroll in the garden, and was in my own room, sitting on a single-backed easy-chair, leisurely dipping into *Vanity Fair*. While turning over the pages in search of some favourite passage, I became aware of an abnormal and quite indescribable sensation. My chest and breathing seemed inwardly oppressed by some ponderous weight, while I became conscious of some presence behind me, exerting a powerful influence on the forces within. On trying to turn my head to see what this could be, I was powerless to do so, neither could I lift a hand or move in any way. I was not a little alarmed and began immediately to reason. Was it a fainting fit coming on, epilepsy, paralysis—possibly even death? No, the mind was too much alive, though physically I felt an absolutely passive instrument, operated upon by some powerful external agent, as if the current of nerve-force within seemed forcibly drawn together and focussed on a spot in front of me. I gazed motionless, as though fascinated, on what was no longer vacant space. There an oval, misty light was forming, elongatory, widening—yes, actually developing into a human face and form! Was this hallucination, or some vision of the unseen, coming in so unexpected fashion? Before me had arisen a remarkable figure, never seen before in picture or life—dark-skinned, aged, with white beard, the expression intensely earnest, the features small, the bald head finely moulded, lofty over the forehead, the whole demeanour instinct with solemn grace. The hands, too, how unlike any hands I knew, yet how expressive! They were dark, long in fingers and narrow in palms, the veins like sinews, standing out as they moved to and fro in eager gesture. He was speaking to me in deep tones, as if in urgent entreaty. What would I not give to hear words from such a figure! But no effort availed me to distinguish one articulate sound. I tried to speak, but could not. With desperate effort I shook out the words, "Speak louder!" The face grew more intent, the voice louder and more emphatic. Was there something amiss in my own hearing, then, that I could distinguish no word amidst these deeply emphasized tones? Slowly and deliberately the figure vanished, through the same stages of indistinctness, back to the globular, lamp-like whiteness, till it faded into nothingness. Before it had quite faded away, the face of a woman arose, indistinct and calm. The same emphatic hum, though in a subdued note, indistinct and dim. The same paralysis of voice and muscle, the same strange force, as if it were overshadowing me.

With the disappearance of this second and far less interesting figure, I recovered my power of movement, and arose.

"My first impulse was to look round for the origin of this strange force; my second was to rush to the looking-glass to make sure I was myself. There could be no delusion! There I was, paler than usual, and greatly agitated; I walked hurriedly to and fro. True, there had been nothing alarming in the apparition itself, but the sensation preceding had been vivid in the extreme. What was it? Was it night, or had I been in some strange sleep? Certainly not! Was I in my right mind? I believed so. Then, if so, and the conditions being the same, would it be possible to bring back this strange phenomenon that I might know it had really existed, whether subjectively or objectively? Like an inspiration I determined that, if this experience had a basis in objective or subjective fact, it might certainly recur. I would sit down in the same position, try to feel calm, open a book, and remain as still and passive as I could. To my intense interest, and almost at once, the strange sense of some power operating on the nerve-forces within, followed by the same loss of muscular power, the same wide-awakeness of the reason, the same drawing out and concentrating of the energies on that spot in front, repeated itself, this time more deliberately, leaving me freer to take mental notes of what was happening. Again rose the same noble, earnest figure, gazing at me, the hands moving in accompaniment to the deep tones of voice. The same painful effort on my part to hear, with no result. The vision passed. Again the woman's face, insignificant and meaningless, succeeded it as before. She spoke, but in less emphatic tones. It flashed upon me I *would* hear. After a frantic effort, I caught two words—"land," "America"—with positively no clue to their meaning.

"I was wide awake when the first apparition appeared, and in a highly excited state of mind on its reappearance."

This case strikes me as particularly interesting, for the reason that it illustrates the possible manner of the externalization of forces, and the possible manner of their guidance and manipulation by outside intelligences, as postulated in *Eusapia Palladino*, p. 300. Here we see the process actually at work, as it were, described by a careful observer, who was perfectly conscious all the time of the phenomena going on within him. This is, to my mind, a human document of no little importance.

It appears quite credible, therefore, that a "fluid" of some sort does exist, and that its liberation, under certain peculiar conditions, should produce odd physical phenomena; and this conviction has been rendered almost a certainty by the unique experiments of Dr. Ochorowicz with his medium, Mlle. Tomczyk. A brief summary of that case will make this apparent.

For many years experiments of the kind here recorded have been in progress, but the path has always been blocked by fraud and innumerable difficulties. Dr. Ochorowicz did, however, apparently succeed in obtaining photographs of human radiations, of thoughts, and even of materialized hands! What are they? Are they the hands of "spirits," inhabitants of the "Great Beyond"? Are they astrals or elementals? Are they projections from the body of the medium? Of what can they consist? Who directs and guides them? And how can a thought be photographed?

These newer researches into the fields of science have been undertaken, for the most part, by French investigators, who have progressed very far in their demonstrations and speculations in this direction—much further, it may be said, than either the English or American investigators have advanced—assuming, of course, the accuracy of their conclusions!

Dr. Ochorowicz had been known for thirty years to all researchers as a careful investigator. Professor Charles Richet of the University of Paris spoke of him in the highest terms, and regarded him as "an exceptionally careful and cautious investigator." His book, *Mental Suggestion*, which was published early in the eighties, is considered an authority, and his general erudition and scientific attainments no one could question. For many years he was professor in the University of Lemberg.

Several years ago a young girl, Mlle. Stanislaw Tomczyk, then about eighteen years old, was sent to Dr. Ochorowicz for medical treatment. She suffered greatly from nervousness. In order to bring about relief Dr. Ochorowicz hypnotized her, inducing somnambulism; and in this state she displayed, quite spontaneously, a number of "mediumistic" phenomena. This proved to be the beginning of her mediumship. She possessed a power unknown to herself; and it probably would have remained for ever unknown had she not fallen into the hands of a man such as Dr. Ochorowicz. By the average physician she would, most probably, have been treated as hysterical or insane; but careful analysis and training caused her to become, instead, one of the most remarkable psychics the world has ever known.

Her early trials and tests were simple enough. A glass clock, possessing a pointer, was hung up in the centre of the room, and Mlle. Tomczyk was told to will that the pointer, when set revolving, should stop at a certain number. Generally she pointed with her finger at the indicator, keeping her hand a few centimetres distant. The indicator generally, though not invariably, stopped at the number desired—at any rate, a far greater number of times than Dr. Ochorowicz or any other person could cause it to stop when trying the experiments themselves. The clock belonged to Dr. Ochorowicz, and was innocent of trickery.

The next experiments consisted in raising or "levitating" small objects from the table—by placing the medium's hands on either side of them. Sometimes the object would be raised from Dr. Ochorowicz's hand instead—while he was holding it. Of course the natural supposition is that a thread or hair of some sort was employed, but this possibility was eliminated in a number of ways.

It must be remembered that all these manifestations took place when the medium was in a state of induced somnambulism. She remembered nothing when awakened of what had occurred. But now something curious and interesting demanded special attention. A distinct personality, calling itself "Little Stasia," began to develop. This personality asserted that she, and not the medium, was responsible for the physical manifestations we have recorded. She said (through the mouth of the entranced somnambule) that she was not an independent spirit, but a creation, an individuality, similar to the "alternating personalities" so well known to us. There would be no difficulty in accepting this estimate, were it not for the awkward fact that this little being was photographed on one occasion and seen to be a small, independent creature, existing apart from the medium! This is how it came about.

Through the entranced medium instructions were given to focus a camera upon a certain chair—having first placed a shawl over the back. This was done. Dr. Ochorowicz and Mlle. Tomczyk then left the room together. At the end of a certain length of time they returned, developed the plate, and upon it was found the distinct imprint of a small child's face, apparently belonging to a body, seated in the chair, and swathed around with the shawl in question! The experiment was performed in the hotel where they happened to be stopping; the photographic camera and plates were Dr. Ochorowicz's own, and the medium was out of the room, in the doctor's company throughout. It has never been explained.

Such is a brief account of the more interesting experiments conducted during the early years of this medium's development. In later years her powers, under the skilled guidance of (the late) Dr. Ochorowicz, took another turn and provided some of the most interesting and striking manifestations in the history of this subject, as, for example, his experiments in the photography of "fluidic" or "materialized" hands, and also in thought-photography.

These photographs of fluidic hands Dr. Ochorowicz calls "radiographs," because they can only be explained by supposing that the fluidic hand, which is placed upon the photographic plate, is in some way radio-active during the process. In no other way can the facts be explained. Even supposing, for the sake of argument, that the psychic could in some way have placed her own hands on the plates, they would not have produced the results obtained—as any one can prove to his own satisfaction.

These impressions upon photographic plates were obtained "mediumistically"—that is, in more or less complete darkness, and without any apparatus. Not only were all known forms of radiation thus excluded, but the impression was direct, and obtained without camera, focussing, etc. The impressions of hands obtained were of various shapes and sizes, both larger and smaller than those of the medium (who, of course, was the only other person present), peculiarly deformed hands and partially formed hands, according to the degree of success of the experiment, and the desire of the medium.

These hands can only be produced in the presence, and with the assistance, of a good "physical medium," in more or less darkness, and are taken by means of a peculiar light which the hands seem to create for themselves. Sometimes the hands were visible to both the medium and Dr. Ochorowicz, sometimes visible only to the medium, sometimes invisible to both. We are assured that in the series of tests under consideration the impressions were obtained only when the psychic was deeply entranced, and then only at certain times.

On a number of occasions the psychic placed her hand upon the plate, and its impression was left upon it. The hands were photographed by means of a form of light radiating from the hands themselves. On one occasion, Dr. Ochorowicz held the plate against the medium's ear; the ear itself was not photographed, but the side of the head, the hair, and particularly the hairpins were. On two occasions a leaf was placed between the hands and the plate, and the outline of the leaf was left upon the latter. From these experiments it was concluded that the rays—whatever they might be—were emitted by the "etheric body" (the "astral" body, the "double") and not by the physical body, since their intensity did not seem to correspond in any way to the anatomical distribution of the nerves.

These rays may be centred and concentrated by the action of the will of the subject. They radiate from the surface of the skin and reproduce a simulacrum, as it were, of the surface. They throw a shadow of any object placed between the subject and the photographic plate. They are more penetrating than the rays discovered by M. Darget, and brought to the attention of the French Academy several years ago. Interesting analogies may exist here between these rays and the so-called "Black Light" of M. Le Bon, which he describes at length in his work, *The Evolution of Forces*.

It was now determined to attempt more interesting and startling experiments. The medium was requested to hold her right hand in the air, where it could be seen plainly, against the faint red light in the room. It was not moved throughout the experiment. In his own laboratory Dr. Ochorowicz then procured a fresh plate and held it in the air, at some distance from the hand of the medium. The latter then said: "Ah, I see another right hand detaching itself from my arm and approaching the plate. How it pains me! Yes, it is placing itself over the plate—it is done."

Dr. Ochorowicz then took the plate with him at once to the dark room and, when it was developed, there was found the outline of an unformed hand—one apparently in the process of condensation. It was, as it were, a hand in embryo. It had apparently become detached, or had detached itself, from the medium, and remained sufficiently solid to leave an impression of itself upon the plate, held about half a metre from it. It was, in fact, a form of materialization, but of so shadowy a texture that it remained often quite invisible to the onlooker.

A long series of experiments is then described, which might be condensed somewhat as follows:—

"The somnambule said that she did not see the double's hand leave hers, but saw it placed upon the plate. It was placed upon it at an angle of ninety degrees from the position taken by her own hand. At my request the thumb was made particularly distinct, the whole hand being quite different in contour from that of the medium.

"I take another plate, and hold it some distance from the medium's hand. She makes an effort to impress it, with the result that an immense finger, superhuman in size, is seen upon the plate when developed. Upon the next plate, which I hold about twenty-five centimetres from her hands, three fingers appear, non-luminous—the light seeming to come from behind the hand, and shining through the spaces between the fingers.

"I now hold a plate at a distance of one metre from her right hand, which is held up in front of her. The red light is turned slightly low. The somnambule sees a shadowy hand detach itself from hers, which is at the same time, also, attached to a very long, thin arm, and which approaches the plate. The hand is very large, she says, and is a right hand. It places itself over the plate, which I thereupon remove and develop. A large hand is distinctly visible upon it. Finally, I hold a plate two and a half metres away from the medium's hand. The somnambule shivers and feels cold in her lower limbs, despite the fact that my laboratory is very warm. She again holds out her right hand, and a left hand, attached to a long, thin arm, is seen by her to detach itself and place itself over the plate held in my hand. Upon being developed, the impression of a very large left hand was found upon the plate—so large that only a portion of the hand could be seen! The whole of the medium's hand can easily be placed upon the plate. These are very similar to the enormous hands frequently seen in the Palladino séances, and said to be those of 'John King.'

"From the above facts I think we are justified in arriving at the following tentative conclusions:

"1. That the hand of the double can be larger than that of the medium.

"2. That a left hand can be projected from a right arm, drawing its force from the entire body of the subject, this being accompanied by a chilly feeling in the extremities and by congestion of the head.

"3. That the arm of the double appears to shrink in size according to its distance from the medium's body.

"4. That it is easier for the fluidic hand to imprint itself upon the photographic plate (negative) in white than in black.

"5. That in the case of the large and shining thumb it is surrounded by a clear halo of light.

"6. The etheric body of the medium, the 'double,' behaves as though it were an independent spirit."

In a second series of experiments very small hands were produced by request. These hands terminated abruptly at the wrist, but it was found by a series of independent experiments that any hand would appear to do so if the illumination came from a certain direction. In one case the photographic plate was placed on the sofa, three feet from the entranced somnambule. Dr. Ochorowicz took his seat by her side. A fluidic hand was seen to approach the plate, then retreat into the medium's body, avoiding the red light. Upon the plate being developed, the imprints of two small hands were seen, somewhat resembling the hands of the medium, though smaller. They were not typical children's hands. The medium had, in fact, made two distinct efforts to impress the plate and have the fluidic hand place itself upon it. These semi-materializations are very interesting, since they form the connecting link between true materialization, which is solid and substantial, and so-called thought photography.

After this Dr. Ochorowicz wished to try another experiment. A pencil and a sheet of paper were placed on the floor under the bureau by Dr. Ochorowicz. The medium sat in her chair entranced. Soon the sound of writing was heard; then the fall of the pencil. Upon the sheet of paper being removed a word was found scratched across it—

"STANISL—"

The psychic then desired to obtain writing in full view of Dr. Ochorowicz, so he placed another piece of paper upon the floor, and upon it the pencil.

The medium then exerted herself; the pencil stood on end, and attempted to write. In this, however, it failed, and fell to the floor. This was repeated several times, when the medium had to give up further attempts, owing to her extreme fatigue.

The question now arises: Can these fluidic hands, which are thus exteriorized, move of their own volition, or must they remain stationary? To this question Dr. Ochorowicz addressed himself in a later series of experiments.

In the first experiment, the somnambule saw a finger upon a plate, which was self-luminous, and seemed to be writing. A large "J" was seen to be traced upon it. In the second trial, neither the medium nor Dr. Ochorowicz saw anything, but the letters "J. O." were seen to be imprinted upon it when developed.

This proved that the intelligence guiding the finger at least possessed memory and intelligence. The finger was to some extent self-luminous. From these experiments Dr. Ochorowicz concluded that:

The actinic action of the emitted rays is feeble, comparatively speaking; and that the visible light of the fluidic hands is less actinic than the invisible light.

The relation of these rays to ordinary light is thus an interesting question. It is well known that all mediums shun light, and there are sound physiological and psychological reasons for this. Daylight has been found to be more destructive to the success of phenomena than any form of artificial light; moonlight is far better than sunlight. It has lately been shown that light exerts a powerful physical pressure, and is a disruptive agency, destroying protoplasm and many of the lower forms of life. We only have to see the effect of sunlight upon a photographic plate to appreciate its power. The absurdity of assuming that light plays no part in such manifestations—where very delicate, subtle, and little understood forces are in operation—is thus manifest.

Still, the fluidic hands emit a light of their own; and the question is, Can this emitted light penetrate solid substances—"matter," as we understand it? As the result of a number of experiments, Dr. Ochorowicz ascertained that, in the majority of cases, these rays, like ultra-violet light, did not penetrate solid substances, as do the X-rays; yet their actinic action was found to be far stronger! Here is a field for long-continued observation and experiment. In thought photography, on the other hand, it has been ascertained that the rays can pass easily through solid matter, like the X-rays.

The next question of interest which presented itself for solution was this: To what extent can the fluidic hands change their form, size, and contour at will? Experiments were first tried in the reduction of the size of the hands, upon request.

Three plates were prepared and laid in a series upon the table at some distance from the medium. Through the entranced somnambule the "double" was then informed of the experiment, and asked to place its hand upon the three plates in succession, willing on each occasion to make the fluidic hand smaller. This was done. An impression of the same hand was obtained on each plate, but it can be seen that, on each occasion, the hand is smaller in size. This was all accomplished within a few seconds.

Of these experiments Dr. Ochorowicz says:

"We are therefore justified in arriving at the following conclusions:

"1. At first, the double's hand is larger than that of the medium.

"2. It tends to decrease in length and general size.

"3. The palm of the hand, especially, tends to decrease.

"4. Only the little finger remains without appreciable change.

"5. The change is that of several millimetres, but not enormous.

"6. The fingers of the double tended to close nearer together, as well as become smaller—just as an ordinary hand would probably do."

The light which supplied the necessary illumination for these photographs seemed to have been emitted from a sort of "egg," near the wrist of the hand, which was intensely luminous. This was not expected, and came as a surprise. Two suggestions as to its nature at once present themselves: (1) that it is a self-created mediumistic light; and (2) that it is a mass of matter from which the hand derives its material sustenance.

In a further series of experiments, during which Dr. Ochorowicz was repeatedly touched by a cold hand, impressions of large left hands were left upon the plates—the medium's left hand being, meanwhile, a long way removed from the plate. The fingers were very large, the thumb enormous and abnormally shaped at the end.

Summing up the conclusions which, he thought, could be drawn from his researches, Dr. Ochorowicz said:

"1. Fluidic hands are detached more or less rarely—according to the condition of the subject's "forces." When these are strong, hands may even be produced unknown to the medium.

"2. The direction and character of these hands are determined by the subconscious mind of the medium; but also partially by the conscious mind.

"3. The properties of the fluidic hands are not constant; they change frequently.

"4. These changes represent transformations of energy—certain forms of energy being transformed into other forms. When the conditions are good, the forms of available energy are multiplied; when weak, they are lessened. They alternate, but do not blend. The mechanical effects are produced chiefly by the invisible hands, while the visible hands are inactive.

"5. I have never seen more than two hands formed by one medium at one time, and more usually only one. When there are two hands, however, they may be quite dissimilar, one from the other.

"6. There are several degrees of materiality, which succeed each other rapidly. The hands are so fugitive that it is almost impossible to seize them. When the imperfectly formed hands are grasped, however, they are cold, slippery, and unpleasant to the touch. The better materialized hands, on the contrary, are warm and life-like.

"7. The well-materialized hands can be photographed; even the poorly-developed hands can give radiographs.

"8. The ultra-violet light necessary to produce these photographs can be produced by the hand of the medium or by the double itself.

"9. Radiographs are difficult to obtain; a materialization generally loses its luminosity.

"10. The hands are sometimes like, and sometimes unlike, those of the medium.

"11. The fluidic hands can be moulded plastically, and altered as to their dimensions."

To resume the experiments: Dr. Ochorowicz desired to see whether the fluidic hand of the double could pass through a very small hole or space. He accordingly proposed placing a rolled-up film in a bottle, leaving only the small hole at the top, and see whether the hand could impress itself under these circumstances. Upon this being proposed to the medium, she exclaimed: "Make it more difficult than that; you will make the double lazy! Cork up the bottle!"

Dr. Ochorowicz accordingly cut a film, rolled it into a small roll, placed it in the bottle, and held the latter between his two hands, the right-hand palm acting as a cork, the left supporting the bottle; the medium placed her hands on either side of the bottle, on the outside. She soon complained that her hands were paining her, seeming to swell and get larger. She was soon after seized with cramps, and the experiment was at this point discontinued.

Dr. Ochorowicz tried to draw the film from the bottle, but failed; he was finally obliged to break the bottle to extract it. The film was then developed, and upon it was the imprint of a hand—larger even than his own, to say nothing of the medium's—clearly formed. Fraud was absolutely out of the question. There seems only the alternative choice of invoking the fourth dimension, or assuming that the fluidic hand could curve itself round and round the film after having entered the bottle in some manner! The facts seem incredible; but I give them as recorded.

The question now arises: is the fluidic hand two-dimensioned? It could hardly have any thickness, to accomplish the last experiment. Dr. Ochorowicz determined to try a novel experiment, to test this theory.

Two photographic plates were placed face to face, separated by small pieces of cardboard at the corners. The "double" was requested to insert its hand between the plates when the medium was entranced. Upon the plates being developed, the imprint of a hand (the same hand) was found on both plates; i.e. a photograph of the top, and of the under side of a hand. This was repeated again, under more stringent conditions. The hand again appeared.

It was then decided to repeat the experiment with the rolled film in the bottle. The experiment was again made; the film was developed when the medium reclined on the couch on the opposite side of the room, and a very large hand was again found to have impressed itself upon the film. It had evidently succeeded in curling itself round the rolled film in the closed bottle!

The question is: First, Do the facts occur? And if they do, what is the cause of them? What is the nature of these fluidic hands? To whom do they belong? Of what are they constituted? Are they the hands of a spirit, or mere exteriorizations from the body of the medium—materializations, only partially independent?

Without attempting to answer these questions in this place, I will conclude by pointing out two facts, which seem to me of considerable importance. The first is that many nervous and mentally abnormal patients may be mediums were the pains taken to ascertain that fact. I know of one famous alienist who confided to me his belief that a very large percentage of mediumistic cases could be found in hospitals for hysterical patients or in wards for the mentally unbalanced. The trouble is that experiments tending to ascertain the truth of such a theory are never tried. Had not Dr.

Ochorowicz been interested in things psychic, Mlle. Tomczyk would simply have been cured by him in the general routine manner and dismissed. The world would thus have been deprived of one of the most remarkable mediums on record!

In the second place, these fluidic hands are almost identical in many ways with those presented by Eusapia Palladino at her best. The materialized hands, of varying degrees of density and formation, attached to long, shadowy arms, are exactly like the hands so often materialized at her séances—hands which are at times small, and at other times enormous. They no more resembled the hands of the medium than chalk resembles cheese.

16. This brings me to a final reflection, which I should like to mention before leaving this branch of our discussion. It concerns the question of darkness and its effect upon genuine mediumistic phenomena. Whether this effect be primarily physical, physiological, or psychological, the *fact* remains that it exists; and the researches of Dr. Ochorowicz have tended to confirm this very strongly. His work has shown us (or rather confirmed us more strongly in the belief) that the question of *light* is a highly important one, and that the greater the degree of darkness, *ceteris paribus*, the better and the more startling the phenomena.

Now, there has always existed a sort of *a priori* assumption that this should be so. Light, as we know, does bring about chemical reactions, and even exerts a definite physical force or pressure. Even so gross and so powerful a form of physical energy as wireless telegraphy is greatly interfered with by reason of the sun's rays (ultra-violet rays), and, of course, photographic plates are at once rendered useless by an instant's exposure to the sun. Again, it is known that sunlight has a more or less destructive influence upon all forms of animal and vegetable protoplasm, and it is very soon fatal to many of the lower forms of life. This being so, it has always appeared to me perfectly reasonable to suppose that the energy of the light-rays should interfere most seriously with the delicate and subtle forces and forms of energy which are liberated in the séance room. The old objection: "Why must these things always be done in the dark?" has appeared to me very short-sighted and inconsistent with all the facts above mentioned.

But, further! It is highly probable that life of any kind can only originate in the dark. Certainly, conception invariably takes place in complete darkness, and the whole period of embryonic development is passed in that condition. Again, inter-stellar space is, of course, absolutely black and devoid of any form of light save the faint twinklings of the far-off stars. Without the surface of some globe to reflect the sun's rays, no light of any kind would be possible; so that if life were conveyed across space, from star to star, upon infinitesimal specks of dust, under the influence of light pressure, as postulated by Arrhenius (*Worlds in the Making*, pp. 212-30), this life must exist, and in a sense originate, in the blackness of inter-stellar space.[10] And, finally, if life on our globe originated, as many think, in the ocean's depths,[11] this must have been in the densest darkness, since light penetrates but a few fathoms below the surface of the ocean. Below that all is blackness, complete and eternal. No light penetrates to that depth—nor has it for millions of years! Yet it is in this region that life is thought to have originated! As G. W. Warder expressed it (*The Universe a Vast Electric Organism*, pp. 60-1):

"During this period of primeval 'darkness upon the face of the waters' the resistless electric waves of the sun were beating upon the cloud-enwrapped surface of the planet. It was the formative period of elementary life, and the descendants and successors of that mighty host of living beings have to this day to lay the foundations of their being in similar conditions of darkness. *Creative energy in its first stages of living form operates in dense darkness*, and the first life upon the planet began and perfected itself in the age when midnight gloom enveloped the globe."

This fact—that life originated in darkness, and that the power of life can only be exercised in darkness—is, it seems to me, a most significant one when viewed in the light of our studies, and seems to point to the conclusion that the "darkness" said to be essential at spiritistic circles is indeed necessary; and that, when delicate and subtle forms of life and energy are being manifested, they are likely to become disrupted by the sudden introjection of a coarse and powerful form of energy, such as light, so that this "condition," said to be necessary by all mediums, is probably in reality essential; and their claim, far from being absurd, is well founded, and in accordance with well-established scientific facts.

17. So far as to the physical phenomena. We must now turn to the mental manifestations, and discuss one or two points in connection with them before concluding.

Hitherto we have considered the process of communication (granting such to exist) solely from the physical and physiological sides, and not from the psychological. There is a great deal to be said in this latter connection, however, though I shall endeavour to be as brief as possible.

Take, for instance, the question of *symbolism*.

Our dreams, as we know, are largely symbolic, the work of Freud and others having proved this beyond all doubt. It is highly probable that the ravings of delirium are also of this nature, though no one, so far as I know, has yet devoted any serious attention to their study. Certainly it is true in mediumistic phenomena; for, in trance conditions, a larger number of messages, tests, and visions seen are of this nature and character—the symbolism often being so elaborate that the original thought is not perceived. As Mr. Coates remarked: "When a 'psychometer' places a geological specimen to his forehead, and describes an 'antediluvian monster,' roaring and walking about, no one but a very shallow individual would imagine for a moment that the psychometer was actually seeing the original," but rather that he obtained a faint and dream-like impression of the world at that epoch, and his subconscious impression was symbolized in the creature seen. A better example is, perhaps, furnished by the following: a gentleman of my acquaintance visited a certain trance-medium, and, among other things, she described a large key. This meant nothing to him at first; but later, and after some apparent effort, the medium succeeded in catching (and conveying) the idea that the key was symbolic of success—unlocking the door of happiness, etc.—whereupon all she had said fell naturally into place.

Why this symbolism? The probable answer to this question is that the "message" cannot be given *directly*, and that this symbolic method of presentation must be resorted to in order to get the message through at all. There is good evidence to show that a pictorial method is resorted to, very largely, by the *soi-disant* spirits—mediums seeing what they describe, very often, when the more direct auditory method is not resorted to. The "spirit" presents somehow to the mind of the medium a picture, which is described and often interpreted by the medium. Often this interpretation is quite erroneous—resembling a defective analysis of a dream. Because of this the message is not recognized. Yet the source of the message may have been perfectly "veridical."

Let me illustrate this a little more fully. Suppose you desired to tell a Chinaman, who spoke not a word of English, to fetch a certain object from the next room. It would be useless for you to say "watch," because he would not know what the word meant. Probably you would tap your waistcoat pocket, pretend to take out a watch, wind it, look at the hands, etc., in your endeavour to convey to him your meaning. If this was not recognized, for any reason, you would have the utmost difficulty in conveying your meaning to him—and equal difficulty in telling him to fetch the watch from the next room.

Now, suppose these antics—or somewhat similar ones—were resorted to by a "spirit" in his attempt to convey the word watch—perhaps to remind the sitter of a particular watch he used to wear. The medium might well proceed as follows: "He taps his stomach, and looks at a spot over his left side.... He seems to wish to convey the impression that he suffered much from his bowels—perhaps a cancer on the left side. Yes, he seems to be taking something away from his body; evidently they removed some growth, and he wishes to convey the idea that something was taken from him.... Now he is examining his hands; he is looking intently. He is doing something with his fingers.... I can't see what it is ... a little movement. Was he connected with machinery in life? Now he is pointing to the door ..." etc.

Such an interpretation of the facts, it will be observed, while describing all his actions, is wholly misleading in interpretation; the symbolism has been entirely perverted and misconstrued. And inasmuch as the subject probably never died of cancer, had no bowel trouble, underwent no operation, and was never connected with machinery, it is highly probable that the "message" would be put down wholly to the medium's subliminal, or even to guessing or conscious fraud. Yet, it will be observed, the message was, in its inception, wholly "veridical"—the fault lying in the erroneous symbolic interpretation of the medium.

There is evidence to show that other forms of symbolism are adopted also—applying to the auditory as well as to the visual presentation of the messages. *Names* afford some of the best evidence for this; e.g. in the sitting of Mrs. Verrall with Mrs. Thompson, November 2, 1899 (*Proceedings*, xvii. pp. 240-41), "Nelly," the control, gave the names "Merrifield, Merriman, Merrythought, Merrifield," and later went on: "I am muddled. I will tell you how names come to us. It's like a picture; I see school-children enjoying themselves; you can't say Merrimans, because that's not a name, nor merry people...." (Mrs. Verrall's maiden name was Merrifield.) If I remember correctly, there was similar symbolism with regard to the name Greenfield at another sitting.

18. Here, then, we see the full play of symbolism and its possible extension to cover proper names. But there is another and a very simple reason why names should be hard to recall and give clearly by "spirits." Names are proverbially hard to remember, even in this life—and we know that some persons naturally remember names far better than others. (This may account, to a certain extent, for the differences in the ability of communicators to give proper names.) But, with all of us, names are hard to recall. We all resort to "what's-his-names," and "thing-o'-my-jigs," on occasion, in our efforts to discover within us the name in question. And there are good physiological reasons for this. We learn names only after many other parts of speech—which means that the brain-cells corresponding thereto are laid down or brought into conscious activity *last*; they are therefore more ephemeral and less fundamental than others— hence the first to "go." This accounts for the increasing difficulty in the aged for remembering names—theirs is a physiological rather than a psychological defect. By analogy, therefore, there is every reason to believe

that proper names are hard to recall—every reason for thinking that they should be—by "spirits" after the shock and wrench of death. The necessary psychical mechanism would be so shaken and disturbed that it would be impossible to recall names and events, which seem quite straightforward and simple to the sitter. The possibly pictorial method of presentation of proper names would greatly add to the difficulty, as we have seen, and would be liable to lead to misrepresentation and error.

19. Dr. Hyslop, in his second report on Mrs. Piper, (*Proceedings*, Amer. S.P.R., pp. 1-812), calls attention to certain analogies which may be drawn from everyday psychology, rendering the process of communication far more intelligible, and the difficulties within the process far clearer to our perception and appreciation. For example, he calls attention to certain analogies with aphasia, which are most instructive. He says, in part:

"The two traditional types of aphasia are motor and sensory. Sensory aphasia is the inability to interpret the meaning of a sensation ... motor aphasia is the inability to speak a word or language, though the ideas and meaning of sensations may be as clear as in normal life.... This latter difficulty is apparent in several types of phenomena purporting to be associated with communications from spirits. I have found them illustrated in four different cases of mediumship, and they may be represented in three types. They are: (*a*) The difficulties with proper names; (*b*) The difficulties with unfamiliar words; and (*c*) The inability to immediately answer a pertinent question....

"The analogies with aphasia, of which we are speaking, may comprise various conditions affecting both medium and communicator. Thus the abnormal physical and mental conditions involved in the trance may affect the integrity of the normal motor action. Then the new situation in which death places a communicator, in relation to any nervous system, may establish conditions very much like aphasia. Then there may be difficulties in the communicator's representing his thoughts in the form necessary to transmit them to and through a foreign organism."

Dr. Hyslop then offers the following diagram as a possible solution of certain difficulties involved:

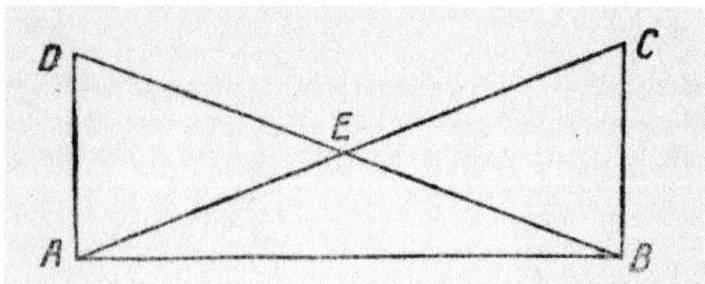

A B C represents the normal consciousness; A B D the subliminal consciousness. They intersect at E, which point represents the "equilibrium of the controls." "The area A E B shows the condition in which all sorts of confusion may occur, incidental to the infusion of controls, and this confusion will vary with the relation with the supraliminal and subliminal action of the mind." As one advances, the other recedes. As one gains a greater control over the organism, the other loses it, and *vice versa.*

Extending this conception to cover the cases of spirit "possession," in which this varying and fluctuating control is also manifested, we might represent this by the above diagram, in which normal consciousness is left out of account, for the sake of clearness, and the trance condition (subliminal) only represented. The spirit control of the organism takes its place in the diagram.

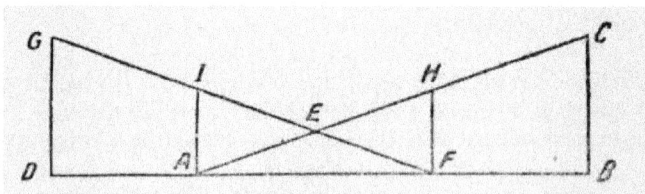

Here A B C represents the trance state—the subliminal consciousness. G D F represents the sphere of the spirit's control. It does not begin at all until the point F be reached. The space A E F represents the area in which all kinds of confusion is possible, and it is within this area that most of the mediumistic messages come. E is the "point of balance." A F H represents the amount of subliminal action accessible to the control, on the one hand, and related to the discarnate, on the other, in its *rapport.* A F represents the amount of the discarnate personality which is accessible to communication, so we have two fields which are wholly inaccessible to each other, and are respectively represented by B C H F and D G I A, the former a portion of the subliminal personality of the living and the latter a portion of the discarnate personality which cannot reveal itself.

This intermediate area, in which the control is liable to vary, and be thrown on to one side or the other, also has an analogy in the *hypnoidal state* of Boris Sidis—this being an intermediate state (so it is thought) which is convertible either into ordinary sleep, on the one hand, or into hypnotic sleep on the other. It all depends upon how this state is handled and controlled. It may be the same here; the medium may sink into internal reverie, or introspective trance; or she may be converted into a genuine "medium" by some influence exerted upon her from without.

20. On this theory, the deeper the trance the greater the control by the "spirit," and this corresponds very well with what has been said before. There are always a number of obstacles to clear communication, and the degree to which these are overcome would represent the degree of clearness of the communications. The process of transferring a mental picture to the medium may be attended with all kinds of difficulties of which we know nothing. Assuming, for the sake of argument, that there is a sort of etheric body, or double, and that this is in any way involved in the process, we might have the following "difficulties" to encounter: The difficulty in picturing the event clearly in the communicator's mind; difficulty in transferring it to the light; difficulty in getting this transferred to the medium's physical body; the difficulty of manipulating the latter. We know that we often have great difficulty in manipulating our own bodies properly; and, in paralysis and kindred affections, we are unable to do so at all. Yet we are thoroughly familiar with our own bodies, and know how they work. How much more difficult would it be if we were suddenly transplanted in *another* person's body, and had to manipulate *that*? We should have to "learn the ropes," so to say; and all the little automatic tricks, and habits, and slips of speech, and what not, would be liable to slip out without our consent and before we knew it. We should "inherit," in fact, its whole psychological and physiological "setting." This being the case, we may readily see how difficult it would be for a discarnate spirit to manipulate another organism; and how likely it would be to allow certain tricks and habits of the medium herself to slip through, without being able to control them. As one communicator said, through Mrs. Chenoweth: "I do not like those 'don'ts'; they are hers, not mine." Here is a clear recognition of the difficulty involved in controlling the organism, and this is greatly accentuated when we remember that all such communications must be given when the *soi-disant* communicator is in a constrained mental attitude—"gripping the light," "hanging on to the medium's body," while giving the communications. There is a double strain involved; and, as Dr. Hyslop said: "With what facility could I superintend the work of helping a drowning person and talk philosophy at the same time? How well could I hold a plough in stony ground and discuss protection and free-trade?" It is

small wonder that the messages should be fragmentary and incomplete, were any such difficulties as these experienced!

The three chief difficulties involved in mediumistic messages may be summed-up under three headings: (1) intra-mediumistic conditions; (2) intra-cosmic conditions; and (3) the mental conditions of the communicators.

Under the first head may be placed all those difficulties which are liable to interfere between the communicator and the amanuensis. If the communicator is naturally a good visualizer this may help his visual communications, but impede the others; an audile might be better in some instances. Again, the impulse may come in some motor form, in which case neither of these types would be that best suited to control the organism of the medium. Whether the communicator is a good visualizer or not may affect the communications to a great extent. Whether or not he had a normally good memory would also have a great influence. In fact, the whole construction of the mind might have great influence upon the results. This is a subject which deserves to be studied very carefully one day, when the mere fact of communication is established.

As is well known, both Drs. Hodgson and Hyslop wrote strongly in defence of the theory that the communicator, at the time of communicating, was in an abnormal mental condition, somewhat resembling trance or delirium or secondary personality. They were, at least, not in full control of their thoughts; and this was said to be established by the statements of the communicators themselves; and by a study of the messages communicated, wherein it was found that they became dreamy and vague; that they showed the same rapid change of imagery and subject which is manifested in dreams; an automatic tendency to capricious and confused association, a general indifference to personality, etc., as manifested in delirium. In dreams and sleep we have practically no control over the body at all, any more than if we were dead; and Dr. Hyslop contended that probably "somnambulism and hypnosis, dreaming, sleep, trance conditions, and death are all simply different degrees of the same state." Dr. Hyslop during his later years modified his views upon this question, and came to the conclusion that other conditions play a greater share in the results than the state of the communicator's mind. But there can be no doubt that this has its results.

Then, too, the medium's subliminal has a great and very decided influence upon the content of the messages. This was very small before Dr. Hodgson's death, but increased very much after that time. In a letter to me, dated January 27, 1908, Mrs. Ledyard, an old Piper sitter, said:

"DEAR MR. CARRINGTON,—... All sorts of false statements don't necessarily tell against the spiritistic hypothesis. If you get other evidences of personality, the false statements only confirm R. H.'s belief that "they" are in a sort of dreamy, half-trance state and *very suggestible*. My own opinion of the Piper trance is that, since R. H.'s death, when Mrs. P. has been less carefully guarded in many ways, and allowed to have so much voice in what she would and would not do, that there is much more effect of Mrs. Piper herself on the trance—and more *leaks through* from Mrs. Piper—though I have, so far, seen no special evidence that it leaks the other way, and that what is told her by sitters during the trance gets into the normal consciousness. But it does affect her normal life, just as an hypnotic suggestion does, on which the subject acts quite unconscious of its source...."

But Rector's[12] business seems to be more far-reaching and more complicated than this. I quote from Dr. Hyslop's second Piper report (p. 197) the following interesting passage:

"I may notice a remark Dr. Hodgson once made to me regarding the office of Rector in the phenomena of Mrs. Piper. It was not only as control that he exercised an influence over the results, but also both as intermediary between the communicator and the sitter, and as an inhibitor of the influence of the sitter's mind and the subconsciousness of Mrs. Piper upon this same result.... His view was that Rector inhibited the thought-transference from the sitter to Mrs. Piper's subliminal, on the messages, so far as that was possible...."

From this it will, at all events, be seen that the relationship, and the whole system of inhibitions and influences at work in the Piper case is very complicated. It must be remembered that, on any theory, the "messages" must come *through* the medium's subliminal, which acts as a sort of matrix in which the whole mould of the supernormal is cast; and, this being the case, it is only natural to suppose that the results would be most complicated and inextricably mixed in their relationships and influences. If spirit communications influence the subconscious, we have a right to suppose that the subliminal influences the communications in turn. And this is apparently proved by the facts.

21. Now a few words as to the psychological processes of communicating, and the interplay of minds one with another, which figure in this process. Writing of this, Dr. Hyslop says:

"Psychology distinguishes between what it calls visuals, audiles, and motiles. A visual is one in which visual experiences receive such emphasis, and which prove to be of such predominant interest to the subject that his habit of thinking about objects is expressed mentally or mnemonically in visual terms—that is, in the memory pictures of vision.... An audile is one in whom the sense of hearing is predominant. [In motiles the impulse is towards motor action.]

"Suppose the psychic is a visual and the communicator an audile, might not that difference make a marked difficulty in the adjustment necessary for communicating clearly?... A visual might see apparitions more easily, and have more difficulty in automatic writing; and an audile might easily hear voices and write with more difficulty, etc.... A proper name is purely an auditory concept. It has no visual equivalent whatever, except the letters which form it. If, then, the process of communication at any time involves a dominant dependence on visual functions of the mind, the sudden attempt to interpose an auditory datum might meet with the difficulty of prompt adjustment to auditory conditions for its transmission, and it might even be that the psychic could not, from habit in visual methods, adjust herself to all the needs of a proper name, except by converting it readily into visual terms, as the spelling of the name would express....

"In the lighter trance it is clear that visual phenomena play a most important part in the communications. With Mrs. Piper the phenomena seem to be more auditory. Mrs. Piper never sees apparitions or phantasms in her normal state; none have been reported of her as systematic experiences, as I have observed them in Mrs. Chenoweth....

"What we gain in clearness of consciousness in the communications when the message comes through the active subliminal of the medium, we lose in the accuracy and specific value of the message, while what we gain in the specific definiteness of the messages through Mrs. Piper, where the subliminal, if intermediary at all, is passive and automatic, we lose in the dream-like and disturbed mental state of the communicator."

22. Another difficulty must be referred to in this place; and that is the probable loss of control over the stream of thought by spirits, such as we exercise in this life. Here, the checks and inhibitions are easily accomplished, unless disease in some manner prevents them; but there are strong indications that a "spirit"—at least when communicating—cannot control his stream of thinking to the same extent; and that, if it is constantly interrupted—by questions, etc., as it usually is—it tends to break up and become automatic, echolalic, or useless. That even experienced and careful psychic researchers will interfere with the flow of consciousness in this manner I know to be a fact; I myself, though I had been especially warned against doing so, did the same thing in my Piper sittings! Some of these difficulties I endeavoured to make clear in a letter, which I wrote to the English *Journal S.P.R.*, and which appeared in March, 1908. In it I said:

"For the sake of argument, let us assume that the intelligences that communicate through the organism of Mrs. Piper—and perhaps of some other mediums—are spirits of the departed, and that they temporarily 'possess' the organism of the medium (at least in part) during the process of communicating. That is the generally-held theory, I believe, and the simplest one to account for the facts. If this be true, it is to be supposed that the normal consciousness of the medium is in some manner removed, superseded, or withdrawn, and that only some "vegetable consciousness" remains, as it were, sufficient to keep the organism going until the return of the normal consciousness and normal control by the medium. Meanwhile, the controlling intelligence is, by supposition, influencing the nervous mechanism of the medium's body—directly or indirectly through some etheric medium—and influencing it to write out letters and words by the usual slow and laborious process. That they *do* find it slow and laborious is evidenced by the fact that all possible abbreviations are adopted—'U.D.' being used for 'Understand'; 'M' is frequently written 'N,' and so on. Even in our normal life we know that thoughts frequently flow faster than we can put them on to paper, and this would almost certainly be the case with spiritual intelligences who have no material brain to hinder their flow of thought. It is probable that the brain is as much an inhibitory organ as anything else; and when this inhibition is removed, it is natural to suppose that the flow of thought would be far less controllable and far more automatic than it is with us. It would be impossible for spirits to check and go on with their stream of thought at will, as we do on this hypothesis; they would be far more automatic and less under the control of the will. If this were true, it would account for much of the confusion present in the communications. Suppose a spirit is trying to communicate some fact or incident in its past life. It is endeavouring to force this thought through, in the face of great difficulties, and while trying to retain its grasp of the organism. Now, let us suppose that this stream of thought is suddenly interrupted by the sitter asking an abrupt question—referring to another incident altogether, and perhaps related to another time in the communicator's life. Is it not natural to suppose that, labouring under these difficulties, and lacking the inhibitory action of the brain, the communicator's mind should wander, and that he should either think aloud to himself as it were (all this coming through as confused writing, be it understood), or that the spirit should lose its grasp of the organism altogether and drift away? The mind cannot retain two vivid pictures at the same time; either one or the other must grow fogged and dim; and this would certainly be so in the case of any communicator, where we may suppose a certain amount of mental energy—corresponding to a mental picture perhaps—is necessitated in the very process of holding the control of the organism. If communications take place at all in reality, we may well suppose that the difficulties of communicating would be so great that all clear, systematic thinking would be impossible. People seem to imagine that the process of communication is as simple as possible, instead of the most delicate and complicated imaginable—the very difficulty being evinced by the rarity of the intelligible communications coming through. If any one were to try the simple subjective test of closing the eyes and attempting to conceive his spirit controlling some *other* person's organism, he would very easily perceive the tremendous difficulties in the way of controlling an organism other than his own!

"However, my object in writing this letter is not to point out difficulties of this character, which are probably well understood by the majority of the readers of the *Journal*. It is to draw attention to another fact, and an analogy. Let us take a man in good health, whose brain and mental functions are normal. Let this man be all but killed in a railroad accident. In the jar and shock of the collision this man was thrown (let us say) against an iron post, and his head badly cut and bruised. He was knocked insensible, and it was several hours before he returned to the first dim consciousness of his surroundings. Gradually he would revive. Objects would present themselves to his eyesight vaguely, indistinctly; he would "see men as trees walking." Sounds would be heard, but indistinctly; there would be a vague jumble of noises, and no definite and articulate sounds would be recognized at first, and until consciousness was more fully restored. Tactile sensations, smell and touch, would probably come last, and be least powerful of all; they would not be even distinguishable until consciousness was almost completely normal. All intellectual interests would be abolished, only the most loving and tender thoughts would be entertained or tolerable, and these would be swallowed up, very largely, in the great, central fact that the body and head were in great pain; that the memory was impaired, and that anything like normal thinking and a normal grasp of the organism was impossible. Thoughts would be scattered, incoherent, and only the strongest stimuli would focus the attention on any definite object for longer than a few moments at a time, and perhaps even these would fail. But if oxygen gas were administered to such a person, in moderate doses, he would recover and rally far more quickly and effectually than if no such stimulant were employed. He would rally more quickly, and be enabled to think more clearly and consistently—at least *pro tem*. In shocks to the living consciousness this would almost certainly be the case.

"Now, when we come to die, the departure of the soul from the body must be a great strain and stress upon the surviving consciousness, and must shock it tremendously—just as the accident shocked it in the case given above. Certainly this would be so in the case of all *sudden* deaths, and in those cases which 'die hard'; and it is natural to suppose that it would be true also, more or less, in every case of death, however natural—since the separation of consciousness from its brain must be the greatest shock that any given consciousness could receive in the course of its natural existence. But after a time the spirit is supposed to outlive and 'get over' this initial shock, and to regain its normal functions and faculties. In its normal life, it is then supposed to be once more free and unhampered by any of the bodily conditions that rendered its manifestations on earth defective. But when this consciousness comes once more to communicate, it seems to again take on the conditions of earth life, i.e. those conditions which were present when the person died, and this would account for the fact, often observed, that mediums 'take on' the conditions of certain spirits who are communicating, i.e. they suffer *pro tem.* from heart or bowel trouble, pains in the head, etc. Further, this seems to extend to the mental functions and conditions also. Idiocy and insanity, e.g., are supposed to gradually wear off in the next life, and a gradual return to normal conditions ensue. This is, at least, the statement made through several mediums, and it is only natural to suppose that such should be the case. The spirit gradually returns to a normal mental condition; but when any attempt is made to return to the 'earth plane,' and especially to communicate, these conditions return with greater or lesser force—varying with and depending upon the length of time such a person had been dead, and other considerations. On any theory, the consciousness must undergo some sort of temporary disintegration, while communicating, and must be scattered over a wide field of recollection, while at the same time attempting to 'hold on' to the organism. It must also be remembered that the flow of thought is far more automatic than with us. All this being so, we can readily understand that any attempt at communication would be attended with the greatest difficulties, and such a consciousness, if it were constantly interrupted by questions, etc., would tend to go to pieces—to lose its grasp of the organism, and to drift away—only confusion and error coming through. This consciousness might be strengthened and rendered clearer, perhaps, by the presentation of some object belonging to the person when alive—as, no matter how explained, this seems to clear the communications. Any means that can be adopted to render clearer the mind of the communicator, on the one hand, or improve the condition of the nervous mechanism of the medium on the other, should therefore be of great utility and should at least be tried. This being so, I now come to the heart of the matter, and offer a suggestion which, if followed out, might improve the physical body of the medium, and hence render the conditions better from *this* side—as the presentation of objects might be supposed to render the conditions better from the other side.

"I have pointed out before that, in certain cases, when it is desirable to restore the consciousness and to render its renewal more certain and clear (after an accident, e.g., that has knocked a person senseless) a mixture of oxygen gas is sometimes administered to the patient in order to produce these results. This being so, I ask: why may it not be a good idea to administer a diluted mixture of this gas to the medium when she is in a trance state—and when a communicator is attempting to convey his thought to the sitter by means of automatic writing? Might not such an experiment be tried, since no *harm* could come to the medium if the oxygen were diluted and only sufficiently strong to effect the desired results? And might not its administration tend to improve the tone of the nervous system *pro tem.*, and render clearer the consciousness that is trying to use it and manifest through it—just as one's own consciousness might be rendered clearer by the same device? Of course such a process might have the effect (especially at first) of breaking the trance altogether, and of reviving the medium. But if the medium understood the experiment beforehand, and the process were also explained to the controls, it is reasonable to suppose that—after some trials at any rate—the trance would not be broken, and that better, clearer results would follow. At all events, when some of our physicians in America are experimenting upon the effects of various electrical rays upon mediums in a trance, might not this far simpler and better-understood method be tried with more or less impunity? I at least suggest that it be so tried."

23. It must not be thought that this "possession" theory of the Piper and similar cases is the only one which has been held in the past. On the contrary, as we know, there have been several others—Mrs. Sidgwick's telepathic theory—from the discarnate; Mr. Andrew Lang's theory of telepathy *à trois*; Mr. Podmore's theory of simple telepathy; the theory held by Andrew Jackson Davis and other clairvoyants, that there exists a sort of mirror-like sphere, upon which all thoughts and acts are recorded, and which the medium is somehow enabled to "read" during the trance state; the theory that discarnate spirits somehow project their thoughts upon a wax-like surface of astral substance, and that the medium is enabled to reinterpret them in some mysterious manner; the Theosophical theory; the theory of the occultists and mystics; the Catholic theory—that these manifestations are all the result of evil, lying spirits—these are but a few of the hypotheses which have been advanced in the past by way of explanation of these phenomena. I may say that this latter theory has some respectable evidence in its support, by the way, a few very remarkable cases having come under my own observation, which I hope to detail at some future time; and Dr. J. Godfrey Raupert has cited some impressive cases in his *Dangers of Spiritualism, Modern Spiritism,* and *The Supreme Problem.* This is assuredly a side of psychic investigation which demands close study and prolonged investigation; and, in spite of the masterly analysis of some of these cases by Professor Flournoy in his *Spiritism and Psychology* (chap. iii.), I

cannot but feel that there is yet much to be learned as to the nature of the intelligence manifested in these cases. And this was, as we know, the opinion also of Professor William James, for he wrote (*Proceedings of S.P.R.*, vol. xxiii. p. 118): "The refusal of modern 'enlightenment' to treat 'possession' as a hypothesis to be spoken of as even possible, in spite of the massive human tradition based on concrete experience in its favour, has always seemed to me a curious example of the power of fashion in things scientific. That the demon theory (not necessarily a devil theory) will have its innings again is to my mind absolutely certain.... One must be blind and ignorant indeed to suspect no such possibility...." It must by no means be taken for granted, therefore, that the intelligences operating through Mrs. Piper and other mediums are all that they claim to be, even if their externality to the medium were proved.... We must be extremely cautious in accepting any messages coming through mediums until the most certain and convincing proofs of identity be forthcoming—and *then* we should be cautious!

The only plausible theory which in any way accounts for the Piper and similar phenomena—short of the spiritistic—is one based upon the existence of independently fluctuating strata of the medium's mind, acquiring their knowledge by means of telepathy, clairvoyance, and other supernormal means. This view of the case is held and defended with extreme ingenuity and persuasiveness by Professor Flournoy in his *Spiritism and Psychology*—a book which I myself think should be read by every one interested in psychics or inclined to "dabble in spiritualism." The complete isolation and individuality of the various personalities involved could only be explained, it seems to me, by postulating a series of subliminal strata, between which there would be no memory connection—very much like Mr. Gurney's strata obtained by him and described in his paper on "The Stages of Hypnotic Memory" (*Proceedings*, vol. iv. pp. 515-31). In this way alone could we account for the facts; but even so, are they explained?

When psychical research becomes a recognized science there will be ample room for "specialization," and for many years of study in each branch of the work. Consider, for instance, the many ramifications and possibilities which would be thrown open to the researcher! A man might become a "specialist" in haunted houses, in the investigation of such cases, and in their "treatment" and "cure." He would then have to investigate the nature and character of the phenomena which occur in them, and of the intelligences which manifest themselves. The nature of the figures seen in such houses would form a special branch of research, and the degree of their objectivity or subjectivity in any particular case. Numerous experiments might be tried, such as crystal-gazing, automatic writing, séances, induced dreams, etc. Experiments should be tried in photographing the apparitions, and in getting them to register their presence upon delicate and sensitive instruments of all sorts. Phonographic records of the "footsteps" of the ghost (if such occur) should be made, and a record taken of all the sounds and noises which occur in the house. Clairvoyants should be sent on "trips" to ascertain the character of the haunting, if possible, in order to "check off" their descriptions against the experiences of those living in the house. Communication should be established with the "haunting spirits," if possible, by means of raps, table-tipping, etc. The character of the phenomena should be studied, and the *physical* separated from the *mental*. The nature of the intelligence "haunting" the house should be investigated psychologically. The dreams of those who sleep in the house should be recorded and analysed. Animals should be taken to live in the house, to see whether or not they perceive anything unusual. The effect of suggestion, exorcism, etc., should be tried and noted. Experiments in hypnotism, "magnetism," etc., should be conducted in the house. Red lights and lights of other colours should be tried, to see whether they affect the phenomena in any manner. These are but a few of the many tests and experiments that might be made, and which would doubtless suggest themselves to the mind of the investigator as soon as the legitimacy of the subject were once granted.

Again, in the case of telepathy. Once the facts were proved, the fascinating study of the laws and causes would begin. Under what mental, physical, and, possibly, spiritual conditions does telepathy operate? What is the best mental condition of the agent? of the percipient? What would be the effect of hypnotic trance? What of dreams? (These are not original ideas, but they have never been followed out as they should be, and might be, if the subject were pursued scientifically as other questions in science are.) Again, might not telepathy be facilitated if we chose individuals of the same general temperament? If we chose two individuals to whom the same chord on the piano appealed (say the common chord of G minor or C sharp), and this chord were struck repeatedly, might not telepathic transmission be facilitated under such conditions? If both subjects were hypnotized, and the agent were told to "will" certain figures, etc., might not the percipient receive them more easily? If both agent and percipient were placed in a strong magnetic or high-tension electric field, might not this in some way influence communication? Again, these are but a very few of the experiments which might be tried, once telepathy became an accepted fact.

In the case of clairvoyance the field is even greater, but here more original work has been done, owing largely to the fact that many of the experiments have been conducted upon subjects in the hypnotic trance, and hence more fully resembled "laboratory experiments." Still, much remains to be done, particularly in the realm of the *explanation* of clairvoyance, and in the investigation of the neural and general physiological concomitants of the condition.

In the field of "thought-" and "spirit-photography," the possibilities of research and experimentation are obvious and almost unlimited. The recent researches of Dr. Ochorowicz in "radiographs," and of Commandant Darget in thought-photography and the so-called V-rays, are of extreme importance, if true. Here is a field which any one may invade; and, with the aid of a camera and specially sensitive plates, might accomplish really valuable and striking results. Very rarely have attempts been made to photograph apparitions (probably because they were too fleeting and unexpected), and the forms at séances have been photographed on only a few occasions. The human "aura"—granting it exists—should certainly be capable of being photographed, under certain conditions, as well as the radiation said to issue from magnets, crystals, etc., as explained by Reichenbach.

The human "aura" itself should be made the subject of special study. Here is a perfectly tangible thing, so to speak, which physicists can work on to their hearts' content, without becoming "contaminated" by the general run of psychic manifestations! Is the aura a form of physical radiation? Does it affect the atmosphere? Can it be photographed? Is it connected with the phenomena of exteriorization of sensitivity or motivity? Will it affect the galvanometer needle, or other delicate electrical or physical instruments? Is it connected with the "astral" or "etheric body"? What is its condition when the subject is asleep? Can it be altered at will? Is it affected by passing a high-tension current through the body of the subject? (We know that these high-tension currents will themselves create an electric aura around the body.) What becomes of the aura after death; and what changes, if any, does it undergo at the moment of death? Such are a few of the questions which the psychic student might ask himself, and which certainly call for solution.

Once more: is "psychometry" a fact? If objects can retain certain "influences" within them, what is their nature, and how are they retained? How does the sensitive perceive these impressions? Is there not a connection between these phenomena and haunted houses? or between the "charging-up" of a table or planchette board before it proceeds to answer questions and behave in the manner it is often reported to do?

What is the nature of the "cold breeze" which is so often experienced, not only at séances, but during very many psychic phenomena, both of the experimental and spontaneous types, in all parts of the world? Is it a physical breeze, or is it purely "psychical"? Could it be collected and analysed, as was suggested in the case of the cold breeze issuing from the scar on Eusapia Palladino's forehead? What is its source? And what is its object? On this subject alone much suggestive and valuable research might be undertaken.

Take the simple phenomena of *raps*. What produces them? What is the bond between the hand of the medium which makes a gesture in the direction of the table, and the table itself? What is the nature of the physical impact upon the table? Are these raps due to exteriorized vital force? If so, does this energy exude from the nerve termini, or is it connected only with the etheric body or double? Can these raps be controlled at will, or directed and controlled when the subject is under hypnosis? Can this energy be directed at will? Could it not impress delicate physical instruments? Might not a connection be thus established between these phenomena and the impressions of hands and faces, etc., occasionally seen in the presence of Eusapia and other mediums?

Then the phenomena of materialization! Here is a wide field for study indeed! How can such an organism be built up? Out of what materials is it constructed? What degree of density can be attained? What is the power which manipulates this matter? and what is the structure of the matter itself? How can *will* plastically mould matter in space? On what framework, so to speak, is the body constructed? What is the nature of the vital drain upon the medium and the sitters? What is the nature of the intelligence animating the materialized figure? What is the connection between so-called "thought-forms" and materialized phantoms?

These are but some of the questions which would suggest themselves, and call for solution when "psychics" is recognized as a legitimate science, as it surely will be one day. These are problems mostly on the physical plane; but the psychological problems are just as many and just as alluring! I have referred to some of these elsewhere; and would content myself with again saying, that only when the *facts* of psychical research are recognized will their real, scientific study begin.

FOOTNOTES:

[1] The copy of this book in my possession is the copy once owned by Dr. Hodgson—having his name in the front, and the date, April 1881. This passage is marked with a thick red pencil stroke, showing the importance which Dr. Hodgson attached to the point here made.

[2] Might not this account for the fact that trance or "spirit control" practically never occurs during the hours of sleep? Even "obsessed" patients find peace and rest during their sleeping hours. Is this not, in all probability, due to the fact that the mind is, at such times, forced in upon itself; as it were—instead of being directed outwards—away from the

centre of being, as it is daily, during conscious life? It is probably nature's protective device—ensuring the stability and integrity of the psychic "self."

[3] Kilner, *The Human Atmosphere*. I myself have conducted a number of interesting experiments in this direction, which I hope to make public at a later date.

[4] Townsend, *Facts in Mesmerism*, p. 215.

[5] *Metaphysick*, bk. iii. ch. v.

[6] *Body and Mind*, pp. 299-300.

[7] *Eusapia Palladino and her Phenomena*, pp. 293-301.

[8] *Vitality, Fasting and Nutrition*, p. 41. For discussions of this question from a variety of different points of view, see *Life and Matter*, by Lodge; *The Riddle of the Universe*, Haeckel; *The Correlation of Spiritual Forces*, by Hartmann; "Consciousness and Force," *Met. Mag.*, Oct. 1910; the article on "Consciousness and Energy," by Professor Montague, in *Essays in Honour of William James*, and pp. 283-5 of *The New Realism*, etc.

[9] Bulwer Lytton, with his usual remarkable foresight in things psychic, clearly perceived this. In his story, "The Haunters and the Haunted," he says: "In all that I had witnessed, and indeed in all the wonders which the amateurs of mystery in our age record as facts, a material human agency is always required. On the Continent you will still find magicians who assert that they can raise spirits. Assume for a moment that they assert truly, still the living, material form of the magician is present, and he is the material agency by which, from some constitutional peculiarities, certain strange phenomena are represented to your natural senses.... Accept again as truthful the tales of spirit manifestation in America, produced by no discernible hand—articles of furniture moved about without visible human agency—or the actual sight and touch of hands to which no bodies seem to belong—still there must be found the "medium," or living being, with constitutional peculiarities capable of obtaining these signs. In fine, in all such marvels, supposing even that there is no imposture, there must be a human being like ourselves, by whom, or through whom, the effects presented to human beings are produced."

[10] It should be said, however, that—apart from its innate difficulties—this theory has recently received its death-blow by the discovery of the fact that space is filled with ultra-violet rays, which would soon prove fatal to all forms of life.

[11] See, especially, Duncan, *Some Chemical Problems of Today*, pp. 63-83 and 97-104.

[12] "Rector" is the name of Mrs. Piper's chief control and amanuensis, during her trance sittings.

CHAPTER II

INVESTIGATING PSYCHICAL PHENOMENA WITH
SCIENTIFIC INSTRUMENTS

It is generally conceded that Aristotle possessed the greatest single intellect the world has ever known; yet any schoolboy today knows more of the structure of our universe than did Aristotle! The reason for this is that Science has more fully penetrated the secrets of Nature, and we now know approximately the constitution of matter and a good deal concerning life and mind. How has this progress been possible? Only in one way. Improvement in the *mechanical instruments* by means of which we study Nature. We might "speculate" as to the constitution of matter for a thousand years, but we should never have arrived at our present positive *knowledge* had it not been for the delicate and sensitive instruments which are today in the hands of the physicist and the chemist, and employed by him in his laboratory.

Doubtless much the same law will be found to apply in the realm of "psychics." Until we can apply definite "laboratory methods," and study psychical phenomena by means of physical instruments far more delicate than our senses, it is probable that the present state of things will continue to exist; but it is my firm belief that, were a laboratory fitted up with physical and electrical apparatus, suitable for this work, and if we could by their aid study a promising case of "psychic" or "mediumistic" phenomena, we should (within ten years or so) arrive at some definite conclusions! We should then know something about the *laws* and conditions under which telepathy, clairvoyance, telekinesis (the movement of objects without contact), et cetera, operate, and not until this is done, I believe, will such positive conclusions be reached.

Of course the reader may object, just here, that I am assuming such phenomena to be *true*—while the tendency of many present-day scientists is to regard them as unreal, hallucinatory, and the result of fraud. I cannot spare the time in the present place to argue the point. While I admit freely that a very large percentage of such phenomena *are* so produced, and while I freely admit that probably 98 per cent of so-called "mediums" are fraudulent; I am equally emphatic in declaring that a residuum of genuine phenomena exists—that supernormal manifestations *do* occur, and that every one who investigates *carefully enough* and *long enough* will find them. This has been not only my own experience, but that of every person who has investigated this subject with an impartial mind for any length of time. As Sir Oliver Lodge said, in writing of this very question:

"The result of my experience is to convince me that certain phenomena, usually considered abnormal, *do* belong to the order of Nature, and as a corollary from this, that these phenomena ought to be investigated and recorded by persons and societies interested in natural knowledge."

Based on this conviction, Sir Oliver Lodge wrote, as far back as 1894, in a paper entitled "On Some Appliances Needed for a Psychical Laboratory":

"If the investigations are to go on easily and well, special appliances must be contrived and arranged conveniently for use, precisely as is done in any properly fitted laboratory. It has already doubtless been realized that one of the needs of the future is a *psychical laboratory*, specially adapted for all kinds of experimental psychology and psycho-physics...."

Sir Oliver Lodge suggested at the time, among other necessary appliances, a delicate registering balance,—so adjusted that it would record the medium's weight, unknown to her, at all times during the séance—the fluctuations in weight, if any, to be recorded on a revolving drum. Means ought also to be provided for studying the temperature, pulse, muscular exertion, breathing, etc., etc. The lighting of the room should be carefully attended to and capable of the slightest gradation. Means should be provided for obtaining moving pictures of the séance from without the room, unknown to the medium. Were the sittings held in complete darkness, these photographs could be obtained by means of ultra-violet light, with which the room might be flooded. In addition to these devices, we may add others—such as X-ray tubes, high-frequency currents and a delicate field of electric force,—while instruments for testing the ionization of the air (if it exists) in the immediate vicinity of the medium, during a séance, should also be employed,—together with the more strictly psychical instruments and devices which have been utilized of late years.

Electrical apparatus *has*, in fact, been utilized on several occasions to test so-called "physical mediums" in the past. Italian investigators, particularly, have excelled in this. In a series of séances conducted in Naples, the following apparatus was employed. (Fig. 1.)

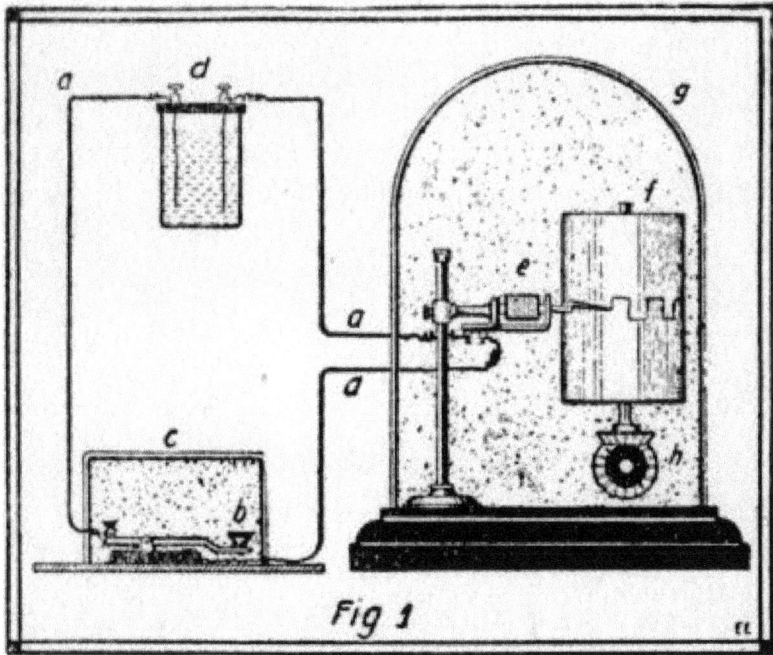

Fig 1

A telegraphic key (b) was connected by wires (a,a) to a battery (d) and to two screws, connecting them with an electro-magnet (e) to the opposite end of which was attached a needle. The point of the needle touched a revolving drum (f), with a smoked surface, driven by two interlacing, cogged wheels. The whole of this registering apparatus was enclosed under a glass bell-jar (g). The telegraphic key itself (b) was covered by a cardboard box (c). The "powers" manifesting were asked to press the telegraphic key *without* tearing the cardboard box (that is, *through* it). When the key was depressed, this would be instantly communicated to the electro-magnet, and cause the needle to oscillate,—these oscillations being marked upon the smoked surface of the revolving drum. A number of successful tests were conducted by means of this apparatus.

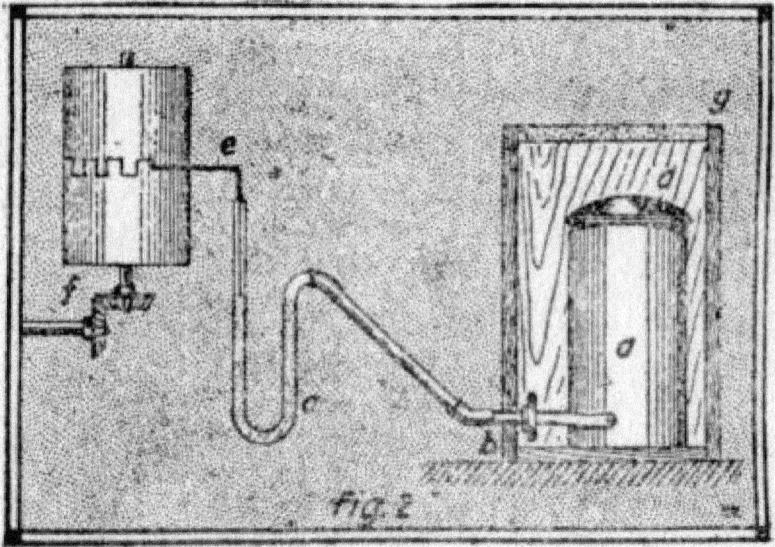

fig 2

A variation of this was then employed (Fig. 2). A cylinder filled with water (a) was connected by means of tubing (b) to a U-tube, or manometer (c), filled with mercury. Upon the further side of this tube floated a bent wire (e) inserted into a small cork. The point of this wire, again, was so adjusted as to come into contact with the smoked surface of a revolving drum (f), driven as before. The top of the cylinder (a) was covered with a rubber cap (d), and this whole apparatus was inserted under a wooden box (g) having a cloth top.

Now, if the rubber covering (d) were pressed upon, this would force some of the water, in a, along the tube, b, and the added air-pressure would depress the column of mercury in the manometer, causing the floating needle to rise on the opposite side, and scratch upon the revolving drum. Fig. 3 shows some of the tracings which were obtained in this way—the force acting through the cloth top, g.

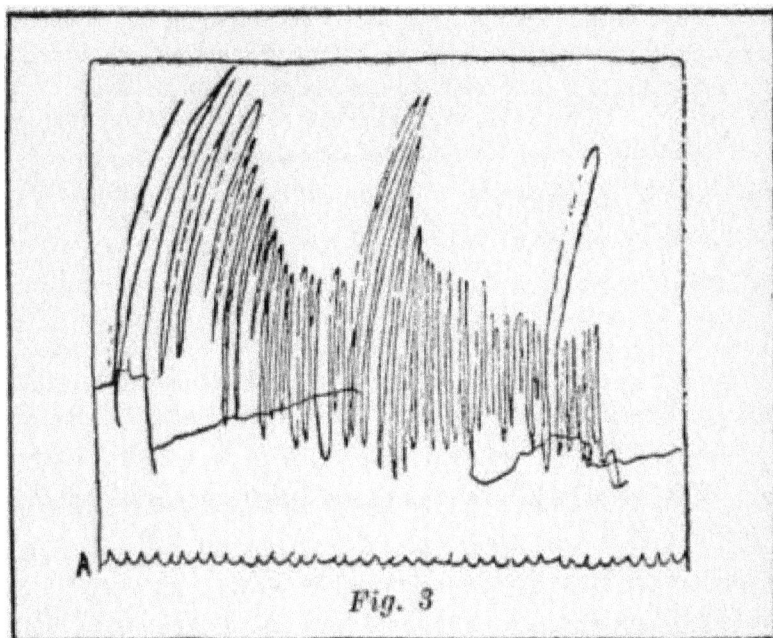

Fig. 3

The instruments thus recorded a *definite physical, intelligent force.*

It may interest my readers to know that, at the time of his death, M. Curie,—who had been completely convinced of the reality of these phenomena,—was busy devising an instrument which would register and direct *psychic power* liberated from the body of a physical medium when in trance.

Dr. Imoda, the assistant of Professor Mosso, has also conducted a number of experiments in the discharge of an electroscope, by means of "rays" issuing from the medium's body. It was found that, if the medium held her fingers at a distance of an inch or so from the knob of the electroscope, some form of energy, apparently *radio-active* in character, issued from her fingers, and *gradually discharged the electroscope.* This is the "radiation" or "emanation" issuing from the body, which has been studied extensively by students of the occult. Dr. Imoda concluded—as the result of his experiments—that "*the radiations of radium, the cathode radiations of the Crookes' tube, and mediumistic radiations are fundamentally the same.*"

Some other very interesting facts have been observed by means of the electroscope. For example, Dr. W. J. Crawford (D.Sc), in his experiments, noted that:—

"... In séance rooms where tables are moved without physical contact, I found that after a sitting was well started, I was always *unable* to charge an electroscope, even though I tried to do so in the corner of the chamber farthest from the medium. In order to charge it I had to take it outside the room. I asked the 'operators' (intelligences 'directing things,' apparently, in the séance-room) if there was any 'power' in the séance-room so far away from the medium, and they answered in raps that there was. By 'power' I understand them to mean particles of matter taken from the medium...."

Again, in his *Reality of Psychic Phenomena*, he says:

"I took the electroscope to the table in the corner; then placed it in the circle near the medium. I asked the operators to touch the disc of the instrument very gently. They did this almost at once, the 'touching' consisting of a metallic scraping upon the brass disc, quite audible, similar in type to the imitation of the floor being rubbed with sand paper, a phenomenon I quite often observed.

"Result:—On examination, the electroscope was found to be completely *discharged!*

"I took the electroscope to the table in the corner of the room and tried to recharge it, but found I was unable to do so even after repeated trials. Accordingly I asked the 'operators' to put back into the body of the medium the matter they had taken out (for the production of the sledge-hammer blows) and to give a few raps when they had done so. In a minute or two some *very light raps* were given, and when I asked if the process was complete I received *no raps in reply at all*, which seemed to indicate to me that all the matter used for rapping had been returned to the medium. At any rate, I found that I could now charge the electroscope; which done, I placed it on the floor as before within the circle, and asked that the disc should be touched lightly. After a little time, there was the metallic scraping as before, and on examination the electroscope was found to be completely *discharged.*"

It will be at once apparent to the reader that two problems confront the investigator, when once he is called upon to solve such problems as the above: (1) the *physical miracle* itself; and (2) the nature of the *intelligence*, lying behind and directing or controlling the manifestations. This latter is purely a *psychological* question, which, immensely important as it is intrinsically, does not enter into the *physical* problem. It need only be said that this is *the* baffling question in psychical investigation, and the most puzzling. Whether it be an independent "spirit," as it claims to be; or the subconsciousness of the medium; or whether it is a sort of compound consciousness, made up of the collected minds of those forming the circle at the time; or whether some other interpretation is open to us—this is all a moot question, which is referred to here, merely to draw attention to the fact of its existence.

It will be at once apparent to the reader, also, that physical and electrical apparatus have played an important part in such investigations, in the past, and are certainly destined to occupy a far more important place in the future. These curious phenomena—like all others in our world—depend upon invisible forces or energies for their production. Those interested in electricity should realize, more than all others, the power of the invisible; and the fact that *the invisible is the real.* Anything that we see consists merely in a bundle of "phenomena"—of *effects.* The real cause is always behind, and is always invisible.

There is nothing inherently absurd or impossible, therefore, in these odd manifestations,—however bizarre and unusual they appear to us at first sight. An unusual combination of circumstances might bring them about. Stones do not ordinarily fall out of the air; yet at times they *do* (meteors). Water does not usually rise above its own level, yet it can be made to do so. The curious freaks of lightning are well known. There is nothing inherently impossible, therefore, in supposing that a table can be "levitated" into the air, under unusual conditions; it is simply the manifestation of an unknown energy—of which, doubtless, there are many. We can manipulate and control the electric current; but we do not know yet precisely what it *is.* Similarly, we can study the effects of many of these curious biological forces, without understanding their true nature. Above all, it behooves us to keep an open mind, and not to cry "impossible," just because we have never seen such facts, or because they appear to us innately improbable.

Here, as elsewhere, we depend upon hidden and unknown energies. Could we but find an *energy common to the two worlds*—the spiritual world and the material world—we should have here a means of direct communication, possibly by instrumental means. *Delicate physical and electrical apparatus may be the means, after all, by which such communication will ultimately be established!* At all events, when subtle causes and forces are in operation (as they doubtless are during a séance) it is only natural to suppose that instruments, *far more delicate than our senses,* should be the logical method of detecting them, and, as yet, such experiments have rarely been attempted.

When we take into consideration, finally, the electrical theory of the nature of matter; when we remember the many striking analogies between electricity and the life-force; when we remember that the science of electricity is yet in its infancy, it should hold out to us the hope that, *here,* we may find a solution of many of these obscure problems, and that further investigations in the field of electricity may serve to explain to us many of these unknown and mysterious secrets of our inner nature, and the still more mysterious secrets of the séance-room. No more interesting and profitable researches could be attempted than those which endeavour to establish a connection between known and unknown phenomena; between physical and electrical manifestations, on the one hand, and these curious "psychical" phenomena, on the other. The crying need of the day is a "Psychical Laboratory," wherein such experiments as these could be conducted. It is my sincere hope that, some day, I may assist in the foundation of such a laboratory.

CHAPTER III

LIFE: AND ITS INTERPRETATION

(In the Light of M. Bergson's Philosophy)

The philosophy of life which M. Bergson advocates is more than a mere philosophy—more than a metaphysical doctrine; for, in so far as it endeavours to account for the "phenomena" of life, it entrenches upon biology; and M. Bergson himself is the first to acknowledge this. His own books are filled with interesting scientific data, which he has interpreted most ingeniously; and no broad-minded biologist can afford to neglect his work in the future. Two points of his theory call for special mention, however, it seems to me, and are subject, not to criticism but to discussion. One of these is that M. Bergson has not gone far enough in his interpretation of the facts; in the other he is, I believe, wrong in his interpretation—though his is the one commonly advanced and accepted. A few remarks on these two points may not, perhaps, be without interest.

It is apparent to any student of these problems that the interpretation of life which M. Bergson has adopted is very different from that usually held. The *facts*, the phenomena of life, are the same on either theory, the difference lying in their explanation. All the facts of life are the same; they may be interpreted equally well on either theory. It is important to bear this in mind for reasons which will become apparent as we proceed.

Now, the difference between M. Bergson's theory of life and that commonly held is this: that, whereas one[13] regards life as created or resulting from the total functioning of the body, the other regards it as something separate and distinct—merely utilizing the body for the purposes of its manifestation. In the one case, life is, as it were, made; in the other, it exists apart from the body it animates, and is merely associated with it. To sum up in two words, one is the *production* theory of life; the other is the *transmissive*. One theory leads direct to materialism; the other allows all sorts of possibilities, which are readily perceived by any student of these questions.

Thus stated, the situation at once reminds us of the controversy which raged some years ago as to the relation of brain and mind, as the result of the publication of James' lecture on *Human Immortality*. He then showed that it was quite possible to accept all the facts as to the relation of brain and consciousness, yet interpret them in a different manner; that there might be a transmissive function of the brain as well as a productive or secretive function; and that the undoubted fact of the inter-relation of the two sets of phenomena might just as well be interpreted in one way as in the other. The mere facts proved no theory true. As James so well said: "The psychologists noticed a connection, and at once assumed that it was the only possible *kind* of connection"—which was not at all the case. Mere coincidence, in two sets of phenomena, does not prove that they are *causally* related; that one produces the other. They may be quite separate from one another (psycho-physical parallelism), or both may be aspects of something else, etc. It is all a matter of interpretation, not of fact. But this is a view of the case which is seldom perceived, it seems to me, by psychologists generally. Seeing a coincidence, they at once postulate causal relation, and then proceed as if this had been thoroughly and scientifically established!

I have spoken of this analogy, drawn from psychology, because it bears upon the problem before us in the clearest possible manner. Just as consciousness is usually conceived to be due to the functioning of the brain; so life is conceived to be due to the functioning of the body; but just as mind can be shown to exist apart from brain, and merely manifest *through* it, in the same way, M. Bergson suggests, life may exist apart from matter, and merely animate it in its passage through it. It is all a question of interpretation.[14]

Is the interpretation correct? As Hamlet said: "That is the question!" To use the words of the Right Hon. A. J. Balfour (*Hibbert Journal*, October 1911, p. 18):

"M. Bergson regards matter as the dam which keeps back the rush of life. Organize it a little (as in the protozoa)—i.e. slightly raise the sluice—and a little life will squeeze through. Organize it elaborately (as in man)—i.e. raise the sluice a good deal—and much life will squeeze through. Now this may be a very plausible opinion if the flood of life be really there, beating against matter till it force an entry through the narrow slit of undifferentiated protoplasm. But is it there? Science, modesty professing ignorance, can stumble along without it, and I question whether philosophy, with only scientific data to work upon, can establish its reality."

It would seem to me that the only way to settle this question one way or the other is to bring forward certain *facts* which can be accounted for more fully and rationally on one theory than on the other. If facts could be produced which one theory could not account for at all, the alternative theory might be said to stand proved. Do such facts exist which tell in favour of M. Bergson's theory as against the other? I believe they do. Before coming to them, however, I must draw attention to certain weaknesses in the generally held theory of life, which are, it seems to me, also shared by M. Bergson's theory. Until these are disposed of, I do not believe that any definite forward step will be taken towards proof either in one direction or in the other. So long as certain fundamental tenets are held, it seems improbable that any one theory of life will be proved more than any other theory. M. Bergson has gone part of the way, in his demonstration, but he has stopped there instead of carrying his train of argument to its logical conclusion. At least so it appears to me; for I think it obvious that the chain of argument which M. Bergson adopts can be carried much further than he has carried it, in his various writings.

The view which M. Bergson adopts is somewhat as follows: Life is directive and creative; it utilizes the chemical and physical forces of the body for the purposes of its manifestation. It is the "spark" which sets off the explosive; it is the "hair-trigger" which liberates the enormous energy contained in the cartridge, etc. To apply the analogy: life utilizes and directs the energy obtained from food (by a species of chemical combustion) so that the bodily energy, as such, is, so to say, a "physical" energy, and subject to the law of conservation; while the power that guides, controls, and directs it is conscious life—the power of choice, the guider, the controller.

This view of the case is, I believe, unsound, and for two reasons. In the first place, it does not, I think, go far enough in its interpretation; and, in the second place, we are face to face with a paradox—the problem of no-energy affecting energy. Let us take the second of these objections first.

If a solid body, a fluid or a gas, be moving in a certain direction, a certain amount of energy must be exercised in order to divert its course—for otherwise it would continue in a straight line. Similarly, any energy will continue to exert itself in one direction, unless its course of activity be diverted into another channel; and this "divertion" constitutes a pressure, as it were, upon the energy; and this "pressure" can only be brought about by a "physical" force or energy—and so be within the law of conservation. No matter how *slight* this pressure—this guidance—may be, it is nevertheless *there*; and in so far as it directs the flow of energy, it must itself *be* energy—for otherwise it could not direct or divert it. Even the analogy of the banks of a river fails us, because in that case every atom of the banks is acting upon the body of the water by a material pressure; and hence the banks as a whole are. Either life must be energy, or it must be no-energy. If the first of these suppositions be true, things would be intelligible; but if the second were true, they would not be, because no-energy cannot effect or guide or control energy without itself being energy; and this would either make life a "physical" energy, or remove its power of guidance altogether. I do not see how these alternatives are to be avoided.

M. Bergson apparently tries to evade this issue by supposing that life only affects the energies of the body (derived from food) *very slightly* by a sort of "hair-trigger" action, which releases a vast amount of energy, quite disproportionate to the energy of direction applied. But surely this is a mere begging of the question! One is reminded of Marryat's character, who asked to have her illegitimate baby excused "because it was such a little one!" No matter how *slight* the amount of energy may be, if it is capable of affecting energy at all, it *is* energy, and hence subject to the law of conservation. Life, as energy, must lie wholly outside the law (in which case all talk of "control" and "guidance" must go by the board), or it must lie wholly within it (in which case life becomes a purely "physical" energy, like any other, and cannot well be thought to exercise this "guidance").[15]

We have thus seen that the second of our two alternatives (that life is no-energy) is untenable. Let us now return to the first—that life *is* energy—and see whither it leads us.

If life be a form or mode of energy, it might affect, guide, and direct other modes of energy, or the matter of the body (and, through it, of the inorganic world) readily enough. It would affect them, but blindly. It could have no intelligent action. If life be an energy, it must be like all other energies in this respect; it must fall within the law of conservation and be non-intelligent. Otherwise it would be something different from all other forms of energy; and so we should have energy, plus intelligence, in the case of life; and only energy for all other forms. But in that case life could not simply be converted into or derived from any other mode of energy; because we should have "intelligence" left over, in our equation—which was created *de novo* whenever life was derived from other energies, and plunged into extinction and nothingness whenever life passed into any other mode of energy—in the course of our daily lives. But this is contrary both to experience and to all legitimate scientific thinking! Life, therefore, cannot be an intelligent or a directive energy. And so this argument also goes by the board, and we have left to us only the old materialistic conception of a non-intelligent, blind, life-force, or energy, derived from food, by a process of chemical combustion, and essentially no more mysterious than any other energy. This, therefore, is the conclusion to which we seem driven.

But such a conclusion is not only contrary to M. Bergson's philosophy, but to daily observation and scientific knowledge; for we know that life *is* directive, purposive, and progressive, and if evolution teaches us anything, it tells us that it must have been so always. We are thus driven into this dilemma: life must be an energy—but, as such, it cannot be purposive! Life *is* purposive, yet it must be an energy—for otherwise it could not affect the bodily energies and the material world! Here then is an apparent paradox—a flat contradiction—incapable of solution or further elucidation.

M. Bergson (and before him Sir Oliver Lodge and others) has attempted to meet this difficulty by supposing that the energy of the body is a "physical" energy, derived from food, and, as such, blind and subject to the law of conservation. This energy, they assert, is however manipulated and directed by the power of life or consciousness, which makes "use" of it, directs, and guides it. But this theory is, it seems to me, refuted by the arguments just advanced, which show that life and consciousness cannot affect energy in this way unless they themselves be energy; and thus we are in a "vicious circle" again, with no hope of ever getting out.

The whole difficulty has arisen, it seems to me, because of the conception of the nature of life usually held. Were this altered these problems would be found to have a ready solution. M. Bergson has gone half way toward finding this solution, but has stopped there; he has clung to the most fallacious part of the theory, and for this reason has been unable to emerge altogether from the difficulties above mentioned. Only when we change our conception of the nature of the life-force will these problems become clearer—these questions find their true solution.

Have I, then, any theory to offer as to the nature of this power of life which is essentially new to physiology and biology? I believe that I have—not new as to facts, but as to the interpretation of facts (the latter remain the same on either theory).

In order to make the theory which follows plain in as few words as possible, it will be necessary to refer for a moment to the current conception of vital energy—of life—in the human body. It has been stated by Bergson himself with admirable clearness (*Hibbert Journal*, October 1911, pp. 35-36; *Creative Evolution*, pp. 253-54, etc.), and is briefly this:

Food, when broken down and oxidised in the body, gives forth or liberates energy—just as coal liberates energy when burned in the engine. In both cases energy (contained in the food or the coal, as the case may be) is liberated, and this energy is utilized to drive our engine—the human body or the steam-engine (it makes no difference to the argument). The energy thus gained is, it is contended, again given off as heat and work—muscular and mental work in the case of the human engine (the body); mechanical work of all sorts, and heat, in the case of the steam-engine. Thus one is essentially no more mysterious than the other—the body no more so than the steam-engine—vitality no more so than steam! Both are "physical" energies, subject to the law of conservation, and as such transmutable one into the other. This is the generally accepted theory, which likens the human body to a steam-engine, and is the theory all but universally adopted by scientific men, held as proved and adopted without question by M. Bergson!

But such a view of the case is, I believe, essentially untrue. It is *one* interpretation of the observed facts, truly; but not the only interpretation. The facts remain equally true on either theory; the difference lies in their explanation. It is the old error of confusing coincidence with causation— and not only that, but a particular *kind* of causation, and "treating it as the only imaginable kind." Just as the psychologists reasoned upon the acknowledged facts of the relation of brain and consciousness; so do the physiologists, in our own day, reason upon this question of the causation of vital energy by food. In both cases there has been one-sided and partial reasoning.

If, however, we reject the prevalent notion of the causation of vital energy by food, we must have another theory to offer in its place. It is, I know, presumptuous thus to run counter to the whole of accepted teaching, in this respect, and my excuse must be that I believe my theory represents the truth, while that universally held does not! Again, I must emphasize that I speak, not of facts, but of inferences drawn from facts. With this apology, I shall state my own view of the case as follows:

Instead of comparing the human body with the steam-engine, it should be compared with and likened to the *electric motor*. Just as the motor is recharged, or receives its energy from some external source, just so, I believe, is the human nervous system recharged from without, during the hours of sleep. It is placed into a peculiar, receptive condition, in which this "recharging" process takes place. Our energy is derived through sleep, and not from food. Food merely replaces broken-down tissue (and, if you will, the animal heat) but never supplies or creates its vital energy. This depends upon its nervous mechanism, and upon sleep, and not upon the muscular system and chemical combustion. What differentiates the steam-engine from the human organism is the fact that one needs sleep while the other does not (in other words, one is living and vital, and the other is not), yet, in spite of this obvious difference—which is so great that it really destroys all the analogy—physiologists have continued to disregard it, and to treat the human body as a mere machine—such as a steam-engine—which requires no sleep, and derives its energy solely by combustion! To my mind, this is one of the most curious paradoxes of modern science.

To place the theory in as clear a light as possible, then, it is this: Food supplies or replaces broken-down tissue (and heat) to the body; but not vitality, or the power of life, which comes only from rest and sleep. No matter how much food we may eat and perfectly oxidise, there comes a time, nevertheless, when we must go to bed, and not to the dining-room, to recuperate our strength and energies. During sleep, vital energy flows into us (our nervous systems), and all animals need sleep—this fact differentiating them, at once, from any form of mechanical engine. Life, vital energy, is not due, as is universally thought, to chemical combustion, but to vital replenishment. No energy is *created* within the body; it is merely *transmitted*. The body, in fact, acts as a means of transmission—as a sort of "organic burning glass" which transmits and focuses the sun's rays on one focal point. And just as any crack, or blur, or clouding, or other accident to the burning glass would interfere with its power and capacity from transmitting the rays, so, any accident or disease or pathological state of the organism would interfere with or altogether prevent the passage or flow through it, of the life or vital energy. "The more perfect, the better these conditions, the greater the influx of vital force, and vice versa. We must see that all the electrodes and avenues and channels are bright and clear, so that there shall be as little hindrance as possible to either the inflow of energy in the form of power, or to its outflow in the form of work done." My theory of the relation of body and bodily energy is, in fact, an extension of James' "transmission theory" of consciousness to the *whole* of our life and vital energy. And I believe the one is as defensible as the other.

But, I shall be asked, is there any evidence for such a theory? There is much evidence, there are many facts, which I have adduced in full elsewhere.[16] This is not the place to discuss the physiological intricacies involved, and I can only refer those interested to the work in question. At present, I shall assume its accuracy—or at least its validity—and proceed to show in few words why it is that this theory is not contrary to any known facts, but is capable of explaining them just as fully as the generally accepted theory, and other (disputed) facts far more readily.

The facts upon which the current theory is founded are well known, and, apparently, thoroughly established. Briefly, they are these: So much food, oxidised or burned outside the body, can be shown to yield so much heat and energy. The same foods, oxidised within the body, yield approximately the same amount of energy. Further, the energy which the body expends (in conscious and unconscious muscular activity, thought, emotion, and as heat, etc.) is, it is contended, practically equivalent to the energy which is thus supplied. There is, therefore, an equivalence, a balance, between income and outgo of energy: so that the recently conducted experiments in calorimetry are held to prove beyond question the causation of vital energy by food.

I shall not in this place stop to question the accuracy of the figures obtained—to point out that the results do not always tally; that far too little allowance has been made for mental and emotional states, etc. I shall assume that the figures are accurate and prove all that they are held to prove. The question then arises: Do the figures prove the causation of vital energy by food? Apparently they do, no doubt, and they are held to do so by the majority of experimental physiologists; but I do not believe that this is at all the case. Admitting the facts, admitting far greater accuracy than the figures really show, we have to consider the question of their *interpretation*. And this brings us back to the remarks made at the beginning of this paper—that coincidence does not prove causation; and that the same set of facts may often be interpreted in an entirely different manner—one which would show that life is not directly dependent upon food combustion at all, as is generally supposed. The alternative method of interpreting the facts would be as follows:

Life is a *power* which acts upon organized matter, under certain conditions, in a variable and fluctuating manner. Whenever energy acts upon substance, substance wastes. Whenever work of any kind is done by the body, therefore, the tissues are broken down, and to supply this waste, this destruction, food material is needed. The more waste, the greater the need for repair, and *per contra* the less waste, the less the need of repair. So far as the material equivalent (food) is concerned, therefore, it will be seen that this is only what we should expect on either theory; and tells no more in favour of one than the other.

But what of the energy? The greater the expenditure of energy, the more work done, the more tissue destroyed. The more tissue destroyed, the more food needed, and the more ingested. But this does not prove that the extra amount of food has *created* the extra energy! That would be putting the cart before the horse with a vengeance! And yet this is what is universally done by physiologists in considering these experiments! Perhaps I cannot do better than to quote, just here, a portion of the excellent Introduction which Dr. A. Rabagliati, F.R.C.S., F.F.C.P., etc., wrote to my book, and which really states the case more clearly than I stated it myself. He says in part:

"To take an analogy: It seems to me it would be as pertinent to argue that because the strings of a violin or harp waste in proportion to the quantity of music evolved through or by means of them, therefore the waste of the strings is the cause of the music, while in fact it is the hand of the player, and even the spirit behind the hand, which is the real and efficient cause of the music. So the form of the infinite and universal energy, which we may call erg-dynamic, is the cause of the waste of the body through which it works; and this is at once made good by the increased trophic metabolism which occurs, to replace the waste—this increased trophic metabolism showing itself in increased O_2 intake and coincidently or correspondingly with increased CO_2 output. If the strings of a musical instrument were self-repairing, we might perhaps be induced to think that the material which fed the strings was the *cause* of the music, since in that case some measure of the waste would probably be discoverable in the *débris* emitted; and we might imagine that the *débris* was the measure of the music, while what it really was, was the measure of the waste of the strings, when they were made the instrument of the music. If a spade is used in digging, the spade wastes in proportion to every spadeful of earth it is made to lift. The more it digs, the more it wastes. If we could arrange that a stream of fine steel particles flowed into the spade, to replace the waste caused by each act of digging, we might perhaps come to think that these fine steel particles were the cause of the digging, especially as the quantity of them required would always be exactly proportioned to the amount of work done. Nevertheless, this would be a very inconsequent assumption. Yet this is the assumption invariably made by modern scientists."

It will thus be seen that another interpretation might easily be placed upon the observed facts, and that, while the latter are accepted without question, it is yet possible to conceive the relationship as quite other than usually imagined; and consequently of life as an energy independent of the food supply,[17] and outside the law of conservation—a force absolutely distinct, separate, *per se*. M. Bergson has gone so far as to speak of life as a "power," as a "vital impetus"—utilizing matter for the purposes of its manifestation, etc. I have merely extended this conception in what appears to me a logical and necessary direction. It appears to me certain that life is a sentient power—different from any other mode of energy of which we have any knowledge, and as such no longer subject to the objections raised earlier in this paper (to other conceptions of life), which might also be advanced, it seems to me, against M. Bergson's theory. Were the theory of life here defended true, it would not only enable us to account for life in a satisfactory manner, but it would render clear many obscure and sporadic phenomena which the current theories are quite incapable of explaining (and hence often ignore!); and it would also practically assure us continuity of life beyond the grave—after the dissolution of the body—because mind and consciousness are shown to be independent of physical energy, even in *this* life! This, however, is a subject which requires special and lengthy treatment, and I cannot touch upon it now. All that I can aim to do at present is to show that there may be a spiritual source even for our *physical* life and energy here. And, were this true, psychic phenomena might readily be accounted for—since there would no longer remain any valid objection to their occurrence.

FOOTNOTES:

[13] The orthodox, scientific theory.

[14] See *Mind Energy*, chapters 1 and 2. This view has also been adopted by Mr. W. Whately Smith (see his *Theory of the Mechanism of Survival*) where he says (p. 114): "This latter (the transmissive theory) is the view held by M. Bergson, by Mr. Carrington and by myself."

[15] It might be contended that life is an *intelligent* force—both a physical energy and intelligence; but if that were the case we should simply have energy *plus* something, and the "plus something" would constitute the whole mystery. We should be no better off than we were before. All the energies known to us are certainly non-intelligent, and if you superimpose anything else on the energy you at once differentiate it from all other energies—which you are not entitled to do (see below).

[16] See my *Vitality, Fasting and Nutrition*, pp. 225-350.

[17] The question has been asked, What becomes of the potential energy contained in the food, if it is not converted into bodily energy? I reply, it is given off or imparted to the body as heat (not energy), but this heat is again given off by the body. The more imparted to the body, the more is again given off. We know that the body possesses a self-regulating apparatus which keeps the body, when alive, always at a constant temperature. (When dead, of course, the "corpse" cools to the temperature of the surrounding air.) The equivalence is again maintained, it will be observed, because the more heat we impart to the body the more it in turn gives off.

CHAPTER IV

THE HUMAN WILL IS A PHYSICAL ENERGY

AN INSTRUMENT WHICH PROVES IT

PART I

THE FACTS

That the human will is a definite physical energy, which can be registered by means of a scale or balance, may appear so incredible that the bare statement of the case would seem to carry with it its own refutation! Yet I firmly believe that this is a fact; that the energy of the will may be registered by means of an instrument I am about to describe; and that any one can prove this,—any one, i.e., who cares to take the time to repeat these experiments, and to try a sufficient number of subjects until the right ones be found—who are capable of affecting the balance in the manner described.

Such a fact—if fact it be—is of the utmost importance to science and to philosophy; even more important and more far-reaching in its implications than may at first sight appear. Not only is the fact itself of extraordinary interest, but the very origin and structure of our universe is called into question—and shown to be capable of an interpretation very different from that usually offered by modern science. And, further, if it be true that the human will is a physical energy, we have here the discovery of a *new force*—a force just as new to science as magnetism or electricity—and vastly more interesting, since it is intimately associated with all of us, and subject to our direction, guidance, and command—a force for us to wield and manipulate—for weal or woe!

It may be thought, by some, that this is no new discovery; that the human will is a physical energy is a fact of common observation; and that we all feel the liberation of this energy whenever an act of volition is performed. I may reply at once to such critics that (common sense as it may appear) this is not at all the attitude of modern psychology; and that, by *savants* the will is not considered an energy at all, but rather a choice of actions or an effort of attention. It is a state of consciousness merely, possessing intrinsically no more energy than any other state of the kind. This may, perhaps, be made clear by the following brief quotation from James' *Psychology*:

"We can now see that attention with effort is all that any case of volition implies. The essential achievement of the will, in short, when it is most "voluntary" is to attend to a difficult object and hold it fast before the mind. The so doing *is* the *fiat*; and it is a mere physiological incident that when the object is thus attended to, immediate motor consequences should ensue. Effort of attention is thus the immediate phenomenon of will." (p. 450.)

This, then, is the attitude of psychology. It contends that the will is by no means an energy, in the sense in which physicists use that term; but rather that it is a mere state of mind, or of consciousness. As such it is, of course, helpless; a mere witness of the drama of life, incapable in itself of affecting or changing the external world. So far as the physical world is concerned, it is a mere by-product, a useless adjunct—the feeling of energy-expenditure being delusory. Such is the attitude of modern psychology, and a very hopeless and unattractive belief it is!

As opposed to this view, I propose to show that the human will *is* a definite physical energy, which forms an essential part of our human personality—and forms, indeed, the very core of our being, so far as its expression into the physical world is concerned. This view of the case, I may say, is not altogether new; several competent neurologists have, of late, defended this conception in no measured terms. Thus, Dr. William Hanna Thomson, in his *Brain and Personality*, says:

"An important conclusion is led up to by these facts, namely, that we can *make our own brains*, so far as special mental functions or aptitudes are concerned, if only we have wills strong enough to take the trouble. By practice, practice, practice, as in Miss Keller's case, the Will stimulus will not only organize brain centres to perform new functions, but will project new connections, or, as they are technically called, association fibres, which will make nerve centres work together as they could not without being thus associated.... It is not the power of the brain, it is the masterful personal Will which makes the brain *human*. It is the Will alone which can make material seats for mind, and, when made, they are the most personal things in a man's body.... Man can always do what he chooses, or, in other words, wills. Therefore this very different thing, his Will, makes man different from every other earthly living thing."

Such a view of the case certainly gives a far greater dignity and power to the will; but is it true? That is the question; it is a mere matter of interpretation, without any means of settling the facts one way or the other. It may be "pleasant" to believe this or many other things; but that does not make them true!

It is obvious that arguments such as this might go on for ever. The nature of the human will would never be settled by such means. We desire a more definite and concise method—one capable of settling the case one way or the other—and settling it, not by argument, but by fact. Arguments convince no one; facts every one! It is only by an appeal to fact, therefore, that this question can be settled one way or the other. The difficulty has been that, until now, no direct method has been devised capable of solving the problem. This has now been rendered possible for the first time, by means of the instrument described in this chapter. The experiments herein narrated settle, to my mind, the question of the nature of the human will; they prove it to be a definite physical energy—as much so as any other energy we know. The majority of these facts have been before the scientific world for some time; and why their philosophic interpretation and implications have not been seen is to me a great mystery. One can only account for it by assuming that most scientists are not at the same time philosophers; they do not see the full *meaning* of the facts they observe. Only in this manner can one account for the apathy with which the scientific world has, so far, accepted the facts in question—why it has utterly failed to see their tremendous philosophic and even religious value and significance.

My attention was first drawn to the instrument in question by Professor Th. Flournoy, of Geneva, the author of *From India to the Planet Mars*, *Spiritism and Psychology*, and other works, well known to English readers. Immediately I learned of the experiments in question, I wrote to Professor Alrutz, and obtained from him one of his instruments, by means of which the experiments described below were performed. Writing of the early results obtained by him, Professor Alrutz says ("Report to the Sixth Congress of Psychology," etc.):

"In spite of the knowledge we have gained of the electrical and chemical phenomena of the central nervous system, we must confess that we know little indeed of the inner nature of the psycho-physical processes. What is happening in the brain—especially in the psycho-motor centres—when we move an arm by means of an act of will? What are the forms of nervous energy which are employed? Are these entirely electrical and chemical forces, the neural impulses being mere electrical currents? Or are there other forms of energy which experimental physiology has not as yet brought to light? Might there not be, perhaps, some form of energy more closely allied to the psychic acts, constituting a sort of bridge or transition between psychic phenomena, on the one hand, and electrical and chemical phenomena, on the other?

"When we wish to study the electrical charge contained in any body, we obtain exactitude only when we succeed in transferring this charge to another body; we may then study the nature of the charge under varying circumstances, and establish the influence of the two charges upon one another. It is only in this way that experimentation becomes truly fertile.

Should we not apply the same laws to the phenomena of the nervous system, and institute a similar mode of experiment for the nervous energies? Under what conditions can we conceive this transference?

"The most natural supposition seems to be that it would occur, if at all, in labile organizations; in those subjects which, according to Janet (*Les Névroses*, p. 339), possess an excessively unstable personality; and whose psychic life is characterized by great suggestibility, by instability, and a certain peculiar mobility. Such individuals are also characterized by the great facility with which the functions vary and react upon one another. Binswanger has said that the nervous system of these individuals is characterized by the variability of the dynamic cortical functions; that is to say, by the fact that the nervous segments of their cerebral cortex present a *mélange* of greater or lesser irritability...."[18]

Professor Alrutz goes on to say that, guided by this idea, he constructed an instrument designed to test his theory—based in part, but not wholly, upon the earlier instruments employed by Hare, Crookes, etc., to test the same thing. As is well known, these experimenters spent much time in their investigations—both of them coming to the conclusion, after years of patient research, that physical apparatus could be definitely influenced and moved by the will of certain persons, when exercised in the direction of their movement, and without sufficient contact to account for the observed facts. Crookes' experiments, in particular, are very conclusive in this direction—his apparatus being very similar to that designed by Professor Alrutz. He employed a board, one end of which was attached to a spring balance, while the other end of the board rested upon a solid table. The subject placed his hands upon the board, and a definite pressure was registered by the balance—far more than could be obtained in any normal manner. These experiments of Crookes are classical, and have never been "explained away." With the present instrument, there seems every likelihood of confirming these earlier experiments.

The apparatus employed is of the simplest possible construction. A solid board, some 10-1/2 by 13-1/2 inches, and 1 inch thick, forms the base of the apparatus. In this, at a distance of some 6 inches, two holes are drilled, into which are inserted pegs, 3-1/2 inches long, and sharpened at their top edges to a fine knife-edge. This constitutes the fulcrum—the upper board resting on these knife-edges, and being unevenly balanced on them. (See Frontispiece.)

The upper board, resting on these edges, is some 19 inches long by 13 inches broad at the lower end, and 10 inches broad at the upper end. The narrowing takes place about 6 inches from the end of the board (broad end), in the form of a rapid inward curve. It is here that a groove is cut, and, 7-1/2 inches from the broad end of the board, two pointed grooves are also cut, which allow the board to rest nicely upon the knife-edges of the two pegs below it. In this position the board would naturally assume a downward slant, owing to the greater length of the board on one side of the fulcrum than on the other. (See Frontispiece.) When the long end of the board is supported, by means of a piece of string, to a letter scale, however, the board is made to assume a horizontal attitude, parallel to the table top. In this position the board weighs just 5 ounces, and if the balance registers more than 5 ounces, it shows that a weight or pressure or force has been applied to the long end of the board. If force be applied on the *short* end of the board (where the hands rest), it would have the effect of merely depressing this end of the instrument, and causing a *lessening* of weight, as registered by the balance. This is noted invariably whenever pressure of the hands is made upon the board near the sitter.

With this little instrument, Professor Alrutz tried a number of experiments, on several occasions, which he divided into groups or series. The history of his initial experiments is, as briefly as possible, as follows:

1st Series.—No results.

2nd Series.—The board, after a short interval, lowered, showing a pressure of 40 grammes. This was at the first trial. It descended slowly, remaining at this point for about 5 seconds. It again descended several times, making at one time a depression of 120 grammes. On another occasion the board was depressed, and showed a pressure of 100 grammes, which lasted for 35 seconds. On other occasions lesser depressions were noted, but for longer periods of time. On several occasions the balance registered a downward pressure for two minutes or more. This was in good light, and was carefully observed by two physicians, as well as by Professor Alrutz. The "subjects" were, in this case, ladies of good Swedish families, who had never seen or heard of the instrument before. They were, however, during the experiments, treated as professional "mediums," and every precaution was taken to prevent fraud. The following were some of the precautions observed:

The light was sufficiently good to enable the observers to *see* that no threads or hairs were attached to the board or any part of the apparatus or balance. They also ascertained this with their hands. It was also seen that none of the subjects lifted the board by slipping their fingers under the edges of the board and pulling it upwards. (It may be remarked in this connection that even had they done so this would not account for the results noted; since, in several instances, the downward pressure recorded was more than the weight of the entire board.) As the eyes of the observers were close to the board and to the fingers of the subjects, it was clearly seen, however, that nothing of the sort took place. Besides, as before said, the subjects who tried the board were ladies, and not professional "psychics" in any sense of the word.

It was also ascertained that no sticky material was upon the fingers of the subjects; they were carefully examined both before and after each experiment. Further, to test this hypothesis fully, thin strips of wood (shavings) were on several occasions introduced between the subjects' fingers and the board, which was depressed. Had they lifted their fingers, therefore, they could not possibly have lifted the board, which would not have adhered to them under these circumstances.

3rd Series.—Two "functionaries of state" attended this series, the principal subject tried being the wife of one of these dignitaries. He himself was extremely sceptical of his wife's ability to move the board, and remained so until convinced by the facts! The board was lowered, and the balance showed a pressure of from 70 to 100 grammes. The subject was extremely fatigued after these tests, and went to sleep almost immediately. Others who tried the board could obtain a registration of only 2 or 3 grammes.

4th Series.—Several very successful trials were made in this series with two ladies as subjects. Both placed their hands on the board together, and the depressions were of very long duration. In these experiments sooted paper was placed under the hands of the experimenters. It was noted that better results were obtained if one of them cried "Now!" when the board was to be depressed. The desire to sleep was strong after these trials, and in one instance the subject really did fall asleep during the experiment! An odd fact which should be noted in this connection is that no results were obtained unless the subject *looked* at the long end of the board while the "willing" was in progress.

5th Series.—This series of experiments was attended by a well-known physician and a psychologist. The light was good as before. From 40 to 50 grammes were registered by the balance on several occasions, the downward pressure lasting from 20 to 30 seconds. Clearly, therefore, none of these depressions could be attributed to mere oscillations of the board, but denoted a definite and persistent downward pressure.

Nausea and a strong desire for sleep were experienced by the subjects in this series of experiments, as before.

The above is a very rapid summary of the report drawn up by Dr. Sydney Alrutz, and read to the Sixth Psychological Congress, which met at Geneva in August 1909. Professor Alrutz also attended the Congress in person, and brought with him one of his instruments, which he desired to try upon some of the members in the presence of a number of psychologists. In several instances these attempts were entirely successful; and Professor Flournoy, editor of the *Archives de Psychologie*, was enabled to say of these experiments:

"Professor Alrutz invited me to assist in two séances, in which we experimented upon some of the feminine members of the Congress who desired to try it. The first, in which the subject was Mme. Glika, yielded nothing conclusive. But at the second, at which Professor Alrutz attempted to increase the force by adding two other members of the Congress (strangers who had appeared to him to possess suitable temperaments), it succeeded fully, and I was able to prove conclusively after three trials, and under conditions precluding all possibility of fraud or illusion, that the will of these ladies, concentrated upon a certain material object with a desire to produce a movement in it, ended by producing this movement as if by means of a fluid or an invisible force obeying their mental command." (*Spiritism and Psychology*, p. 291.)

So much for the testimony of Professor Flournoy and Professor Alrutz. In view of the facts and the well-known caution of these investigators, we may assuredly take it for granted that there is here no room for doubt, and that the manifestations really took place as recorded.

My own experiments with this board have not, unfortunately, proved nearly so conclusive as those of Professor Alrutz—owing, doubtless, to the rarity of good "physical mediums" or those capable of exercising their will in the desired manner. It must not be thought that any one possessing a "strong will" can manipulate the board—as Professor Alrutz has pointed out. It is only a peculiarly endowed person who can move the board, one capable not only of exercising the necessary will power, but also of externalising it—a very rare power. Hence the small number of successes. Out of all those tried, I have found only two who could (apparently) move the board at all, and even in their cases the results were far less striking than in the cases reported by Professor Alrutz. In one case a number of slight depressions were obtained; but these were so fleeting, and lasted for so short a time, that it was almost impossible to be certain that the results were not due to mere oscillations of the board. In the second case, however, more definite results were obtained. On several occasions, depressions of half an ounce were noted; and, on two occasions, of more than an ounce, lasting for several seconds. I was enabled to assure myself at the time that these depressions were real, and were not the result of fraudulent manipulation of the board. Although these results are few and meagre compared with those of Professor Alrutz, still they tend to confirm his views, and add to the testimony adduced by him and by Professor Flournoy, in favour of the reality of the facts—of the actual physical pressure by the Will upon the board in question.

In view of these results, then—of this apparently mutually confirmatory testimony—it seems impossible to doubt the fact that we have here definite and conclusive proof that the human will has succeeded in depressing the board in question—in being registered upon the balance, and, consequently, that it is a physical energy, capable of affecting the material world just as any other physical energy does.

PART II

THEORIES

It may be contended, however, that in thus postulating the human will as a physical energy I have not taken into account the alternative explanation of the facts which might be adopted or assumed. This theory contends that it is not the will itself which causes the movement we observe, but the cerebral activity which corresponds to it, and is its physiological counterpart. It has frequently been pointed out before (*cf.* Ribot, *The Diseases of the Will*, pp. 5, 6), that when we will to move our arm, e.g., it may not be the will at all, *per se*, which affects the movement, but the brain-state or neural activity which accompanies the act of will. In other words, mind or will never affects matter (as we feel it does), but it is always one portion of the body which affects another portion—the will or state of consciousness being merely coincidental with this observed action.

This has been one of the classical objections to the doctrine of inter-actionism; and it must not be thought that I have failed to take into account this alternate theory. But opposed to this view of the case we have the facts—(1) that the state of consciousness, and not the brain-state, is surely here the important factor; and (2) that, even were the supposition true, this nervous action or influence must cease at the periphery of the body; for, were this not the case, we should already have exceeded the limits of the orthodox physiological theory, which contends that one portion *of the body* affects another portion (only), and does not contend or pretend that this action may extend beyond the surface of the body; for, if it did so extend, we should have a nervous current without nerves—an appalling fact, and one totally opposed to accepted physiological teaching!

In order for nervous energy or life force to exist independent of the body (upon the functionings of which it supposedly depends), it would be necessary for us to reconstruct the mechanistic interpretation of life, since it would show that life is not dependent upon the body for its existence, but might exist independently of it, which is the very point in dispute. It cannot logically be contended, therefore, that the energy which we here see in operation lies in the nerves or in the brain-centres, but rather that it is a separate force, which physiology, as taught today, cannot account for.

Introspection and experiment seem to unite in telling us that this energy is none other than the human Will.

But if it be granted, on the other hand, that the will is a physical energy, we immediately encounter certain difficulties which must not be ignored. In the first place, if the will be a physical energy, it is subject to the law of Conservation, and, consequently, must be included within the cycle of forces which that law encompasses. Light, heat, chemical affinity, etc., are supposed to be mutually convertible and transmutable; and, according to the present hypothesis, Will must also be included in this series! But every energy we know in the physical universe is a non-intelligent energy, and, as I have pointed out elsewhere, if we make the human will thus subject to the law of Conservation, it seems to form a unique exception to the law. For we know (if our consciousness tells us anything) that willing is an intelligent act, and we should consequently have this conscious act or intent left over in the equation. For we have, in all other cases, purely physical energy, and in this case physical energy *plus something* (conscious intent). The law of Conservation tells us that one energy is derived from another, and is converted again into another form of physical energy, when it is expended. But if will, *ex hypothesi* a physical energy, is derived from another physical energy (by a process of combustion, or what you will), we have here a case of the lesser including the greater—of a thing giving rise to something greater and more inclusive than itself—which is contrary to all accepted thinking. The will, therefore, cannot be *entirely* subject to the law of Conservation, but appears to draw upon an additional fund or source of energy, which is infused into it, as it were, from without. This "thing" which is infused or super-added, this "something" which is the "plus" in our equation, appears to be the directive element, the life element, the sentient element—which is thus shown to lie outside the law of Conservation, as many physicists and philosophers (Lodge, Crookes, Bergson, etc.) have for some time past contended it must or might lie.

One significant fact, in this connection, is that while the law of Conservation is doubtless true, so far as it goes, there is also in operation another law, well known to physicists, called the law of the Degradation of Energy, which asserts that energies of a higher order are constantly being converted into energies of a lower order. This law maintains that energies of a lower order cannot be reconverted into energies of a higher order. All other energies are being slowly but surely converted into heat—the lowest of all forms of energy. And this heat is gradually being dissipated, or radiated away, into space, so that, at some distant day, our universe will be cold and lifeless, like the moon.

Now it is a significant fact that the single exception to this rule consists in, and is constituted by, *life*, or vital energy, which is constantly building lower forms of energy into higher forms. Life is certainly the highest form of energy which we know in this world, and all energies are below this in rank—as may readily be proved by an appeal to the facts of nutrition and metabolism. And, as life is constantly being added to or infused into the world (as the population increases), it is certainly true that there is here a definite increase of the sum-total of the highest form of energy of which we have any knowledge. Life thus occupies not only an important but a unique position—in that it is constructive instead of destructive; and this fact alone should give us pause, and make us ask whether life is, in its totality, subject to and included within the law of Conservation of Energy.

The establishment of the fact that the human will is a definite physical energy is of importance also, because of its bearing upon the problem of the connection or inter-relation of mind and matter. Theories as to this bond or connection have been propounded since the dawn of philosophy. Aristotle and others wrote and thought deeply upon this subject. As is well known, this question formed one of the central points of debate in the works of Hobbes, Berkeley, Hume, Descartes, Leibnitz, Spinoza, Kant, Hegel, Lotze, and many other philosophical writers—all of whom wrote and speculated at length upon this subject. The theories which have been advanced in the past are briefly as follows:[19]

1st. Crude Materialism.—This doctrine contends that consciousness is merely matter, or energy, or matter in motion. It is not necessary to discuss this theory here, as it is not held today by any scientist of the first rank.

2nd. Epiphenomenalism.—This doctrine found its foremost champion in Huxley. It contends that the important happenings are the brain-changes— which are causally connected—and that our thoughts, or corresponding states of consciousness, merely accompany the brain-changes, just as the shadow of a horse may be said to accompany the horse.

The objections of this doctrine are:—

(*a*) That it is just as inconceivable to believe or imagine that brain-changes generate consciousness as it is to imagine that consciousness generates brain-changes.

(*b*) The law of Conservation is preserved at the expense of the law of Causality. For, if no part of the cause passed over into the effect (the state of consciousness), the law of Causality would be violated.

(*c*) The appearance of consciousness, at some definite point in the course of the evolution of the animal kingdom constitutes a breach of continuity.

For these and other reasons epiphenomenalism is today held by few, if any, philosophers.

3rd. Psycho-Physical Parallelism.—This is the doctrine maintained by Münsterberg and others. It contends that brain-changes and states of consciousness are merely coincidental in point of time, and do not ever influence each other. Their relation is that of mere coincidence or concomitance, and not causation. The two flow along, side by side, without in any way interfering with one another.

As regards this doctrine, it need only be pointed out that, were it true, mind and body could never influence one another, since they are not causally connected. Yet, if there be no connection, how is it that they correspond so exactly?—for, as James said, "It is quite inconceivable that consciousness should have *nothing to do* with a business which it so faithfully attends."

4th. Phenomenalistic Parallelism.—This is the theory maintained by Kant, Spinoza, and others. It maintains that both brain and consciousness (or mind and body) are but two different expressions of one underlying reality—just as the convex and concave surfaces of a sphere are but two expressions of an underlying reality. As to the nature of this reality, Kant and Herbert Spencer were content to call it X or the unknown, while Spinoza maintained that it was God.

Analogies which are held to support this doctrine are, however, extremely defective; but the subject is too lengthy and technical to elucidate in detail here.

5th. Psychical Monism.—This doctrine contends that consciousness is the only reality—the material world being external appearance only. Thoughts are causally connected, but not physical events. (The doctrine is thus the exact inverse of epiphenomenalism.)

In refutation of this theory, it may be pointed out that, if brain-changes are thus caused by, or are the outer expressions of, thought—why not muscular changes, and in fact all physical phenomena throughout the world everywhere? For we cannot rationally draw the line of distinction here. Such is the logical outcome of the theory—and has, in fact, been accepted in this form by Fechner and others.

While many philosophers are inclined to accept this view, it may be stated that the physical scientists are, naturally, repelled by it, and so is common sense!

6th. Solipsism.—The contention of this theory is that nothing exists save states of consciousness in the individual. Neither the material world nor other minds exist, save in the mind of the individual. This doctrine is so opposed to common sense and daily experience that it is unnecessary to dwell upon it.

7th. Inter-Actionism (Animism).—Here we have the world-old notion of soul and body existing as separate entities, influencing each other. Mind is here supposed to influence matter, and utilize it for the purposes of its manifestation.

That there are many facts difficult to account for on this theory cannot be doubted. Heredity and the origin of life must be taken into account; the "inconceivability" of the process has some weight; and the apparent infringement of the law of Conservation of Energy is a serious objection. Further, it may be urged, what evidence have we that consciousness can exist apart from brain-functioning? And, it may be said, apart from the facts offered by "psychical research," so-called, there is no evidence, strictly speaking. Hence the importance of these phenomena, if true. But the greatest objection to the doctrine of inter-actionism is doubtless that drawn from the law of the Conservation of Energy, which says that, inasmuch as mind is a non-physical energy, inasmuch as matter cannot be affected by a non-physical cause, brain-changes cannot result from will, or the activities of the mind.

But once prove that the human will is a physical energy, and this objection is readily disposed of. A physical energy is doubtless quite capable of causing all the changes within the brain which we know to exist within it— molecular, chemical, whatever they may be. It at once removes this classical objection to the doctrine of inter-actionism; and at the same time virtually proves that theory correct—thus solving this problem once and for all!

It may be pointed out, *en passant*, that philosophers and metaphysicians have really attacked this problem from the wrong standpoint—in their arguments concerning the relations of mind and brain—for this is a question which might have been (and in my opinion should have been) determined not by argument, but by *fact*. Instead of arguing, *a priori*, as to the nature of the connection, the problem might have been solved in the same way that all other problems are solved, viz., by an appeal to evidence and fact. The fundamental point made by practically all philosophers, in discussing this question, is that brain-states and conscious states are always found together, and that consciousness can never exist in the absence of brain. In other words, mind cannot exist as an "independent variable" in the world; it must always accompany a human brain.

I pass over, without comment, the fact that, according to the doctrines of idealistic monism and psycho-physical parallelism, this independence is virtually allowed, by the very nature of the doctrine; and shall point out merely that, if consciousness could be proved to exist independent of brain functioning, philosophic theories would have to be remodelled to conform to the evidence; the *a priori* problem could be settled at once by an appeal to actual fact. And again this separate existence of consciousness seems to be established by the facts of "psychical research," which apparently show that mind can exist apart from brain structure. This important fact once established, it would at once alter the whole case and render inter-actionism not only a "respectable" theory, but a proved fact.

So much for the importance of this doctrine (that the will is a physical energy) from the point of view of philosophy, and as applied to the question of the inter-relation of brain and mind. Now let us see if it cannot be applied in another direction.

The present interpretation of the character and nature of the will, and its inclusion as a physical energy, has a distinctly important bearing upon one of the most bitterly disputed points in the whole history of philosophy, viz., the question of the *Freedom of the Will.*

As is well known, there are two opposing views upon this subject—held by opposite schools—the theory of Determinism, on the one hand, and of Free Will on the other. The Libertarians assert that our wills are free—we having power of choice in all our actions. The Determinists, on the other hand, contend that our thoughts and actions are determined by definite, ascertainable causes. They contend that the *feeling* of freedom we all experience is but illusory, and that, in reality, our every action is inevitable—predetermined by its previous cause of causes, and could have been predicted by an intelligence wide enough and possessing a grasp deep enough of human nature to perceive life in all its tendencies. Indeed, one eminent philosopher went so far as to say that a belief in Free Will showed simple ignorance of science and a clinging to superstition!

A great deal has been written upon this subject of Free Will in the past; the point has been bitterly disputed for years. It may be said, however, that, at the present day, practically all philosophers and scientists, with few exceptions (e.g., James, Schiller, Bergson, etc.), believe in Determinism. The arguments for that doctrine are certainly weighty, and may be summarized, briefly, as follows:

1. *The Law of Conservation of Energy* tells us that no energy can be added to or abstracted from the total stock of physical energy in the universe. If the will be a non-physical energy (as it is conceived to be, by psychologists), it cannot affect the physical world, for if it did the law of Conservation of Energy would be overthrown. Hence, the will cannot affect the material world: hence, it cannot be a true cause.

2. *Biology* contends that heredity and environment alone are capable of explaining the actions and movements of the lower organisms, without postulating any "will." Inasmuch as man is connected with these lower

organisms by an unbroken line of descent, why should not these factors explain man's actions also?

3. *Physiology* teaches that in-coming nerve stimuli give rise to certain physical changes in the nerve cells or centres, which, in turn, give rise to out-going (afferent) currents. There is here an arc or loop of unbroken physical causation; and there is no "room" for consciousness, save as an "epiphenomenon," as postulated by Huxley.

4. The *Law of Causation* tells us that an effect must have a cause, and that the cause must, in a certain sense, resemble the effect—since the effect *is*, in a sense, the cause translated. But, inasmuch as the effect is a physical event, the cause must also be physical in its nature; hence will (supposedly a non-physical event) cannot possibly play a part, or be a true cause.

5. *Philosophical Science* contends that Nature is a "closed circle." Mechanical causation holds supreme sway. Everything happens according to law and order. If Free Will were allowed a place in the scheme of things, chance and caprice would immediately be introduced into our world—which could never be tolerated for a moment!

6. *Psychology* holds that every mental state has its equivalent or counterpart in a corresponding brain-state. But each brain-state is not caused by the state of consciousness, but by the preceding brain-state. Here, again, there is no room for "free will" to play any part.

(Inasmuch as we are approaching this subject from a purely scientific point of view, the arguments drawn from sociology, ethics, and theology need not here be discussed. The interested reader is referred to Professor H. H. Horne's excellent little book, *Free Will and Human Responsibility*, for an extremely clear summary of this problem.)

The reply of the Libertarian to these problems is usually somewhat as follows:

1. The doctrine of Conservation has not been experimentally proved with regard to the relation of mind and brain; it is only assumed. Still, granting it to exist, all energy may, in its ultimate analysis, be psychical, instead of physical, in its nature—the doctrine of idealism, which is today gaining wider and wider acceptance, seeming to support this view.

2. That man *resembles* the lower animals does not prove that he is *identical* with them. On the contrary, the observed differences constitute the very differences about which the argument rages. Further, recent theories of organic evolution are tending to prove that interior (spontaneous) forces play a part, as well as exterior forces.

3. If consciousness were a mere "epiphenomenon," having no "use" to the organism, it would soon perish (if it ever appeared) according to the law which says that all useless functions perish. But we know that, as a matter of fact, consciousness has grown more and more complex, as evolution has progressed.

4. The *Law of Causation* is doubtless valid and universal; but to assume that this is invariably physical begs the question at issue. May there not be psychical causation? Only thorough-going materialism can say "No" to this question; but materialism is today out of date.

5. *The Philosophy of Nature.*—This is a strong argument, *a priori*, but is subject to re-interpretation, in the light of new facts, to which it must conform. Facts might be adduced which proved this particular view of nature wrong. It is, in short, only a working hypothesis, subject to revision, as new facts are adduced, tending to alter it.

6. *Psychology.*—Our ignorance of the possible relation of brain and mind is no excuse for our dogmatically asserting that no such connection is possible. It may be a fact, though unintelligible to us. Mental states may influence, partially at least, successive brain-states. We cannot say. If one man asserts that they *cannot*, another may assert that they *do*. Hence every one is at liberty to believe what he pleases! Nothing is proved.

If, now, we glance at the preceding arguments, we find that they may be summarized somewhat as follows:

Arguments 2, 3, 5, and 6 are practically valueless, one way or the other. Both sides might claim a victory; none of these arguments would settle the question.

Argument 4 is certainly valid, to a certain extent, and can only be surmounted by assuming that a non-physical energy can affect physical energy. But I do not think that any physicist would be inclined to admit this. So that this argument cannot be used in support of the doctrine of Free Will.

There remains the first argument, drawn from the law of the Conservation of Energy. This is certainly the strongest of all (to my mind), and is, as it stands, valid. Though idealism may maintain that all physical energy may be, in its ultimate analysis, only psychical energy, I do not for a moment believe that any physicist really believes this, or that any man accepts it as a common-sense doctrine—one which can be acted upon in daily life. It is mere philosophical sophistry and hairsplitting, and we must believe, as a matter of fact, that physical energy *is* really physical, and not psychical, in its nature.

As to the first portion of this argument, although the law of Conservation of Energy has never been shown to be invalid, when applied to the connection of brain and mind, still, every one probably believes that it does actually obtain, and that a brain-state cannot result in consequence of non-physical influences any more than any other physical event could so result. It is tacitly admitted, therefore, that the law of Conservation holds good here also, and that will cannot affect brain, because will is not a physical energy.

We are now in a position to see the tremendous importance of the facts contained in the first part of this chapter. Inasmuch as theory must follow fact; inasmuch as it has been proved experimentally that the human will is a physical energy—this whole question of the relation of brain and mind, of the influence of the former by the latter, and the question of Free Will, must be remodelled in accordance with these facts. The whole Free Will controversy is settled at one stroke (and in favour of Free Will!), and all the books which have been written upon this subject, and all the thought and energy which have been expended in the past are thus shown to be so much waste-paper and wasted effort! For, as we have seen that the whole question resolves itself into the central problem of whether or not the law of Conservation of Energy is valid—whether will or mind can affect brain—it will be seen that the proof that will is a definite physical energy settles the case once and for all. Determinism is routed; Free Will wins the day; and here again, as usual, theory follows fact, instead of dictating what those facts should be! At "one fell swoop" we are enabled to solve and to settle for ever one of the most bitterly disputed points in the whole history of philosophy and metaphysics!

This theory (might we not say, this fact?) that the will is a definite physical energy, at least in part, is thus of great philosophic, no less than scientific importance, if true. It even enables us to recast our conception of the origin of the world, and of all forces, and enables us to reconstruct—in a more or less intelligible manner—the story of Creation, contained in the first chapter of Genesis—an account which has been more ridiculed, perhaps, by dogmatic physicists than any other account in the whole Bible.

Much has been written upon this subject in the past; but it must be admitted that, from the point of view of physics, the whole difficulty lay in conceiving the first initial impulse which started our Universe on its endless way. All matter being but an expression of energy, all energy being (in all probability) but the varying modes or forms of expression of one underlying primal energy, the difficulty has been in accounting for the origin of this primal energy—the initial "push," so to say, which sent the Universe on its way.

Many evolutionists have admitted that, once given this initial impulse, all might readily be accounted for. The difficulty lay in conceiving this primal impetus.

But if Will be also a form of energy—though, as we have seen, only partly within the law and partly beyond it—then it is conceivable that this energy, coming from a source external to that presented by physical nature and physical science, should have infused or imparted enough energy (perhaps only an infinitesimal amount, enough to originate the impetus), which, according to Haeckel and others, is all that need be supposed, to enable us to account for the whole of organic and inorganic nature! This *fiat*, having once gone forth, would originate, or be the source of, the first "cosmic urge"—would, in fact, supply that impetus which modern science has so long sought in vain!

FOOTNOTES:

[18] This explains why "every one" cannot move the board; there must be this peculiar nervous and psychic instability in order to insure the results.

[19] I am indebted to Dr. M'Dougall's excellent work, *Body and Mind,* for the *data* from which I have condensed the following summary.

CHAPTER V

MODERN DISSECTION OF THE HUMAN MIND

Dissection of the mind! Can that too be dissected? We hear much nowadays of dissection of the human body; of organs which have been transplanted and which perform their functions in the body of another animal; of marvellous operations, in which tissues and viscera have been removed, repaired, and replaced—seeming none the worse for their remarkable experience; of operations which have been performed even upon the brain, in which whole segments have been cut away, and other delicate experiments undertaken—all of these marvels we have grown more or less accustomed to, by reason of the ease and certainty with which they are performed. But the human mind; *that* is a different matter. Here is something which, intangible in itself, seems incapable of dissection or of objective experimentation, in the ordinary sense of the word. Yet that is what present-day normal and abnormal psychology has been enabled to do! Shakespeare's adage: "Who can minister to a mind diseased?" can now be answered by saying: "To a certain extent, the specialist in normal and abnormal psychology."

If you shut your eyes, and turn your attention inward, in an attempt to find your real "self," you will probably find a good deal of difficulty in catching it. It will be found as illusory as the proverbial figure of Happiness, which ever flits on before us. The real centre of being, the self, the ego, the person, the individuality, evades us at every turn. Each of us has the feeling, under all ordinary and normal circumstances, that, as James expressed it, "I am the same self that I was yesterday." And one would be most astonished, I fancy, were he to wake up one fine morning and find himself some one else! Like the Arab in the tale, he would be bewildered indeed!

From the solitary desertUp to Bagdad, came a simpleArab; there amid the routGrew bewildered of the countlessPeople, hither, thither, running,Coming, going, meeting, parting,Clamour, clatter, and confusion,All around him and about.

Travel-wearied, hubbub-dizzy,Would the simple Arab fainGet to sleep,— "But then on waking,How," quoth he, "amid so manyWaking, know myself again?"

So, to make the matter certain,Strung a gourd about his ankle,And, into a corner creeping,Bagdad and himself and peopleSoon were blotted from his brain.

But one that heard him and divinedHis purpose, slyly crept behind;From the sleeper's ankle clipping,Round his own the pumpkin tied,And laid him down to sleep beside.

By and by the Arab wakingLooks directly for his signal—Sees it on another's ankle—Cries aloud, "Oh, good-for-nothingRascal to perplex me so,That by you I am bewildered,Whether I be I or no!If *I*—the pumpkin why on you!If *You*—then where am I, and who?"

One can quite appreciate the tangled state of our Arab's mind on awakening under such peculiar circumstances, and, from the point of view of common sense and common experience, such an awakening would be an utter impossibility—fit only for fairy tales and the traditions of savage tribes. Yet, in our own day, here in civilized New York and London, similar cases have been recorded and studied by experts! Under peculiar circumstances, patients have gone to sleep one person and awakened another; and they have remained another, not only during the first temporary moments of bewilderment, but sometimes for days, weeks, and months at a time; and in some cases even whole years have elapsed before the first "self" returned to tenant the body, to look out of the eyes it had looked out of years before; to take up the self-conscious life it had lain down in sleep. And to this there may be the added horror that, during the intervening period of oblivion (for this Self) the same external body, actuated by another "Self," may have performed actions and lived a course of life utterly at variance with the tastes and desires of the primary "Self." The other Self may even have married the common body in the interval— to a man whom the original self had never known—does not know now! There may even have been children; friends, environment, all, all may have been changed in the interim. Like Rip van Winkle, the setting of life may be found to have altered; but in some of these cases, the awakening must be the greater nightmare. The unfamiliarity, even horror, of the situation can be imagined. Yet many such cases exist; and the two Selves alternately usurp and manipulate a common body; the Real Self and the Stranger. Who and what is this Stranger? Apparently it is an alien spirit—another soul, perchance, entangled miserably in the body of some equally unhappy mortal! Yet modern psychology contends that such cases represent, for the most part, mere splits or dislocations or dissociations of the normal personality; and that the two or more Selves we see before us, at such times, are none of them a *real* self; but mere fragments of the primary self, dissociated from it, owing to some shock or accident or disease. Let us see if we can penetrate a little deeper into this mystery of being; and lay bare the secrets of this alien Self, as well as the original Self which owned the body from birth.

The older psychology held that the mind was a *unit*; that it was a separate thing or entity, a sort of *sphere*, which, if it could ever be caught, would reveal all the secrets of True Being. Accordingly, they tried to catch this sphere-of-being, by inward reflection or "introspection." But it was never caught! There are many reasons why this should be so, the chief reason being that a subject cannot be an object also; it is as impossible for a thought to catch itself as it would be to turn a hollow rubber ball inside out without tearing the cover.[20] But the newer psychology studies the mind objectively, from the outside, by means of recording instruments, and does not depend upon introspection for its results. Further, the very conception of the nature of the "self" is different; it is not now considered an entity, as of old; but rather a compound thing, a product, a complex, composed of a variety of elements. Instead of being considered a single gossamer thread, it is now thought to be rather a *rope*, composed of innumerable, interwoven elements—and these, in turn, of still finer threads, until the subdivision seems endless. The mind, in other words, is thought to be compounded of innumerable separate elements; but held together, or compounded into one, by the normal action of the will, of attention, and the grip upon the personality of the true Self. When this will is weakened; when the attention is constantly slackened, when the mind wanders, this single strand of rope separates and unravels. The "threads" branch out in various directions, no longer in control of the central, governing will; the Self has become dissociated or split-up into various minor Selves—all but parts of the real, total self; yet separate and distinct, nevertheless. And if enough of these threads become joined together, or interwoven, one with another, it can easily be imagined that this second strand of rope might become a formidable opponent to the original strand; it might become so large and strong, in fact, by the constant addition of new threads, and the dissociation of these from the first, true strand, that it would assume a more important rôle, and become stronger, and finally even control the whole. What was originally but a single fine, divergent thread has become, in course of time, a successful rival to the original strand of rope.

Now let us apply the analogy. The mind as a whole represents the rope; its elements or component parts are the threads; and, under certain abnormal conditions, these can become torn away from the original Self—like little rivulets, branching off from the main stream of consciousness, forming independent selves. This is an abnormal condition; a splitting of the mind, a dissociation of consciousness. Another fragment of consciousness, distinct in itself, has been formed. Thus we have a case of so-called double consciousness, of alternating personality; or, if there are three or more such splits or cleavages, of multiple personality.[21]

Now we are in a better position to understand the nature of this alien self which has been formed, and which alternately usurps the common body. It is no foreign spirit; it is not a demon or fiend which has entered into the subject; it is merely a portion of the patient's own mind, acting independently a life of its own. It is a portion of the real Self, functioning independently. Let us now see how these splits or dissociations take place.

Often they are the result of some shock to the emotional nature. In one of Dr. Morton Prince's cases, the patient happened to look up and saw in the window the face of a man whom she had known years before, and with whom she had tragic emotional associations. It was storming at the time, and a lightning flash revealed the face in the window. It was a highly dramatic scene, and the shock to the patient's emotional nature caused her consciousness to split-up or become dissociated into various selves; and thenceforward for years these separate "selves" lived independent lives, each ignorant of the life of the other. In this case, there were several such personalities which alternated; and they were only finally unified and the real Self again restored by means of hypnotic suggestion, after a careful analysis of the various selves. This synthesis of the various streams of consciousness, and their ultimate unification into one primary normal self, is one of the most startling, as it is one of the most interesting and suggestive, feats of modern psychological medicine.

The principle upon which many of these cures rest, and the efficacy of suggestion, is thus apparent. By its aid the skilled specialist in abnormal psychology is enabled to gather up the "loose ends" of conscious life, as it were, and unify and consolidate them into one normal, healthy Self. He is enabled to weave them all together, and again restore the "sheath" or "wrapper" of the individual human will, keeping these threads in place henceforth, and restoring the healthy, normal personality; the *mens sana in corpore sano.*

Exactly *how* all this can come about I shall now endeavour to show. Before any of the more complex and complicated disorders of the mind can be understood, it will be necessary for us to discuss very briefly the nature of the subconscious mind—since it is upon this that all modern researches have in a great measure rested—upon the improved understanding of its nature that many of these cures rest.

It has long been known that there is a sort of mind in us, capable, at times, of performing complicated and intelligent actions without the co-operation or knowledge of the conscious mind. We see examples of this daily—in the absent-minded actions of certain individuals, in the dream life, in hypnotic trance, and in many of the cases of normal and peculiar mental action, of which numerous examples might be given, but which are so well known that it is hardly necessary at this late date to elaborate in detail. The idea has been so extensively employed by Hudson in his theory of "the subjective mind," and by others, that the general theory has pretty well saturated the public mind. Hudson's theory—otherwise open to many criticisms—is very lax, not to say erroneous, in its construction, and is not accepted today by any competent psychologist. Apart from the mysterious powers with which he endowed the "subjective" mind, he makes it now synonymous with the *whole* of the subconscious life outside the field of immediate consciousness; now as equivalent merely to the hypnotic stratum; now to a dream-like self, etc., until the term has become so elastic that it means nothing intelligible but everything in general! As understood by the modern psychologist, the term "subconscious mind" must be defined far more accurately before we can proceed to use it as a working hypothesis. What, then, is understood by the subconscious mind? What part of us can perform conscious operations without our being conscious of them? How can we perform intelligent operations without intelligence? It all depends upon the meaning we give to our terms. We must begin by explaining just what is meant by the "subconscious mind"; then, perhaps, we can better understand its operations and aberrations.

There are several theories as to the nature of this subterranean stratum of our being—this hidden self—each of which finds its champion in the modern psychological schools. First, there is the theory that it consists merely in the mechanical workings of the brain—a purely physiological theory, which makes the subconscious mind synonymous with certain brain activities—much the same as a series of complex reactions. It is well known that there is a brain-change corresponding to every thought we think; and the nature of the connection between the two has been one of the most debated points in metaphysics, and is one which, if we thoroughly understood it, would doubtless solve in a great measure the nature of life and of consciousness. Without going into this very complex question, however, there remains the undoubted *fact* of the connection; the thought, which is known by us in consciousness; and the brain-change, which has been verified by ingenious mechanical and electrical instruments, and the effects of which we behold in the chemical changes in the brain-substance itself after severe thinking. This being so, it has been said, Why not suppose that so-called subconscious actions *are* merely brain activities which take place, but which have never risen into consciousness? Professor Münsterberg and others hold this view. It has been conclusively shown, however, by Dr. Morton Prince and others, that this theory fails to explain adequately many of the facts—seems indeed contrary to much experimental evidence; and this view is now given up by all but the most materialistic of the modern psychological school. We have to search deeper yet for the mystery of the subconscious mind; and we shall have to grant it a certain amount of consciousness of its own, apart from all purely brain activity.

A very opposite theory is that advanced by Mr. F. W. H. Myers—that of the "subliminal self." This theory says that the conscious mind is but an infinitely small part of our total self—a mere fragment; that portion best adapted to meet the needs of everyday life. To borrow an analogy from physics, "consciousness is only the visible portion of the spectrum; the invisible, ultra portions are our subconscious selves." I shall not venture upon a criticism of this theory beyond saying that the majority of modern psychologists do not hold to it; and hence, whether it be ultimately true or false, we must disregard it for our present purposes.

Thirdly, there is the theory that the subconscious mind is composed entirely of dissociated or split-off ideas—ideas which have been dissociated or split off from the main stream of consciousness, much as a few freight cars might be shunted on to a side track by the switch-engine. This hypothesis is very similar to another theory, which contends that the subconsciousness consists of dissociated experiences—mental happenings which have been forgotten or passed beyond voluntary recall. For these mental states, or rather trains of thought, Prince has suggested the term "co-conscious," because they are conscious processes in operation at the same time as the normal consciousness. This theory is doubtless far nearer an adequate explanation of the facts than that which contends that the subconscious is merely a portion of the field of consciousness which happens to lie outside the field of *attention*, because *that* is a theory certainly inadequate to cover the facts. This last hypothesis is one which seems to be favoured by Coriat and others, but it is certainly limited in its application.

Now let us see if we cannot obtain a clearer grasp of the facts, in view of the above discussion as to the nature of the subconscious mind. We may sum-up the facts as follows:—

As the result, either of some sudden shock, or by reason of certain subjective psychological practices carried to an extreme, we have a splitting of the mind into two or more separate streams, which function separately and independently, and generally with no memory connection between the two, so that each is ignorant of what the other stream, or self, is doing. This is already an abnormal condition, a pathological state, and its severity depends upon the degree of cleavage between the streams of thought. If this be deep and lasting, we have a well-marked case of hysteria, or other disorders to be noted immediately; if, on the other hand, the cleavage be slight, we have merely absent-mindedness, wandering of the mind, and many lesser symptoms which indicate this tendency to dissociation, and which should be checked at all costs in their inception, since they are symptomatic of the tendency to disintegration of the mind, and which, if unchecked, would lead to grave disturbances later on. It is because of this fact that too much automatic writing, crystal-gazing, meditation, attendance at spiritistic circles, etc., is harmful; they one and all induce a passive state of the mind which favours dissociation and disintegration. Many of the insanities start in this fashion; and all such practices, instead of being encouraged, should be discouraged; and all experienced and intelligent students of psychical research warn those who "dabble" in the subject against the repeated and promiscuous indulgence in such practices— because of the dangerous, even disastrous, effects upon the mind, in many instances.

But we have not yet reached a distinctly morbid state. This dissociation may be slight, and of little consequence; and may even be completely "healed" without the knowledge of the patient; without his knowledge that anything strange has taken place at all—just as tubercular lesions of the lungs may be healed without the patient ever having known that he had suffered from tuberculosis. The co-conscious stream may again be diverted into the main, healthy channel; the threads of the wounded mind may again be bound up, with only a scar to indicate where the delicate protective covering had been ruptured. If such is the case, all is well thenceforward.

But the termination of the accident may not be so fortunate. If, as before said, the cleavage be deep and lasting; and if, instead of attempting to bind up the wounded mind, those practices which caused the original "split" be persisted in; if shock follow shock—to the mental, moral, emotional, or physical nature; if great exhaustion, lack of sleep, or of proper food, or other causes of a like nature, be present—then it is evident that the cleavage must become deeper and deeper yet; and, in a short time, the few stray, wandering thoughts become grouped and bound together, and begin to form a veritable psychological entity. A secondary, an alien self, has been formed. And just as it is increasingly difficult to dam-up a river which has once found its way to some unaccustomed channel, so this secondary stream of consciousness will soon become a rushing, mighty torrent, incapable of being checked or dammed in its mad course.

So long as this split-off portion remains a mass of sporadic thoughts, not much damage has been done; but when they become abnormally linked or associated together, forming groups, then the abnormal conditions have begun in earnest. These masses of subconscious experiences are called "complexes," and give rise to all sorts of trouble. It must not be thought that this complex formation is always harmful; on the contrary, this very process, when normally conducted, is the basis of our educational processes. But when they are thus conglomerated and consolidated outside the conscious mind, and function automatically, involuntarily, by themselves, then they have become dangerous to the mental stability. Their pressure and influence may be felt in the conscious life—in fantastic imaginations, in fears, phobias, and obsessions—in morbid dreams—in morbid emotional and moral reactions throughout the entire psycho-physical life. It is these automatic, self-acting complexes which originate many of the disorders of the mind.

How, then, are we to diagnose this condition when once it has been reached; and, when once diagnosed, how is it to be treated? These are the all-important questions which modern psychological students have set themselves to solve, with more or less success. As briefly as may be, these are the methods.

In the first place, a careful system of observation, question, and experiment will yield many important results. An analysis of the dream life will prove of great value in this connection also. If the dreams cannot be voluntarily recalled, they are brought to light by means of hypnotism, psycho-analysis, or the employment of what is known as the "hypnoidal" state—as induced by Dr. Boris Sidis. This is an artificially induced condition, half-way between sleeping and waking, in which many half-forgotten experiences again merge into the mind; and even thoughts which had *never* been in the conscious mind at all—subconscious observations, etc., or the content of the dream life. These dreams are then analysed. It is a very striking fact that differing or alternating selves may have entirely different dreams; or, on the other hand, different and distinct selves may have a common meeting-place in the dream world. By means of dreams, it has thus been possible to come in touch with the thoughts of the other Self, which had been impossible by any other means at our disposal. A study and analysis of the dream life has thus assumed great importance within the past few years, and bids fair to assume greater and greater importance as the study of the subconscious, and abnormal psychology, increases.

Other methods of tapping the subconscious mental life are: planchette, automatic writing and crystal-gazing. In the former cases, a pencil is placed in the hand of the subject, or the hand is placed on a planchette; and, while the conscious mind is occupied in conversation, or reading aloud, etc., the hand is, nevertheless, writing out an account of its experiences—its thoughts and feelings—which prove highly valuable to the investigator. Or the patient may be asked to look into a crystal, and describe what, if any, visions and pictures form within the ball. These pictures are, of course, hallucinatory; but they indicate, none the less, the content of the subconscious mind; since they are the externalized thoughts and feelings of that stratum of the mind. Here, again, we have a valuable means of diagnosis.

Again, we have a purely experimental method of studying the emotions—by means of the galvanometer. An electric current being passed through the body, variations in the current are detected by means of an electric needle, which fluctuates as the current varies. Now, it has been found that these fluctuations vary in accordance with changed emotional states; and that in certain conditions of the mind, such as dementia, the variations are almost entirely absent, because of the lack of emotional reactions. It has thus been found that this form of insanity is largely a disease of the emotional life. On the other hand, when the emotions are strong, the fluctuations of the needle are very marked and prolonged. We have thus another most valuable method of testing the emotional life—always largely subconscious—by means of purely mechanical instruments.

Finally, we have hypnotism, the skilled employment of which has been found of inestimable value in laying bare the secrets of the subconscious life. By its aid it has been found possible to disclose the secrets of being, to tap the subconscious mind at will, to explore the hidden regions of Self, which would otherwise have remained for ever inaccessible to the experimenter. For, by placing the patient in the hypnotic condition, the subconscious mind is exposed to view, as it were, and its secrets made manifest. The wounds and scars are thus rendered visible to the mental eye of the physician, and he is enabled to treat his case accordingly.

Yes, hypnotism has been found one of the chief means of cure as well as of diagnosis. By its aid the tangled skein of the mental life may be unravelled, the mental knots may be untied, and the threads may be woven and plaited together again into one normal, healthy chain of being. This may be accomplished by means of suggestion rightly applied. When once the hidden complex has been brought to the surface, when its story is told, its secrets laid bare, it seems incapable of doing more damage, of again influencing the mental life detrimentally. Its life, its vitality, seems to have gone; its ammunition has been stolen, it has "shot its bolt," it is incapable of doing more injury to the normal self. Many hidden fears, depressions, and obsessions have been removed in this manner, simply by bringing these hidden fears and thoughts to the surface and disposing of them by means of suggestion. Many seemingly miraculous cures have been effected in this manner. The "demons" have been expelled, the brooding thoughts have vanished. This method of dispelling them is technically known as the cathartic method, and consists simply in a frank and full confession. When this has been brought about, when the brooding thoughts have been brought to light—confessed and discharged, as it were, from the mind—then a cure will be found to have been wrought; the man has again been made whole—a very significant fact if taken in connection with religious conversion, communion, confession, and prayer.

We have somewhat diverged, however, from our main theme, to which we must now return. We have seen that the subconscious mind may become, so to speak, *diseased*—this consisting very largely in the processes of dissociation, complex formation, etc. Further, we have seen that this dissociated, automatically-acting "self" may exist either as a separate stream of thought running alongside of, or rather *below* the main current; or may alternate with it, by rising to the surface and occupying the whole stage to the exclusion of the normal consciousness—when we have those cases of alternating or multiplex personality which have so puzzled psychologists for many years—and the correct interpretation of which we are only just beginning to realize. When this complete change of "self" has taken place, we have those cases of altered personality referred to at the beginning of this chapter—cases which are tragic in the extreme in many instances, but which represent merely extreme types of those losses of memory from which we all suffer, to a greater or lesser extent, even in our normal life. The restoration of lost memories by means of suggestion—the synthesis of the dissociated states—*this* is the key to the mystery, the great secret of modern psychotherapy.

And this theory of dissociation of consciousness has enabled us to explain many puzzling facts hitherto inexplicable. Thus *hysteria*, with its multiform symptoms and its internal contradictions, has long been the stumbling-block of medicine. Now it is no longer thought to be a morbid state (dependent usually upon sexual disturbances), but it is regarded rather as an indication of the splitting of the mind, a dissociation which embraces all the motor, physical, and psychical activities. On this theory, hysteria is easily explained and all its multiplex symptoms understood. In treating it, the self is unified, abnormal suggestibility is removed, and the patient is cured!

Psychaesthenia again, with its obsessions and fears, may be explained in the same manner, and its cure rests upon the same principles. The "attacks" cease so soon as the psychical synthesis is effected and the morbid self-consciousness removed.

Neurasthenia, long regarded as a pathological state, due to auto-intoxication and similar causes, is now thought to be due chiefly to dissociation, caused by excessive fatigue—one of the known contributory causes to this condition. *Psycho-epilepsy*—a sort of fictitious imitation of the real disease—is due to precisely similar causes, and may be cured in a similar manner.

A word of caution may not be out of place in this connection. Inasmuch as hypnotism is itself a method of inducing a passive psychological state—one peculiarly open to suggestion of all kinds—it can readily be seen that its employment may be exceedingly dangerous, save in the hands of a skilled operator. It may be the very *cause* of a splitting of the mind—if improperly administered—if the patient is not thoroughly awakened, the effects of suggestion completely removed, etc. In this lies the great danger—of which we hear so much, usually with so little foundation! The *real* danger in the process is thus apparent; but, properly applied, hypnotism is doubtless of great therapeutic utility and of great practical value to the psychologist.

Just *how* these dissociations of the mind take place we do not yet know with any degree of certainty. We might suppose that certain areas in the brain-cortex become detached in their functionings, as it were, from the general activities, and set up a little "monarchy" of their own—interactions and associations going on within that area, but never extending beyond its periphery; that each one of these centres or areas corresponds to a "self," a personality; and that a cure consists, physiologically speaking, in bringing about a healthy and normal interaction between this "self" and the rest of the brain area, so that associations go on thenceforward in a complete and uniform manner. But this is pure speculation, for which there is no experimental evidence, though it probably represents something of the truth. At all events, the dissociation of the mind is the chief cause of the trouble, and its synthesis the chief means of cure. *That* much has been rendered certain by the newer researches in the field of the subconscious, and by the persistent search for that greatest of all secrets—the MYSTERY OF BEING.

FOOTNOTES:

[20] It can be shown, theoretically, that this is possible in the "fourth dimension," but not in the third. This illustrates the difference between theory and practice—a point it might be well for Christian Scientists to keep in mind!

[21] Although this theory of the "composite" nature of mind is now generally held, Mr. Myers has contended that the Self must have a *fundamental* unity—to enable it to withstand the shock of death.

CHAPTER VI

PSYCHIC PHOTOGRAPHY

(*New Experiments*)

In my *Modern Psychical Phenomena* (Chap. viii.) I reproduced a number of "spirit" and "thought" photographs, the evidence for which seemed to me to be exceptionally good. Since that time, I have received a number of "psychic" photographs, from various sources,—some of them obviously fraudulent, and some of them extremely puzzling, when the circumstances of their production were fairly taken into account. It will be remembered, for instance, that I published a number of curious photographs obtained by Mr. E. P. Le Flohic, on whose plates curious streaks of light were obtained, in a dark room. Since then, I have discussed the matter at some length with Mr. Le Flohic, and I am more than ever convinced that no conscious trickery was involved in the production of these pictures; I have also examined the *negatives* (plates), and am prepared to state that no external markings are upon them, and that they have not been tampered with in any way. In other words, the lights were undoubtedly *in the room* at the time the plates were exposed. Yet no one saw anything unusual! It is a curious and baffling case.

Since then, Mr. Le Flohic has tried other experiments, with almost uniform failure. In a letter dated August 14, 1920, he says:—

"... Since resuming my experiments in psychic photography, I have taken about 25 pictures, and with but two exceptions have had no results whatever. One of these I sent you some time ago, and the last one I am sending you under separate cover. (Reproduced as Figs. 1, 2.) I have not had very favourable conditions for experiments, and discontinued them about three weeks ago. I am going to arrange soon to start a series of experiments, by myself, in my private library, and should I get any results, will gladly inform you."

The curious streak of light noted in Fig. 2 is, on any theory, most remarkable. The central band seems to be *dark* in the middle, surrounded by a band of light, from which a golden "aura" radiates. The sitters saw nothing unusual—either in the dark, or during the flash-light, with which this picture was taken.[22]

Among the newer methods of experimentation I may mention "thought photography"—in which attempts have been made, by individuals, to obtain photographs of their own *thoughts*.

This method of obtaining psychic or thought-photographs is entirely different from that employed in obtaining so-called "spirit-photographs." In the latter case, a camera is focused upon the sitter, who "sits" as usual, and the forms appear upon the plate when developed. In obtaining thought-photographs, *no camera at all is used*; the plates (or films) are carefully wrapped in opaque black paper and sealed up, so as to prevent the slightest ray of light from reaching the plates. These plates (or films) are then placed against the forehead, where they are held for from five minutes to half an hour, or longer, according to the patience of the experimenter and the degree of his psychic power. An intense effort is made to impress upon the plate, by an act of will, a mental picture or image held in the mind. Anything will do—the head of an eagle, the sun, the face of a friend. The plate is then taken into the dark-room, unwrapped and carefully developed. In those cases which have been successful, an image, more or less clear, of the picture held in mind will be found upon the plate.

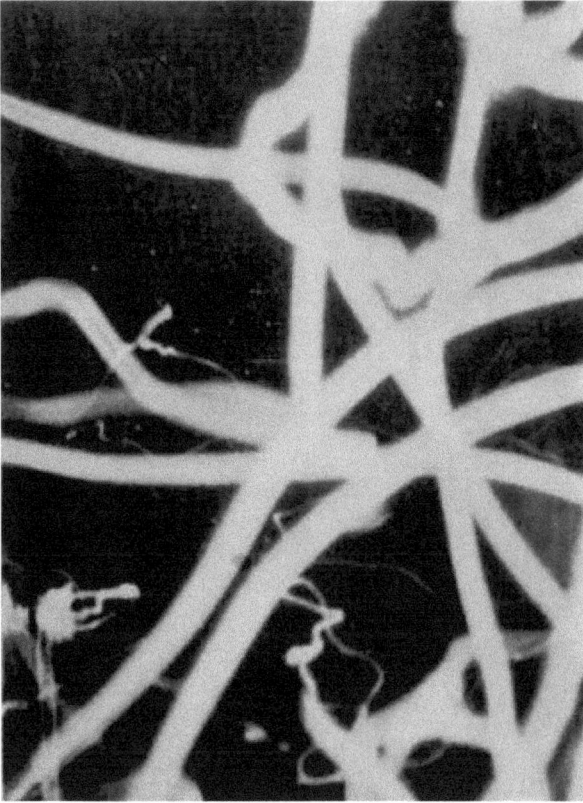

PSYCHIC PHOTOGRAPHS (1, 2)

This will, I have no doubt, appear incredible to the average reader. The facts, nevertheless, remain! Such photographs *have* been obtained—in America, France, Poland, Japan and other parts of the world. A series of careful, simultaneous experiments have proved to us that such photographs *can* be taken, under precisely the conditions I have described.

Commandant Darget, of the French army, obtained a number of very striking photographs in this manner. A number of these are to be found in Joire's book, *Psychical and Supernormal Phenomena*, where we find thought-photographs of bottles, a walking-stick, the head of an eagle and other subjects obtained in this manner. Writing of the impression of the eagle's head, M. Darget says:

"With regard to the eagle, it was produced in this way: Mme. Darget was in my office, lying on my sofa, about ten o'clock in the evening. I said to her: 'I am about to put out the lamp and to try (as I have already done sometimes) to take a fluidic print over my forehead. I will hand you a plate for you to do it as well.'

"I therefore handed her a plate, which she held with both her hands about an inch in front of her forehead. A short time afterwards—it might be about ten minutes—she said to me: 'I think I am going asleep; I am very tired: I am going to lie down.' And feeling her way in the darkness, she handed me the plate.

"I then went to develop it, and was surprised to see this astonishing figure of an eagle. I have called it a 'dream-photograph,' although my wife does not remember having dreamed of a bird or anything else while she held the plate."

Dr. Baraduc, of Paris, likewise asserted that he had obtained psychic photographs of human radiations and of human thought. For instance, calm, peaceful emotions are said to produce pictures of softly homogeneous light, or the appearance of a gentle shower of snowflakes against a black background; whereas sad or violent passions suggest, in the arrangement of the light and shadows, the idea of a whirlpool or revolving storm, somewhat like a meteorological diagram representing a cyclone. If these photographs are really what they are believed to be, they would seem to indicate that, in our ordinary normal condition, we emit radiations which are regulated and flow forth in smooth, even succession; but when violent emotions, such as anger or fear, break through the control of the will and take possession of us, they produce a violent and confused emission.

There is no reason, *a priori*, why the soul should not be a space-occupying body, save for the tradition of theology. For all that we know, the soul might be a point of force, existing within and animating some sort of ethereal body, which corresponds, in size and shape, to our material body. But at all events, there is an abundance of very good testimony to the effect that the shape of the spiritual body corresponds to that of the material body; and, as such, it certainly occupies space, and possibly has weight also. It might and it might not; it is a question of evidence. It will have to be settled, if at all, not by speculations, but by *facts*. Are there any facts, then, that would seem to indicate that the soul might be photographed? Have we any evidence that the soul may be photographed—say, at the moment of death? If so, we should have advanced a great step in our knowledge of this subject.

Before I adduce the evidence on this point, however, it may be well to illustrate the fact that there is no inherent absurdity in the idea, as many might suppose. Of course the spiritual body would have to be material enough to reflect light waves, but where is the evidence that it is not? There seems to be much evidence, on the contrary, that it *is*. It must be remembered that the camera will disclose innumerable things quite invisible to the naked eye, or even to the eye aided by the strongest glasses or telescopes. Normally, we can see but a few hundred stars in the sky; with the aid of telescopes, we can see many thousand; but the photographic camera discloses more than *twenty million*! Here, then, is direct evidence that the camera can observe things which we cannot see; and, indeed, this whole process of sight or "seeing" is a far more complicated one than most persons imagine. As Sir Oliver Lodge has pointed out, there is no reason why we should not be enabled to photograph a spirit, when we can photograph an image in a mirror—which is composed simply of vibrations, and reflected vibrations at that! We are a long way from the tangible thing, in such a case; and yet we are enabled to photograph it with an ordinary camera. Any disturbance in the ether we should be enabled to photograph likewise—if only we had delicate enough instruments, and if the "conditions" for the experiment were favourable. The phenomena of spirit-photography, and especially the experiments of Dr. Baraduc, to which I shall presently refer, would seem to indicate this.

These experiments, as well as those that are about to follow, gain greater credibility when considered in the light of the newer experimental researches in physics, which demonstrate, apparently, that matter can be made to disintegrate and disappear, and can be again reformed from invisible vortices in the ether into sufficiently solid bodies to be photographed by the sensitive plate. In his remarkable work, *The Evolution of Matter*, Dr. Gustave Le Bon has devoted a whole section of his argument to what he has denominated "the dematerialization of matter." He proves by experiments in the physical laboratory that matter can dissociate, and vanish into apparent nothingness. What really takes place, however, is that the solid matter, as we have been accustomed to conceive it, is resolved into its finer constituent parts—not only into the material atoms of which it is composed, but these atoms are in turn dissociated and resolved into a series of etheric vortices, invisible to normal sense perception. Apparently, therefore, matter has ceased to be, as such; and, in fact, it has been resolved into energy! Conversely, Dr. Le Bon proved that, by producing artificial equilibria of the elements arising from the dissociation of matter, he could succeed in creating, with immaterial particles, "something singularly resembling matter." These equilibria were maintained a sufficient length of time to enable them to be photographed.

On p. 164 of Dr. Le Bon's *Evolution of Matter*, are to be found photographs of what is practically materialized matter. This author says, in part:—

"Such equilibria can only be maintained for a moment. If we were able to isolate and fix them for good—that is to say, so that they would survive their generating cause—we should have succeeded in creating with immaterial particles something singularly resembling matter. The enormous quantity of energy condensed within the atom shows the impossibility of realizing such an experiment. But, if we cannot with immaterial things effect equilibria, able to survive the cause which gave them birth, we can at least maintain them for a sufficiently long time to photograph them, and thus create a sort of momentary materialization."

If, therefore, physical science now admits, as it does, that vibrations, or disturbances in the ether, can be photographed, there is no longer any *a priori* objection to these experiments by Dr. Baraduc—which claim, merely, that similar vibrations have been photographed—such vibrations being the external modification or impression left upon the ether by the causal thought.

So much for theoretical possibilities: now for the facts.

In a remarkable little booklet, entitled, *Unseen Faces Photographed*, Dr. H. A. Reid has presented a number of cases of supposed spirit photography, some of which are certainly difficult to account for by any theory of fraud. It is true that the methods of imitating this process by fraudulent means are numerous and ingenious; but practically none of them are unknown. In *The Physical Phenomena of Spiritualism*, pp. 206-23, I have described these fraudulent methods in considerable detail; and have also published an account of a case in which trickery was actually detected in the process of operation. (See *Proceedings of the American S.P.R.*, 1908, vol. ii., pp. 10-13.) But there seem to be certain cases on record that are most difficult to account for by any theory of trickery—partly because of the excellence of the conditions, and partly because of the character of the experimenter. Let us glance at one or two of the cases in which the character of the experimenter would seem to insure the fact that no conscious and voluntary fraud was practised. A résumé of a few such cases is to be found in Mr. Edward T. Bennett's little book on *Spiritualism*, pp. 113-20.[23] I quote in part:—

"The most notable exception to this (rule of fraud) which I am able to quote is that of the late Mr. J. Traill Taylor, who was for a considerable time the editor of the *British Journal of Photography*. The following quotations are from a paper on 'Spirit Photography' by Mr. Taylor. It was originally read before the London and Provincial Photographic Association in March, 1893, and was reprinted in the *British Journal of Photography* for March 26th, 1904, shortly after Mr. Taylor's death. He says:—

"'Spirit photography, so called, has of late been asserting its existence in such a manner and to such an extent as to warrant competent men in making an investigation, conducted under stringent test conditions, into the circumstances under which such photographs are produced, and exposing the fraud should it prove to be such, instead of pooh-poohing it as insensate because we do not understand how it can be otherwise—a position that scarcely commends itself as intelligent or philosophical. If, in what follows, I call it "spirit photography," instead of psychic photography, it is only in deference to a nomenclature that extensively prevails.... I approach the subject merely as a photographer.'

"Mr. Taylor then gives a history of the earlier manifestations of spirit photography, and goes on to explain how striking phenomena in photographing what is invisible to the eye may be produced by the agency of florescence. He quotes the demonstration of Dr. Gladstone, F.R.S., at the Bradford meeting of the British Association in 1873, showing that invisible drawings on white cards have produced bold and clear photographs when no eye could see the drawings themselves. Hence, as Mr. Taylor says: 'The photographing of an invisible image is not scientifically impossible.'

"Mr. Taylor then proceeds to describe some personal experiments. He says: 'For several years I have experienced a strong desire to ascertain by personal investigation the amount of truth in the ever-recurring allegation that figures, other than those visually present in the room, appeared on the sensitive plate.... Mr. D., of Glasgow, in whose presence psychic photographs have long been alleged to be obtained, was lately in London on a visit, and a mutual friend got him to consent to extend his stay in order that I might try to get a psychic photograph under test conditions. To this he willingly agreed. My conditions were exceedingly simple, were courteously expressed to the host, and entirely acquiesced in. They were that I, for the nonce, would assume them all to be tricksters, and, to guard against fraud, should use my own camera and unopened packages of dry plates purchased from dealers of repute, and that I should be excused from allowing a plate to go out of my own hand till after development, unless I felt otherwise disposed; but that as I was to treat them as under suspicion, so must they treat me, and that every act I performed must be in the presence of two witnesses; nay, that I would set a watch upon my own camera in the guise of a duplicate one of the same focus—in other words, I would use a binocular stereoscopic camera and dictate all the conditions of operation....

"'Dr. G. was the first sitter, and, for a reason known to myself, I used a monocular camera. I myself took the plate out of a packet just previously ripped up, under the surveillance of my two detectives. I placed the slide in my pocket and exposed it by magnesium ribbon which I held in my own hand, keeping one eye, as it were, on the sitter, and the other on the camera. There was no background. I myself took the plate from the dark slide, and, under the eyes of the two detectives, placed it in the developing dish. Between the camera and the sitter a female figure was developed, rather in a more pronounced form than that of the sitter.... I submit this picture.... I do not recognize her, or any of the other figures I obtained, as like any one I know....

"'Many experiments of like nature followed; on some plates were abnormal appearances, on others none. All this time Mr. D., the medium, during the exposure of the plates, was quite inactive....

"'The psychic figures behaved badly. Some were in focus, others not so. Some were lighted from the right, while the sitter was from the left; some were comely ... others not so. Some monopolized the major portion of the plate, quite obliterating the material sitters.... But here is the point: Not one of these figures which came out so strongly in the negative was visible in any form or shape to me during the time of exposure in the camera, and I vouch in the strongest manner for the fact that no one whatever had an opportunity of tampering with any plate anterior to its being placed in the dark slide or immediately preceding development. Pictorially they are vile, but how came they there?

"'Now, all this time I imagine you are wondering how the stereoscopic camera was behaving itself as such. It is due to the psychic entities to say that whatever was produced on one-half of the stereoscopic plates was produced on the other—alike good or bad in definition. But, on a careful examination of one which was rather better than the other ... I deduce this fact, that the impressing of the spirit form was not simultaneous with that of the sitter.... This I consider an important discovery. I carefully examined one in the stereoscope and found that, while the two sitters were stereoscopic *per se*, the psychic figure was absolutely *flat*! I also found that the psychic figure was at least a millimetre higher up in one than in the other. Now, as both had been simultaneously exposed, it follows to demonstration that, although both were correctly placed, vertically in relation to that particular sitter, behind whom the figure appeared, and not so horizontally, this figure had not only not been impressed on the plate simultaneously with the two gentlemen forming the group, but had *not* been formed by the lens at all, and that, therefore, the psychic image might be produced *without a camera*. I think this is a fair deduction. But still the question obtrudes: How came these figures there? I again assert that the plates were not tampered with by either myself or any one present. Are they crystallizations of thought? Have lens and light really nothing to do with their formation? The whole subject was mysterious enough on the hypothesis of an invisible spirit—whether a thought projection or an actual spirit, being really there in the vicinity of the sitter—but it is now a thousand times more so....

"'In the foregoing I have confined myself as closely as possible to narrating how I conducted a photographic experiment open to every one to make, avoiding stating any hypothesis or belief of my own on the subject.'"

Let us now return to some later experiments in psychic photography. Two small photographs, one showing a face, the other a series of small starlike markings, were sent to me by a member of the Society for the Study of Psychic Photography, of England. Writing of these prints, my correspondent says:

"A week or so ago we distributed one hundred and ten strips of sensitive film, in light-tight packages, for friends of the members to 'wear.' This was done with the idea of ascertaining approximately what percentage of individuals possessed this gift. We agreed that the films should be carried about for a week, and where possible worn round the forehead at night. The experiment proved more successful than we had anticipated, since six out of the one hundred and ten films were more or less affected. The two best results are those shown on the prints enclosed herewith." (Not shown.)

These results are quite in keeping with some that have lately been obtained in California. In a recent communication which I have received from Mr. Vincent Jones, Vice-President of the California Psychical Research Society,—under whose auspices the experiment was undertaken—he says:—

"Then we tried thought-photography. I bought some ordinary plates, which were opened in the dark-room of an X-ray laboratory. The plate was inclosed within an envelope of opaque black paper and this in another envelope. It was then suspended about twelve inches in front of the eyes of the sitting experimenter....

"This experimenter first wrote down on a slip of paper the thing he was going to concentrate on, folded it and handed it to a committee. Then he sat and concentrated for ten minutes. The plate was then developed, and contained the image, clear and strong and unmistakable, of a *cross*. This proved to be the subject handed to the committee." (See Fig. 3.)

In view of the remarkable character of this experiment—as well as its importance, and taking into account the apparently excellent conditions under which the test was made, I wrote to Mr. Jones, asking him to be kind enough to secure, if possible, the statements of any additional witnesses who might have been present on this occasion, and he sent me, in response to this request, the following affidavit, signed by five of the witnesses who were present at the time:

California Psychical Research Society,
San Francisco, Calif., Nov. 3, 1920.
Dr. Hereward Carrington.
504 West 111th St.
New York City.
Dear Dr. Carrington.

Enclosed is the print I promised you of the "Thought Photograph" taken by a Committee composed in part of members of the Council of the California Psychical Research Society, in May, 1919. The conditions were as follows: I purchased at Hirsch & Kaye, opticians and photo-supplies, a box of one dozen ordinary rapid Seed plates. I took the box unopened to the Committee meeting, which was held at the X-Ray Laboratory of Preston & Huppert in this city. Mr. Henry Huppert, Dr. Frank Collins, Dr. Cecil Nixon and myself went into the dark room, where Mr. Huppert opened the box of plates, took one at random from the centre of the package, enclosed it inside an opaque black envelope, and this again inside another yellow envelope and sealed it. This was taken outside and suspended about 12 inches in front of our subject, who was seated and had previously written down what he would concentrate upon, and handed the memo to Dr. Collins. The subject drew a rough outline of the object of his concentration, gazed fixedly upon it for about 5 minutes, then put it aside and for ten minutes concentrated upon the plate without touching the same. The plate was immediately taken into the dark room and developed, and the image of the cross developed at once, clear and strong. One of the Committee was in the room with the subject during the whole time, and there was no opportunity for any tampering with the plate. The object developed proved to be the one previously written down and handed to Dr. Collins.

Yours very truly,

VINCENT JONES,
FRANK T. COLLINS, D.O.,
J. C. ANTHONY, M.D.,
CECIL E. NIXON, D.O.S.,
HENRY K. HUPPERT.

Thought Photograph (3)

Supplementing this formal report, Mr. Vincent Jones sent me the following letter, in answer to my questions, which I also quote:—

San Francisco, Calif., Nov. 10, 1920.
Dr. Hereward Carrington.
504 West 111th St.
New York City.
Dear Dr. Carrington.

Here is the signed statement I promised you, and the better print of the cross photo. The others who were present at the experiments are not where I can reach them at present, but the five whose signatures are appended to the accompanying statement are the best-known of the eight who were present,—men whose testimony in a court of law would be accepted without question. Dr. Frank Collins is, or was, President of the Osteopaths' Association, a Spiritualist, student of Astrology and mystical subjects, and a member of the Council of the California Psychical Research Society. Dr. J. C. Anthony is a well and favorably known physician, who has practised here for many years, also a member of our Council. Dr. Cecil E. Nixon is a Dentist, best known as a Magician, and as the inventor of "Isis," a wonderful automaton which plays any tune you request of her on the zither. Mr. Henry Huppert is one of the partners in the Preston-Huppert X-Ray Laboratory, a man with scientific training and a student of the Occult.

Such a thing as substitution by the subject of another plate for the one we suspended before him was out of the question for two reasons. First, he was not left alone. Second, he did not know in advance just what was to be the nature of our experiment. When Mr. Huppert broke the seal on the box of plates, in the presence of the Committee of four, in the dark room, and selected one at random from the centre of the box, and enclosed it in the two envelopes, he not only sealed the envelopes but marked the envelopes, so that he would know if they had been tampered with. They could not have been opened without destroying these marks. Furthermore, in the room where the experiment was conducted, there was an ordinary electric light burning, and no substitution could have been made without affecting the plate. It could not have been possible that the subject, being previously unaware of the exact nature of the contemplated experiment, could have provided himself with plates of the same size and envelopes of two colours and of identically the same paper as those used in the X-Ray Laboratory. If anything happened to the plate it happened *through* the paper of the envelopes. But, as I have said, one of the committee was in the room during the whole experiment. The sole possibility of fraud was for the subject to have come prepared with a cross painted with radio-active paint, and to have held this against the envelopes whilst the Committee was off its guard. But the character of the subject is sufficient guarantee to all of us that such was not the case. I admit that to those who do not know him, this would furnish no guarantee, and that for this reason we SHOULD HAVE TAKEN EVEN MORE STRINGENT PRECAUTIONS. HAD WE KNOWN THAT SUCH A RESULT WAS TO BE OBTAINED WE PROBABLY WOULD HAVE DONE THIS, BUT WE WERE JUST A COMPANY OF FRIENDS WHO HAD GATHERED TO TRY WHAT WE MIGHT ACCOMPLISH, AFTER HAVING READ OF COLONEL DE ROCHAS' EXPERIMENTS ALONG THIS LINE. WE TRUSTED ONE ANOTHER, AND SO IT IS BARELY POSSIBLE THAT FOR A MOMENT SOME ONE WHO WAS SUPPOSED TO BE WATCHING THE SUBJECT WAS OFF HIS GUARD. THEREIN LIES THE SOLE POSSIBILITY OF FRAUD IN THIS RESULT, AND, AS I SAID, THIS IS OUT OF THE QUESTION WITH US WHO KNOW THE CHARACTER OF THE SUBJECT.

Yours very truly,

VINCENT JONES,
215 Balboa Bldg.

P. S. The reason we were not all in the room with the subject during the trial was that we were trying to do the same thing ourselves. I was concentrating upon a V, with a film on my forehead, and the others were trying it either with film or plate. Only one other secured anything at all, and that was but a blur. Our subject who did get the Cross result is a very highly developed mystic with remarkable powers of concentration, but modest about his powers and for that reason, and because he is extremely busy, we have not been able to repeat the experiment with him since. V. J.

As might be expected, many of these "psychic photographs" take on the characteristics of "spirit-photographs," in that they show definitely recognizable *forms*. This is especially true of a number of psychic photographs which were recently taken at Crewe, England, in the presence of two non-professional mediums, who have, nevertheless, obtained hundreds of successful photographs in this manner. Regarding their experiments, a correspondent writes me:

"They are not professionals and charge no fee. A nominal charge is made for prints.... I do not know of any one who has sat with the Crewe circle who has not been satisfied that fraud, at any rate, will not explain these things. Those who have *not* been and who know nothing of the subject, say just the opposite.... Many of the results in themselves rule out faking. I have had many sittings with these mediums and have not the slightest doubt whatever regarding their absolute genuineness. In fact, in some of the tests I have carried out with them, faking would have been quite impossible, even had they been desirous of tricking. I speak as an amateur photographer of many years' standing, in touch with photography every working day of his life."

Several photographs obtained at this now-famous Crewe circle are reproduced herewith. Certainly it is true that such photographs might be obtained by means of double exposure, double printing and other devices; but the point is that we have the word of an expert photographer that they were *not* produced in this manner; and when once their genuine character is admitted, they assume very great interest, no matter what view we may care to take as to the results.

Miss Estelle Stead, daughter of the late W. T. Stead, writing of her experiences with this same group of psychics, says:

"I have several times, since he passed on, obtained photos of my father on the same plate I took with me, *under the most rigid test-conditions*—on plates which I have never let out of my sight, save for the few moments they were in the camera for my photo to be taken.

"I also obtained a splendid photo of my brother, who passed over in 1907. He promised that before I went for the sitting he would be photographed instead of Father, if he could manage it. I said nothing of this to the lady who sat with me for the photograph to be taken, or to the photographer. I put my own marked plate in the slide myself, and stood by while it was developed. My brother's face appeared quite as plainly as mine, and has been recognized by many who knew him in life. He was seldom photographed while here, and certainly *never* with his head in exactly the position it is in this photograph, received nine years after his death.

"It is only natural that those who have passed over in the war should, when conditions allow, use this means of establishing their identity, and many have done so successfully! One case of particular interest is that of a boy who was blown to pieces in France last year. His mother wrote in great distress to a friend in Edinburgh stating that the boy had been killed. This friend had not seen the boy since his school-days, but being interested in spiritualism, and able to get in touch with those on the 'other side,' she asked her father, who had passed over, if it would be possible for the boy to be photographed. He said it was doubtful, but they would do their best. She therefore made arrangements to have a sitting with the Crewe mediums, who possess this power which enables those on the other side to manifest sufficiently to be photographed.

PSYCHIC PHOTOGRAPHS (4, 5)

"Two plates were exposed, and on one side, beside the photo of the lady herself, there is an unmistakable photo of the boy. I have seen it, and a photo of the boy taken before he went to France, and there is no mistaking the likeness. She sent the pictures to his parents, who before this had not been believers in the possibility of communication with those who have passed on—with the result that they are now convinced of it, and have received several comforting and assuring messages from their boy."

We see how imperceptibly ordinary psychic photographs shade off into those more definitely spiritistic in character. This is true in nearly all phenomena in this realm. It is hard to draw any hard-and-fast line, and say: "*This* is due to powers within our own being, and *this* is due to external spiritual beings!" They merge one into the other so gradually that it is extremely difficult to draw any line of demarcation between the two.

Certainly *some* of these photographs are due to the thoughts or other psychic activities of the sitter. Thus we can hardly suppose that the "spirits" of bottles, walking-sticks and eagles (as in Darget's experiments) were actually present, and that they impressed themselves upon the photographic plate! Again, some pictures show us a definite *face*, which we cannot attribute to any outside influence. The experimenter merely *thought* of the face, and it appeared upon the plate. This being so, how can we *ever* obtain proof that the forms and faces which appear upon photographic plates are those of discarnate spirits,—even though they appear and are recognized,—since we know that mental images or memories of faces have been photographed in just this manner?

That is indeed a difficult problem: it is very like that which confronts us in the case of any good trance-medium. Inasmuch as telepathy is a fact, and the medium almost certainly derives *some* of the facts from one's mind, or from the minds of other living people, how can we ever prove "survival"— the actual communication of our spirit friends?

We can only apply the same sort of tests in the one case as in the other. We must discount all those facts which might possibly have been obtained normally, or by telepathy, and pin our faith on those which could not possibly, or conceivably, have been obtained in this way. Similarly, we must assume that all psychic photographs represent normal markings upon the plates, or the emotions or thoughts of the sitter, or the vital radiations issuing from his body, until indisputable proof to the contrary be forthcoming. (It may be added that some very striking evidence of identity has been obtained in this manner, from time to time in the past, and is now being obtained in various circles both in this country and abroad.)

Regarding these "vital radiations" issuing from the body, a number of interesting experiments were undertaken in this connection in Poland, Paris and elsewhere. M. Durville obtained imprints of hands, from which emanated streaks of light, as though the hands were radio-active; indeed in no other way can we account for these results.

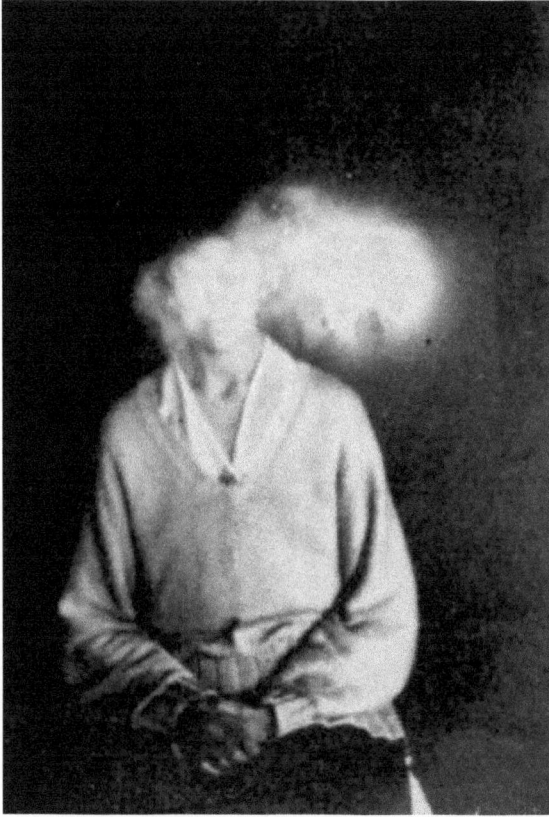

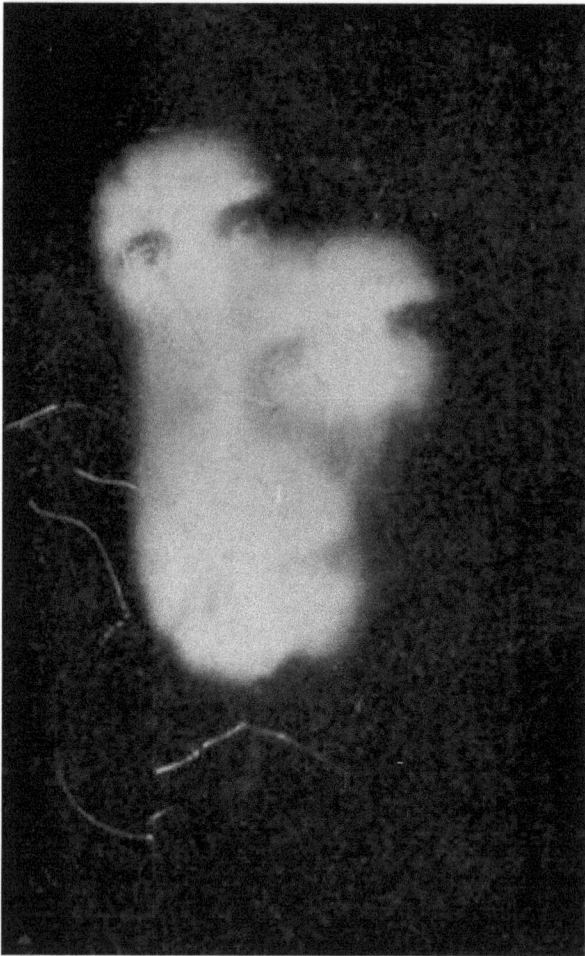

PSYCHIC PHOTOGRAPHS (6, 7)

I next present a remarkable series of photographs, kindly lent to me by Lady Glenconner,—to whom I am indebted for permission to reproduce them. These photographs were taken at the "Crewe Circle," in the presence of Mr. Hope, the medium. Personally, I have never had the opportunity to attend a Crewe séance, and hence cannot speak of the evidential value of these pictures from first-hand evidence. All I can say is that Mr. Hope is not a professional "medium," in the usual sense of the term, since he receives no payment for his services; that no evidence of fraud, in connection with his photographs, has ever been forthcoming; and that rigid test conditions have, apparently, been enforced on a number of occasions, when successful "extras" were obtained upon the plates. In practically all the cases known to me, the sitters provided their own marked plates, placed them in the camera themselves, took them out themselves, and developed them themselves. Such, I understand, were the conditions under which the accompanying photographs were obtained. All that Mr. Hope does is to place his (opened) hands upon the plate-*holders*, after the plates have been inserted therein, and before these are placed in the camera. It is during this period that the psychic "extras," appearing upon the plates, are thought to appear; or at all events it is this "magnetizing" of the plates which renders them susceptible to impressions which would not be recorded upon ordinary plates. How far this belief of the sitters coincides with the actual facts of course I cannot say.

The first photograph shows us Lady Glenconner, seated, with a clearly-defined face over her right arm. This face is enshrouded in the same curious mist-like "clothing," common to "spirit" photographs, and materialized forms, and especially evident in all the Crewe pictures. The face is, I understand, recognizable as that of a lost friend. (Fig. 4.)

The second photograph is one of Lady Glenconner and her son,—a faint, whitish mist appearing over (or on) her left shoulder. This is interesting for the reason that, some time before this picture was taken, a "spirit" had announced through another medium in London that *he would appear in one of Hope's photographs and place his hand on her left shoulder.* Within the whitish mist-like mass, a hand and arm are clearly distinguishable, upon close examination. (Fig. 5.) In photograph number 6 (with a different sitter) the *double* impression of a face is clearly seen, almost obliterating the face of the sitter. These faces appear *sideways*, and represent a woman's face,—wearing glasses! This same woman's face appears in the next picture (No. 7) no less than three times; the uppermost face is the clearest, the one to the right next best, while the lowermost "face" is little more than a misty impression,—in which, however, the eyes are quite clear. This photograph is, on any theory, it seems to me, a very striking and suggestive one, and seems to indicate that the "spirit" attempted three different times to appear and impress the plate, with the greatest strength the first time, and with gradually diminishing energy or power thereafter. This, at least, is the appearance of the facts, and such an interpretation is, it may be said, in strict conformity with the statements made through Mrs. Piper, and other reliable mediums, as to the difficulties actually experienced, in attempting to "communicate." To my mind,—though I do not know the precise conditions under which the picture was obtained—this is a most suggestive and remarkable photograph, strongly indicative of the spiritistic theory.

PSYCHIC PHOTOGRAPHS (8, 9)

In the next illustration (No. 8), a white cloud appears over the sitter's head. There are traces of two "faces" in this cloud, but they are too uncertain to be emphasized. In the next picture, however (No. 9), a face, clearly visible, and enveloped in the usual white mist-like drapery, appears. It is to be noted that the "face" is, in this case, about twice the size of the sitters' heads, as though the "extra" were much nearer the camera. It is, however, still in focus!

Photograph No. 10 shows us Lady Glenconner, and upon the plate a number of "extras" appearing at various "angles" in relation to the sitter's head—some of them at right angles, some of them upside down, etc. (The "cracks" are merely defects upon the plate.) Upon examination, it will be seen that all these faces represent one man, who, apparently, has made a number of separate attempts to "appear" at this sitting. An enlargement of this face is given in photograph No. 11, where the features are quite distinguishable. There are several peculiarities about this face, however, which a closer examination will reveal. The enormous left ear is one of these—mal-formed, or as though in the process of formation. The right side of the head, on the other hand, is partly enveloped in a whitish cloud, through which the outline of the face is faintly perceptible. Further impressions of this same face are shown in photograph No. 12, when several "impressions" were again obtained, all clearly recognizable. In the right-hand photograph, the whitish mass seems to have been just removed from about the head, and it will be seen that part of this still remains, like a thin veil, in front of the *lower* part of the face (under the eyes) and up the left-hand side of the head. This, to me, is a very curious circumstance.

Having thus "cleared the ground," so to speak, let us now consider the more startling statements and experiments by Dr. Baraduc, summarized by him in his work, *Mes Morts; leurs Manifestations*, etc., later on in the account.

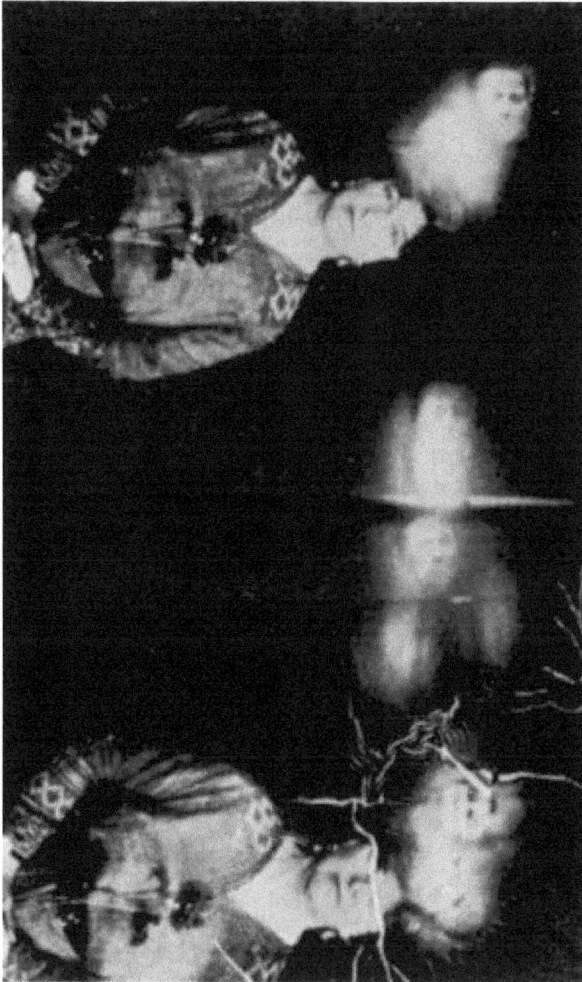

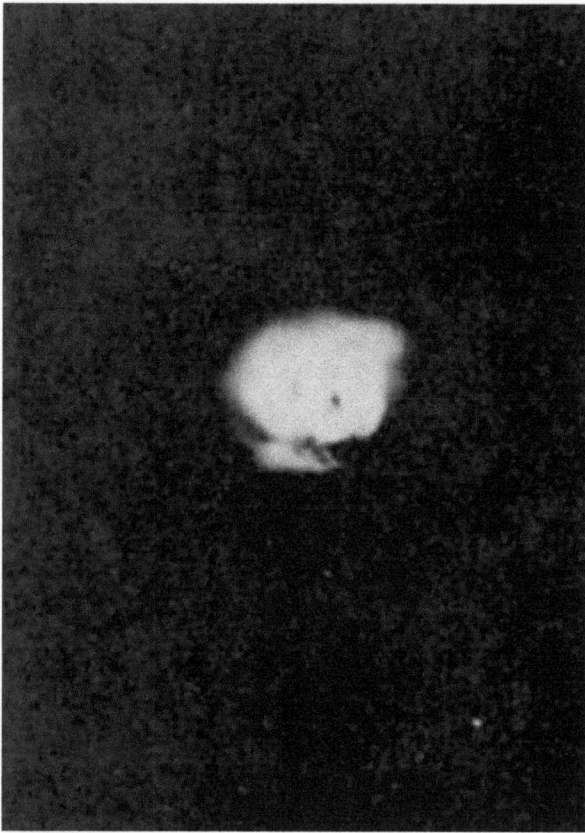

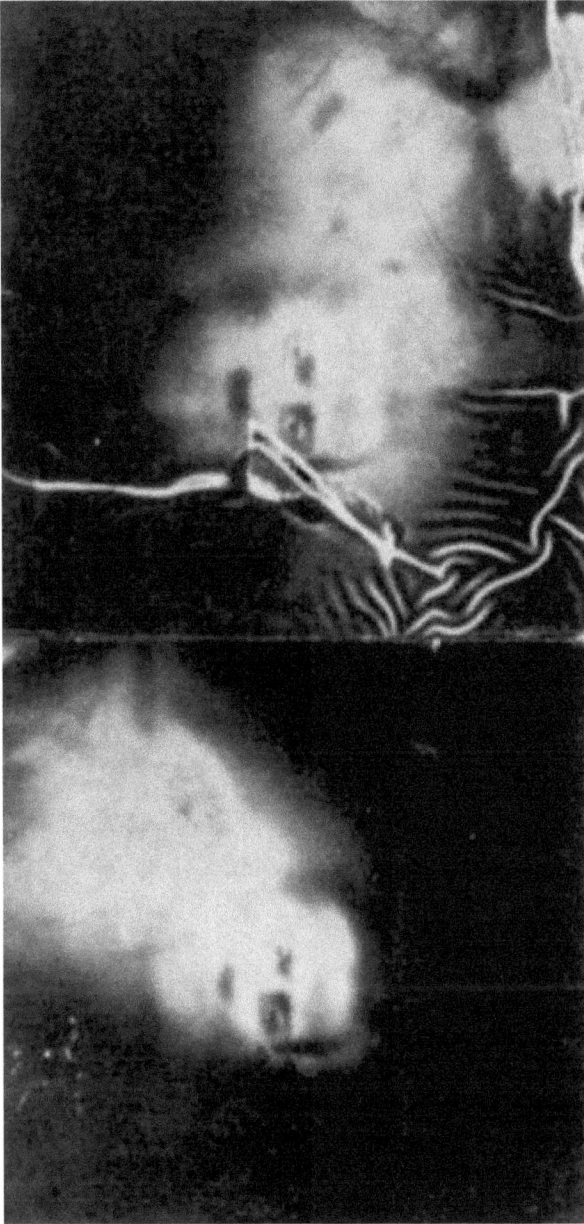

PSYCHIC PHOTOGRAPHS (10, 11, 12)

At a quarter-past nine, on a certain memorable day in April, 1907, died André M. Joseph Baraduc, at the age of nineteen years. Throughout his life there had been a close bond of affection between himself and his father, and we are assured that during the lifetime of the son, telepathic communication had been frequent between them. When he was but nineteen it was discovered that André was suffering from that dread disease, consumption; and henceforward he grew rapidly worse, dying within the year. Toward the close of this year he made two visits to Lourdes, without, however, receiving much benefit in either case, and returning apparently without augmented faith in the cures brought about at that centre. André was exceedingly religious in temperament, as was his father, and both were given to experiments in psychic research. We are informed that, during the lifetime of the son, his "astral" form had been experimentally separated from his bodily frame on more than one occasion. It was only natural to suppose, therefore, that, at the death of this favourite son, the father's grief should be so intense that the emotional reflex found expression in various visions and apparent conversations with the dead boy. For within six hours after the death of André, the son appeared to his father, and thenceforth many apparitions were seen, and several long conversations were apparently held between father and son. Of course, these in themselves would, under the circumstances, have no evidential value, since it is only natural to suppose that hallucinations, both of sight and hearing, would result in a mind so wrought.

These subjective and apparently telepathic experiences of Dr. Baraduc cannot, therefore, be considered of value; but the objective experiences— that is to say, the experiments performed by him are of great interest, since one can hardly suppose that the camera can be hallucinated, because of the grief of the photographer! The impressions left upon the plates, then, such as they are, have their evidential and scientific value, and it is to a consideration of these photographs that we now turn.

Nine hours after the death of André, Dr. Baraduc took the first photograph of the coffin in which the body was deposited. When this plate was developed, it was discovered that, emanating from the coffin, was a formless, misty, wave-like mass, radiating in all directions with considerable force, impinging upon the bodies of those who came into close proximity to the coffin, as though attracted to them by some magnetic force. On one occasion, indeed, the force of this projected fluidic emanation was so great that Dr. Baraduc received an electric shock from head to foot, which produced a temporary vertigo. Emerging from the body are dark, tree-shaped emanations, issuing in formal lines, which gradually diverge, and become more and more attenuated and misty as they recede further and further from the body. Although this photograph[24] does not in itself prove anything supernormal, it is highly suggestive, and it aroused Dr. Baraduc's interest in the subject, and enabled him to pursue his more conclusive experiments immediately upon the death of his wife. (Figs. 13, 14.)

Six months after the death of André, Nadine, Dr. Baraduc's wife and the mother of André, passed quietly away, giving vent, at the moment of her death, to "three gentle sighs." Remembering the result of the former experiments (photographing the body of André shortly after his death), Dr. Baraduc had prepared a camera beside the bed of his wife, and, at the moment of her death, photographed the body, and shortly after developed the plate. Upon it were found three luminous globes resting a few inches above the body. These gradually condensed and became more brilliant. Streaks of light, like fine threads, were also seen darting hither and thither. A quarter of an hour after the death of his wife, Dr. Baraduc took another photograph. Fluidic cords were seen to have developed, partly encircling these globes of light. At three o'clock in the afternoon, or an hour after her death, another photograph was taken. It will be seen from this photograph that the three globes of light have condensed and coalesced into one, obscuring the head of Madame Baraduc, and developing towards the right. Cords were formed in the shape of a figure eight, closed at the top, and opened at the point nearest the body. Thus, as the globe develops in one direction, the cords seem to become more tense, and pull in the opposite direction. The separation becomes more and more complete, until finally, three and a half hours after death, a well-formed globe rested above the body, apparently held together by the encircling, luminous cords, which seemed also to guide and control it. At this moment, the globe becomes separated from the body, and, guided by the cords, floats into Dr. Baraduc's bedroom. He speaks to the globe intensely; the globe thereupon approaches him, and he feels an icy cold breeze, which seems to surround and issue from the ball of light. It then floats away and disappears.

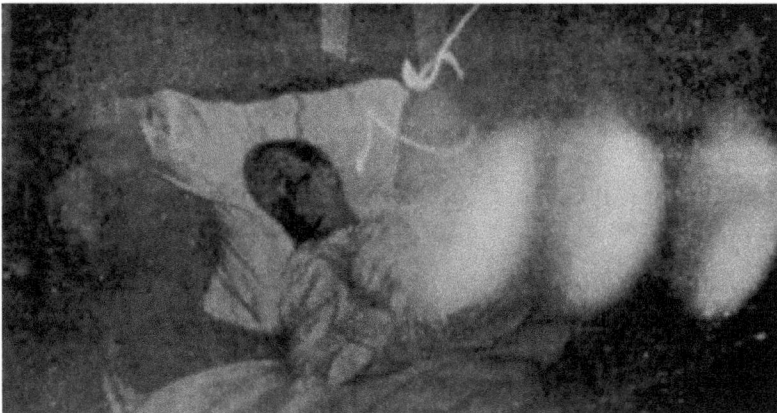

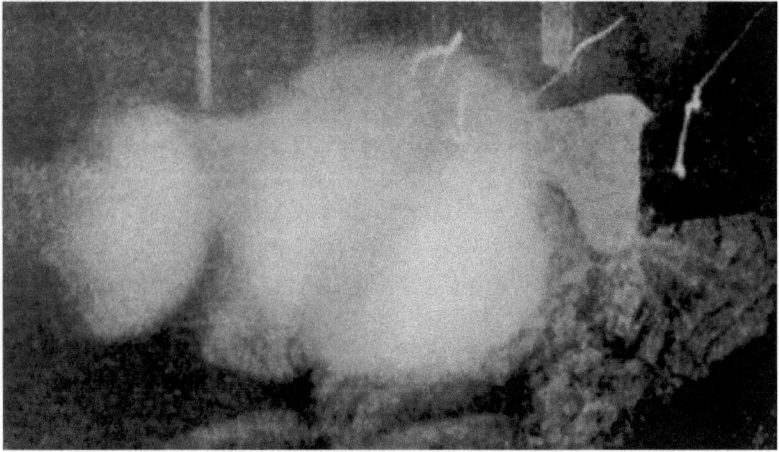
Photographs of the Soul (13, 14)

Frequently, within the next few days after these experiments, Dr. Baraduc saw similar globes in various parts of the house. By means of automatic writing, obtained through the hand of a non-professional psychic, he succeeded at last in establishing communication with this luminous ball, and was informed that it was the encasement of Madame Baraduc's soul, which was still active and alive within it! It was asserted that, as the days progressed, the encircling cords were one by one snapped, and that the spirit more nearly assumed the astral body facsimile of the earthly body. André, however, was seen by him to be a completely developed astral body; and his wife asserted that she too would shortly take her place beside André in her permanent form. As further photographs were not developed, however, there is no experimental evidence confirming these statements.

Although these initial experiments of Dr. Baraduc cannot, of themselves, be considered conclusive, they are nevertheless highly interesting, and should lead to further research in the same direction. The evidence afforded by apparitions, single and collective; by haunted houses; the indirect testimony afforded by the apparent psychic perception by animals; the evidence, such as it is, for "spirit photography"; the recent experiments in thought-photography, and the photographs made at the séances of Eusapia Palladino, all tend to confirm, it seems to me, the conclusions arrived at by Dr. Baraduc, as the result of his preliminary researches. If an astral body of some sort exists, it must occupy space; and, being space-occupying, must, *a priori*, be material enough to occupy it! Whether or not this material is sufficiently solid to reflect light waves, and make an impression upon the sensitive plate of the camera, is an aspect of the problem still open to debate.

Further indirect testimony is afforded by the statements of clairvoyants, and by the direct testimony (taking it for what it is worth) of so-called "spirits" who communicate their sensations and the knowledge they have gained after bodily death. They invariably assert that there *is* an astral facsimile, or spiritual replica, of the physical body. Repellent as the idea may be to some of a semi-material, space-occupying soul, the facts would seem to indicate that such is true. Yet there might be a way out of the difficulty, since we might still suppose that the soul, or seat of consciousness, exists as a point of force within this spiritual organism. Whichever theory is ultimately proved correct cannot, of course, be settled by *a priori* speculation, but by *facts*; and such experiments as those conducted by Dr. Baraduc in "photographing the soul" are, perhaps, the best line of investigation to follow, and one from which,—with the improvements in photography,—the most is to be hoped.

The reader now has the facts before him. I have no theory to offer as to the nature of these photographs, save that they appear to me to be genuine and supernormal from all the evidence and testimony that I have been enabled to obtain. In my *Physical Phenomena of Spiritualism* I have explained a number of ways in which fraudulent "spirit" photographs can be obtained; and in *Modern Psychical Phenomena* I reproduced a number of photographs which seemed to me to be supported by excellent testimony, and which were, so far as I could see, genuine psychic photographs. In that volume I also discussed the various *theories* which have been advanced in the past to explain these extraordinary photographs. The present collection is intended merely to supplement the former, and to present a number of photographs the solution for which is, it seems to me, yet to be found.

FOOTNOTES:

[22] Regarding the earlier photographs, however (those obtained by Mrs. Dupont Lee), further evidence has caused me to modify my belief in their supernormal value, and I should now attach no "evidential value" to them at all, strictly speaking. In an excellent criticism of the Lee photographs, published in the *Proceedings*, Amer. S.P.R., vol. xiii. pp. 529-87, Dr. Walter F. Prince has shown the undoubtedly fraudulent character of the Lee photographs—certainly those with which Keeler had anything to do. The others are still *sub judice.*

[23] T. C. and E. C. Jack, Edinburgh.

[24] Not reproduced here.

CHAPTER VII

HALLUCINATION AND THE PHYSICAL PHENOMENA OF SPIRITUALISM[25]

The discussion begun by Count Solovovo, and continued by Miss Johnson,[26] is assuredly of supreme importance to psychical research. Whether or no many of the alleged "physical phenomena" are genuine, or whether they are merely hallucinatory in character, is a question which involves—not only the phenomena themselves, but psychology and human life in general, and even influences strongly science and scientific experiments in other fields.... The senses are to be relied upon in every science other than psychic research; that seems to be the *dictum* of the world, and strange and even absurd as it may seem, it is, as we know, more or less founded upon fact. In no other science is fraud practised as it is in this; in practically no other line of research are the mental and physical powers so strained out of their usual or normal relations and perceptions as they are in this. It is only right, then, that Caution should be the password, and should be most rigidly employed in all such investigations as these.

While admitting all this, however, one must also admit that it is easy to go too far in the opposite direction, and reject evidence which depends upon the senses simply *because* they depend upon them. This, I think, is invalid reasoning. No one would be more willing than I to admit their fallibility and untrustworthiness—especially when we are dealing with conditions and phenomena where mal-observation is possible; but I do not think that any negative conclusion can be drawn from this. The case is still an open one; nothing is *proved*, one way or the other, and, in such work as ours, proof— and not mere conjecture—must be forthcoming. Very true it is that proof of the sort desired is often impossible; but it is obtained sometimes. If a medium be caught masquerading in a white muslin "robe" and a mask, we are doubtless within our rights in saying that the medium has been *proved* a fraud. But failure to detect such trickery does not prove the phenomena genuine. That would depend upon other considerations, and would only raise a *presumption* in favour of their authenticity. In such a case, "proof" is largely a question of relative probability, and can be obtained only by making the probability in favour of the reality of the phenomena so strong that the negative aspect is rendered logically unsound by the sheer weight of evidence against it.

These trite remarks were nevertheless rendered necessary because of the enormous amount of misunderstanding which exists in connection with these phenomena, and of the general methods and objects of psychic research. The papers that have already been published on the question of hallucination in relation to the physical phenomena should do much to clear away many of these misconceptions, for in them we find (i) a willingness to treat the phenomena seriously; (ii) an admission that the witnesses described what they thought they saw; and (iii) a certain amount of evidence advanced to show that the alleged phenomena were in reality hallucinatory in character, while appearing to be external physical realities to the onlookers. Let us now examine the evidence advanced, and see in how far it is conclusive of the theory entertained—the hypothesis of hallucination.

As both Count Solovovo and Miss Johnson have concentrated their attention upon the phenomena occurring in the presence of D. D. Home, I shall do so likewise in the first part of this chapter. As briefly as possible, I shall review their papers, before passing on to more general remarks— remarks which it is the object of this paper to bring into prominence.

Count Solovovo thinks that it is evidence in favour of the hallucination theory that: "A flower or other small object is seen to move; one person present will see a luminous cloud hovering over it, another will detect a nebulous-looking hand, whilst others will see nothing but the moving flower."[27]

Miss Johnson agrees with this, and in fact goes so far as to say: "If these hands had been completely invisible to some person with normal sight looking directly at them in a good light, we should then have good evidence that they were hallucinatory."[28]

To this I cannot agree. I find myself completely differing from Miss Johnson in my interpretation of such an incident as this. For, while hallucination is one possible theory to account for the phenomena, another equally plausible theory is that the hands were in fact objective and real, but were only perceptible to various individuals in varying degrees. This aspect of the problem is hardly touched upon by Count Solovovo, but is discussed at some length by Miss Johnson. In this connection she says:

"Here [in the hand, i.e.] is a kind of matter which is not only temporary in character—a fact in itself extraordinary enough—but exhibits another quite unprecedented characteristic in the arbitrary selectiveness of its effects on other matter. In order to be visible at all, it must reflect light. How does it manage to reflect light that affects the retina of one person and not the retina of another? We may reply that the difference must lie in the retinae, one being more sensitive than the other. But we do not find the same difference of sensitivity in regard to the light reflected from ordinary objects. It seems to follow then that the light reflected from the spirit-hand is a peculiar kind of light, lying outside the limits of the ordinary visible spectrum. But in that case, why is not the person with the more sensitive retina affected by it? For of course all ordinary objects are constantly giving off radiations outside the limits of the visible spectrum; but our supposed sensitive apparently does not perceive them."[29]

First, as to the matters of fact. Where is the evidence that those with the most sensitive retinae were not the very ones who perceived, most perfectly, the spirit-hand? Were a series of experiments conducted to show which of the onlookers possessed the most sensitive eyes? If so, where are these experiments recorded? It is quite possible that the body is constantly giving off a kind of *aura*—perceptible to some, invisible to others; and the fact that some do not see it is no proof that it is not there. If the experiments of Reichenbach and others go for anything, indeed, there is very good evidence that such emanations do take place—and I venture to think (however rank heresy this may appear) that these experiments have never been completely refuted, and the results obtained shown to be traceable *in toto* to suggestion. The eyes of certain individuals might be attuned to receive vibrations or impressions quite imperceptible to others, no matter how sensitive their retinae to normal perceptions or sensations.

But, quite apart from such purely "physical" speculations, I can quite conceive that these hands were not "seen" in the ordinary sense of the word at all. The physical eyes may have played some part in their perception, but only a small part. It is quite possible that "hands" of the character here seen were active and functioning upon another plane altogether than the sense plane, and were perceived at the time by a species of *clairvoyance*. What "clairvoyance" is I do not pretend to know (unless spiritism be true, in which case I can quite easily conceive its *modus operandi*), but the mass of evidence in its favour seems to place it quite beyond the pale of doubt. But even if this be not granted, I can quite see how a certain *rapport* between the sitter and the hand—or the intelligence behind the hand—might easily enable one sitter to perceive it, and not another. Analogies from trance phenomena and even from experimental thought-transference might be drawn here, in favour of such a theory. The whole theory of apparitions at the moment of death depends upon this established *rapport*, since, if it did not exist, and affect the results, the apparition might just as well appear to Tom, Dick, and Harry as to the percipient—and the percipient is such (supposedly) simply by reason of this pre-established *rapport*.

There might be, then, a certain *rapport* between some sitters and a plane of activity upon which such hands manifest, enabling these individuals to see the hands, while prohibiting others from seeing them. The receptivity or capacity might indicate a greater or lesser degree of psychic capacity—they would be "more mediumistic." That is, the more mediumistic the sitter, the more likely would he be to perceive such hands. And of course we all know in this connection that mediums or psychics in a circle will perceive hands and faces and other forms quite invisible to the ordinary observer. The usual recourse in such cases is to assume that the mediums are fraudulently in league with one another; but when unprofessional psychics experience the same sensations (or perceptions) there is good ground for calling a halt, and asking whether or not the sensations were not possibly genuine in the case of the professional medium also.

In other words, and to summarize this part of the discussion, I can only say that there seems to me no valid reason for thinking that the spirit-hands in Home's séances were probably hallucinatory in character because only some of the sitters saw them. They might just as well be explained by supposing that certain of the sitters were more psychic or mediumistic than the others, and these saw—clairvoyantly or by some similar mode of psychic perception—hands and forms invisible to those less sensitive. It need hardly be said that the carrying about of objects by these hands renders their objective nature and existence far more probable than if such movements had never taken place. These physical phenomena remain, no matter what view we take of the visible (or invisible) hands.

In speaking next of Home's "full-form phantasms," Miss Johnson draws attention to the fact, so often pointed out by Mr. Podmore, that the various witnesses in subsequent accounts do not describe the phenomena in the same terms or in precisely the same manner. The narrative differs in the various accounts, and the phenomena appear far more remarkable in some than in others. The inference is that none of them is right—certainly not the more remarkable ones—and that the inaccuracy of the reports invalidates the records.

Now I have nothing to say against this method *as* a method. But I think it can be pushed too far and wrong deductions drawn therefrom. It is right to discount the value of the evidence, but that is a different thing from discrediting it altogether. If individual records differ when describing any particular phenomenon it is right that the less marvellous be accepted as the more probable; but this is not saying that the phenomenon did not take place at all! Any two accounts of a given phenomenon must necessarily differ—more or less, according to circumstances. But if all the accounts obviously concern a given phenomenon, and if they agree, even in the essential outlines, it is probable that the event resembled the description more or less; and if in all these accounts there is no evidence of fraud forthcoming, and no indications that it existed, we must take it for granted that no suspicious circumstances were noted and no fraud detected—for otherwise it would have found its way into the records. And the fact that it never did find its way into any of them (with one doubtful exception, *Journal, S.P.R.,* vol. iv. pp. 120-21, and Jan. and May 1903) seems to indicate, not that the phenomena were necessarily genuine, but that the central theme of the account, so to speak—the phenomenon—was seen alike by all, and was variously described by the witnesses afterward in the subsequent reports. The minor discrepancies do not suffice to explain away the phenomenon altogether. They serve merely to render it less marvellous. Many psychic researchers, however, seem to imagine that because the various accounts do not agree, the fact recorded probably did not occur at all. That is surely an entirely unwarranted supposition, and were this carried to its logical conclusion, would suffice to disprove the whole of the past history of the human race.

Miss Johnson's discussion of Home's famous levitation out of one window and in at another is surely masterly, and is precisely the kind of criticism which psychic research needs. After reading her account, I can only say that were this case an isolated incident, unsupported by any similar cases of a like nature, it would be so far "explained away" as to lose all evidential value. At the same time I think that Count Solovovo sums the whole argument up when he says that none of Home's phenomena were ever *proved* to be hallucinatory; all that has been done by the discussion is to show that some of them *might possibly* have been so. And there is a great difference between the two. There is a natural tendency in many minds to assume and take for granted that because a given phenomenon might possibly have been produced by fraud, it was unquestionably produced in that manner. That is quite an unwarranted supposition, and fraud should be clearly *proved* in every given instance before a medium be charged with trickery. This is a rule far too seldom observed by sceptical investigators, but an important one nevertheless.

Leaving aside this particular case of Home's levitation, however, it may be said that there are others on record far more conclusive in character, and against which many of Miss Johnson's criticisms could not be levelled. Taken singly, it is probable that no single case of any class of phenomena would prove convincing to a sceptic; sufficient objections could be raised, and sufficient discrepancies in the records pointed out, to invalidate any evidence whatever. Quite apart from any *a priori* objections, any single incident can almost invariably be "explained away." It is the weight of a great *mass* of cumulative evidence which tells the tale. The most expert and exact description of the fall of a meteor would not have forced an acceptance from the scientific world; the relative improbability of the whole of the past experience of the human race would have been so much greater than the fact that the latter would have been discredited. Gradually it would have receded in the mind, and even the original witness might ultimately be persuaded that he had not in reality seen a meteor at all!

And so it is with psychic research; and so it is with the theory under discussion. No single incident, taken by itself, can be said to prove anything; only the great mass of facts, taken together, and all pointing in the same direction, can be said to do so. One can quite see how this would be the case, e.g. in Mrs. Piper's automatic utterances or writings. No matter how conclusive any individual "test" might be, it would prove nothing by itself. No matter how well attested an apparition at the moment of death, singly it would indicate no telepathic communication nor other supernormal factor at work. But together these cases form a strand[30] which becomes too strong to be broken, and which, taken together, practically prove telepathic communication at the moment of death—at least so thought Professor Sidgwick's Committee, of which Miss Johnson was one member. (See *Proceedings, S.P.R.*, vol. x. p. 394.)

In Home's case, then, the evidence for his levitation phenomena rests, not on any one case taken by itself, but on the mass of cumulative testimony offered by scores of witnesses. However completely one case might be explained away, the other cases still remain to us—each case standing on its own merits, and many of them excellently observed, if not so well recorded. For example, the cases mentioned by Sir. William Crookes (*Journal, S.P.R.*, vol. vi. p. 342) are certainly far superior, in point of observation, to the famous case so severely criticized by Miss Johnson. And I think that if one is going to offer any hypothesis at all, it must be one that covers *all* the facts, and not merely one which explains only some of them. The hallucinatory nature of Home's phenomena is certainly not inclusive—it does not include many of the more striking incidents to say nothing of the lesser phenomena. For this reason, it does not appear to me to be conclusive either.

After a brief discussion of Home's fire-tests, which Miss Johnson practically admits are inexplicable by any process either of fraud or of hallucination known to her (p. 498), she passes on to what are called "quasi-hypnotic" effects. To many of the incidents classed by Miss Johnson as due to suggestion, I should be inclined to give an entirely different interpretation. Some of them doubtless resemble hallucinations in a striking degree, but what evidence is there that, e.g., passes made over the heads of the sitters can induce identical hallucinations in all of them; or that, because one of the circle becomes hysterical, the others are thereby rendered susceptible to suggestion? However, I shall defer this question until we come to discuss hallucination in general.

After some wholesome criticisms devoted to the "recognition" of materialized forms, and the very true statement (p. 509) that "a very small error in perception may sometimes lead to a very large error of inference," Miss Johnson ends her remarkably interesting paper with two illustrations—one a hallucination (?)[31] induced by false association of ideas; the other an incident in her own experience, occurring at a séance with Eusapia Palladino. Both of these are of importance, and should be studied carefully.

Count Solovovo on the contrary considers it somewhat in favour of the hallucination theory that hands were found to melt in the sitters' grasp, when they were forcibly retained (p. 441). I cannot agree with this. It is a different thing to say that hallucination might account for the facts, and saying that the facts tell in favour of hallucination. Chance might account for an experimental apparition, but the fact that the apparition occurred does not prove it to be chance. One must be careful to distinguish facts and inferences, in a case of this character. Whether or not the hands were hallucinatory will depend, not upon *a priori* probability, or the fact they were visible to some, invisible to others, (for all this might just as well be accounted for on the opposing theory), but upon the fact that, so far as we know, there is no analogy whatever between this oft-recorded event and any of the phenomena of suggestion known to us. If we offer a theory to explain certain facts, it must not only explain them in a rational manner, but must dovetail into what we know—into *the known*. That is the whole method of science. If, therefore, a man advances "hallucination" as an explanation of such facts as those under discussion, he must show how it is that hallucination might be supposed to work: he must bring forward some analogies and examples of somewhat similar instances in order to have a case at all. In science, we cannot speculate *in vacuo*, but must connect with what is already known, if we wish to be scientific at all. What analogies, then, have we that spirit-hands, similar to those described, can be created by suggestion; and that suggestion can cause a number of investigators, at various times, in various places, to believe that these hands melted in theirs while they were trying to retain them?

I venture to think we have no analogies whatever. It is quite possible that a subject in a hypnotic trance might be induced to believe that he was holding a hand while in fact no hand was there, and, further, that this hand melted away in his grasp while he was holding fast on to it. But I can see practically no resemblance whatever between the two cases. For, in the case we have supposed (i) the hand did not move any material object; (ii) no one but the hypnotized subject saw the hand; and (iii) the illusion was only induced by repeated verbal suggestion to a subject already hypnotized. Where is the analogy in the two cases? Home's hands moved objects; they

- 134 -

were seen by several people at once; and, so far as the records prove anything, they prove that constant verbal suggestions of the sort necessary were certainly *not* given, while there is no evidence whatever that the subjects were hypnotized! On this very subject, speaking of Home's séances, Sir William Crookes has said:

"General conversation was going on all the time, and on many occasions something on the table had moved some time before Home was aware of it. We had to draw his attention to such things far oftener than he drew our attention to them. Indeed, he sometimes used to annoy me by his indifference to what was going on...."[32]

Does this look like suggestion? Is there any similarity between the two cases? Their differences are too obvious to dwell upon. And, apart from the performances of the Hindu fakirs (which I have discussed elsewhere,[33] and which Count Solovovo himself thinks too few and too weak evidentially to require serious consideration), there is no similarity between an hallucination induced in a hypnotized subject by constant verbal suggestion, and one supposedly induced instantaneously in a large number of persons, not hypnotized, without any suggestion. The cases cannot be considered similar, or even as resembling one another in the slightest degree; while the improbability is heightened a thousandfold by the fact that these hands apparently performed physical actions and moved physical objects at the same time. The coincidence would have to be explained as well as the hallucination, in that case.

Both Count Solovovo and Miss Johnson lay particular stress upon the fact that the Master of Lindsay seems to have been extremely suggestible. Assuredly, that is an important point in so far as his own experiences are concerned, but the fact in nowise affects the experiences of *others*. In order to prove that suggestibility played an important part in the phenomena, it would be necessary to show that *all* witnesses of the phenomena were suggestible—for the phenomena were seen by all in a slightly varying degree. Yet there is no evidence that many of the witnesses were suggestible at all: they did not see things Home suggested they should see, while, on the other hand, they saw things quite on their own account, when Home was busily engaged in conversation with some one else. The whole case must be made to hang together, and if "suggestion" be the key to the puzzle, it certainly fits the lock remarkably ill.[34]

In summing-up his paper and the evidence contained therein, Count Solovovo concludes:

"For my own part I lay it down as a general proposition ... that the testimony of several sane, honest and intelligent eye-witnesses is, broadly speaking, proof of the objectivity of any phenomenon. If there are people who maintain an opposite view, let them make experiments themselves" (p. 477).

That is precisely the position I should assume: I do not believe that collective hallucinations of the kind supposed exist at spiritistic séances, except perhaps very rarely, and to special gatherings of individuals. Let me now adduce the evidence in favour of my position, and the reasons for my taking this stand so strongly.

First, then, let us distinguish between *illusions* and *hallucinations*, as this is of the very greatest importance in a discussion such as this. An illusion is a false sensory perception, the basis of which is, nevertheless, real. Thus, if an old coat in a corner of the room be mistaken for a dog, that would be an illusion. A *point de repère* is there—a peg, upon which the mind hangs its false inferences or perceptions. An hallucination, on the other hand, is entirely a creation of the mind, and there is, in this case, no *point de repère*, which exists externally, and serves as the basis of the hallucination. Roughly speaking, this may be said to be the difference between the two. Now, let us apply this to Home's séances, and to spiritistic séances in general.

During the course of my twenty years' constant investigation, I have had many score séances with various mediums—slate-writing mediums, materializing mediums, physical mediums, clairvoyant mediums, *et hoc genus omne*. Speaking now of materialization séances only—of which I have seen many—I may say that in all my investigations *I have never seen one single instance of suggested or spontaneous hallucination*. Plenty of *illusions* were observed, but never the trace of a full-blown hallucination.[35] And I venture to think that, if we examine the evidence in the case of D. D. Home, we find very few cases which could have been illusions—the vast majority of them seem to have been "pure hallucinations"—if they were psychological processes (as opposed to physical) at all. So that we should have to suppose that we find in these séances—not mere illusions, commonly seen at spiritualistic séances, but full-blown hallucinations of a type rarely or never seen elsewhere. In other words, these séances present evidences of psychological processes for which we can find no analogy in any other series of séances, or in hypnotic or any other phenomena with which we are familiar. I venture to think that this entirely *new* order of things cannot be accepted upon such evidence: that the hypothesis of hallucination cannot be said to explain anything whatever, inasmuch as it is entirely unsupported by facts, and finds no analogies whatever in any other psychological processes known to us.

At the very conclusion of his paper, Count Solovovo places his finger upon the vulnerable spot: he there points out the only way to solve the difficulty. It is by the accumulation and study of *new facts*. Discussions as to the historical phenomena might go on for ever and the question still remain unsolved. The only way out of the difficulty is to establish, if possible, the objective or the hallucinatory character of these newer phenomena—if such are obtained—and from them draw conclusions concerning the older manifestations. If these newer phenomena turn out to be hallucinatory—in spite of all the testimony in favour of their being objective—then it is highly probable that many of the older phenomena were hallucinatory also. If, on the other hand, the newer phenomena turn out to be physical and objective, then the improbability of the older manifestations having been hallucinatory is proportionately increased—until it becomes almost a certainty that they were not so. For, if physical phenomena of a genuine character ever do occur, the *a priori* improbability is at once removed, and thenceforward there is but little ground for objecting to the phenomena in Home's case; and not only those, but the phenomena in the case of Stainton Moses, and scores of others less well attested. The props would have been knocked from beneath all logical scepticism of the historical phenomena, once newer manifestations of the same type be proved true. The whole case hinges upon the fact of whether or not such new facts as may be forthcoming tend to prove either the one theory or the other. Let us therefore turn to this newer evidence, and see which alternative is rendered more probable by the phenomena in question.

This newer evidence is, of course, supplied by the case of Eusapia Palladino. Here we find phenomena of a physical character recorded by many men and women—including numerous eminent scientists—not one of whom tolerates for a moment the idea that these phenomena are hallucinatory. Indeed, the photographs of table levitations, of hands and heads,[36] of instruments flying through the air,[37] and the impressions left in cakes of plaster,[38] leave no doubt whatever that, in this case, the phenomena—no matter how produced—are objective. This conclusion is further supported by the fact that registering apparatus has been employed, and has successfully recorded the results of physical movements. From this, it is certain that real, objective facts have been observed.[39] Whether the phenomena were due to fraud or were the results of the operation of some supernormal force, or whatever their explanation, they were certainly not due to hallucination.

Our own sittings, it seems to me, abundantly confirm this conclusion. During the greater part of the time, when phenomena were in progress, Eusapia was passive and silent: when she did speak, she did not suggest anything to us directly, and even if she had done so, it would have been in Italian—a language I do not understand. And yet I saw the phenomena— the movements of objects, the hands and the heads, and felt the touches— just as the others did: in fact, I think I may say *more* frequently than either of my colleagues did. How was this? Eusapia only "suggested" anything to us on three occasions, and on two of these we failed to perceive what she wished us to see! On the other hand, we frequently perceived what she did not "suggest" to us, and which came as a complete surprise to us all. The expression "Oh!" occurring, as it does, at several places in the notes, shows how unexpected the manifestation was. When one's hair is suddenly and forcibly pulled by living fingers, and when one is banged over the head by a closed fist, and when one is grasped by a hand and pulled so forcibly as to almost upset one into the cabinet—it requires a strong imagination to believe that this is nothing but hallucination. Then, too, we all saw the phenomenon at the same instant, invariably; and if one of us failed to do so, it was always because there was a physical cause for it: the curtain intervened, or something of a similar nature occurred. I need hardly point out that this, in itself—looked at from one point of view—is exceedingly strong evidence that the manifestation was not hallucinatory, but objective. The unexpected nature of the majority of the phenomena—when Eusapia was in deep trance, and we were doing all the talking—renders the hypothesis of hallucination quite untenable, it seems to me; at least, if any one chooses to defend it, he must give some analogies and somewhat similar instances of the power of suggestion—a task that will never be satisfactorily undertaken; of that I am sure.

No; whatever be the interpretation of these phenomena, they are certainly not hallucinatory. And if they were objective, it is almost certain that the Home phenomena were objective also—since the parallel between the two cases is often extremely close.

And this, it appears to me, is the only way of approaching this problem that is liable to prove conclusive or trustworthy. Discussions of historical phenomena will never settle anything one way or the other: nothing is *proved* thereby, one way or the other. The only conclusive method, as Count Solovovo pointed out—and I heartily agree with him—is the accumulation of *new facts*; and these new facts, when obtained, have, it appears to me (and to my colleagues also), proved beyond all question that the phenomena were genuine in at least some instances; and, that once admitted, the *a priori* doubts are removed, and the historic phenomena raised to a standard of probability which amounts to certitude. Some of the physical phenomena of spiritualism are objective—real, external facts; and I am assured that they are not due to fraud or trickery. Whatever their ultimate explanation, however, they can no longer be said to be due to any form of hallucination in the sitters.

FOOTNOTES:

[25] The chapter which follows originally appeared in the *Journal* of the American S.P.R. (December 1909), and was critical of the articles of Miss Alice Johnson and Count Solovovo, which had previously appeared in the English *Proceedings*. While the chapter is self-explanatory, it may be well to say that Count Solovovo, in his original paper, considered the "hallucination theory" as a possible explanation of certain physical phenomena—such as those of D. D. Home—and, after a lengthy discussion, came to the conclusion that it would be extremely difficult to believe that hallucination could account for all the observed facts. Miss Johnson, in her reply, inclined rather more to the hallucination theory—at least in some cases—and endeavoured to show how it might have occurred on several occasions. My paper is critical of these articles—chiefly Miss Johnson's; and I have here endeavoured to combat the hallucination theory,—which I do not believe to have nearly so wide a range as Miss Johnson supposes. The interested reader is referred to the original papers, as well as to the discussion which follows; after which he may decide for himself which seems to him the more rational explanation of the facts.

[26] *Proceedings, S.P.R.*, vol. xxi. pp. 436-515.

[27] *Researches in the Phenomena of Spiritualism*, p. 92.

[28] *Proceedings, S.P.R.*, vol. xxi. p. 488.

[29] *Proceedings, S.P.R.*, vol. xxi. p. 487.

[30] Critics are apt to compare psychic phenomena to the links of a chain—each phenomenon being a separate link. As the chain is only as strong as its separate links, it has been pointed out, and as each case, taken by itself, can be shown to be inconclusive, it is obvious that the whole of psychic research comes to naught. This objection is met, it seems to me, by the following consideration. Each separate case represents, not the link of a chain, but the thread of a woven rope, which, taken by itself, is extremely weak, but which, when placed beside hundreds of others, becomes so strong as to be practically unbreakable.

[31] This appears to me to be rather an illusion than a pure hallucination. Miss Johnson's own case appears to me to be an illusion also. See the discussion of this point later on, however.

[32] *Journal*, vol. vi. p. 343.

[33] See *The Physical Phenomena of Spiritualism*, pp. 386-93, and my pamphlet *Hindu Magic*, for a discussion of these performances, and of the theory of hallucination in connection therewith.

[34] See, e.g., Count Solovovo's position which he was driven to accept—that the chair-threading witnessed by him was due to unconscious telepathic suggestion! (p. 469). The position appears to me to be absolutely untenable, in face of the evidence he himself adduces.

[35] An excellent example of an illusion generated by the conditions of a spiritualistic séance is the following, which occurred to myself at Lily Dale, N. Y., during my investigations there in the summer of 1907, and which I reported in the *Proceedings of the American S.P.R.*, as follows:—

"My sister 'Eva' materialized for me. I suggested 'Eva' and she 'came.' I never had a sister Eva, so she was a little out of place. However, she 'came' as a little girl about ten years old, with a hooked nose, bright black eyes, and a fringe of false hair over her forehead. Her doll-like appearance was very manifest. After she de-materialized, I was on the point of walking back to my chair, but was told to wait. I returned to the curtains of the cabinet, and my mother announced herself present, 'who had died from consumption.' The curtains were pulled aside, and I put my face close to the opening, since it was so dark I could see nothing. And there, in the dim twilight of that séance room, I beheld one of the most ghastly, most truly terrifying faces I have ever seen. It was white and drawn, and almost shiny in its glossy, ashen hue. The eyes were wide open and staring—fixed. The head and face were encircled in white; and altogether the face was one of the most appalling I have ever beheld, and it would have required a great deal of fortitude, for the moment, to look steadfastly at that terrifying face—in that quiet, still room, in response to the spirit's demand: 'Look at me!' The distance between our faces was not more than six inches; and after the first shock, I regarded the face intently. I was spurred by curiosity and excitement, and prompted yet further by the spirit form, who grasped my wrist, through the curtain, and drew me yet closer—until I was nearly in the cabinet itself. I remembered that my mother had not died from consumption, and that the present face in nowise resembled hers, and my feeling of terror lasted but an instant; but it was there at the time, I confess. I regarded the face intently, and it was gradually withdrawn into the shadow of the cabinet, and the curtains pulled over it. *I am certain that, had I been in an excited and unbalanced frame of mind at that instant, I should have sworn that the face melted away as I looked at it.* But my mental balance was by that time regained, and I could analyse what was before me. I can quite easily see how it is that persons can swear to the melting away of a face before their eyes, after my own experience. The appearances clearly indicated that, and it was only my alertness to the possibility of deception in this direction, which prevented my testifying to the same effect." (See my *Personal Experiences in Spiritualism*, pp. 31-32.)

[36] *Annals of Psychical Science*, April 1908, pp. 181-91.

[37] *Ibid.*, April-June 1909, pp. 285-305.

[38] Flammarion: *Mysterious Psychic Forces*; Morselli: *Psicologia e Spiritismo*; De Fontenay: *A Propos d'Eusapia Paladino*; De Rochas: *L'Exteriorization de la Motricite*, etc.

[39] Why were Sir William Crookes' experiments with the spring balance not discussed, by the way, in this connection? Here we have indubitable proof of the objectivity of the phenomena; even Mr. Podmore being driven to grant this, and suppose that the manifestations were the result of some trick.—*Modern Spiritualism*, vol. ii. p. 242.

CHAPTER VIII

THE PROBLEMS OF TELEPATHY

"I suppose everybody would say it would be an extraordinary circumstance," said the Right Hon. A. J. Balfour, M.P., F.R.S., in his Presidential Address before the Society for Psychical Research, some years ago, "if at no distant date this earth on which we dwell were to come into collision with some unknown body travelling through space, and, as the result of that collision, be resolved into the original gases of which it is composed.... This is a specimen of a dramatically extraordinary event. Now I will give you a case of what I mean by a scientifically extraordinary event—which you will at once perceive may be one which, at first sight and to many observers, may appear almost commonplace and familiar. I have constantly met people who will tell you, with no apparent consciousness that they are saying anything more out of the way than an observation about the weather, that by the exercise of their will they can make anybody at a little distance turn round and look at them. Now such a fact (if fact it be) is far more scientifically extraordinary than would be the destruction of this globe by some such celestial catastrophe as I have imagined. How profoundly mistaken, then, are they who think that this exercise of 'will power,' as they call it, is the most natural and the most normal thing in the world, something which everybody should have expected, something which hardly deserves scientific notice or requires scientific explanation. In reality it is a profound mystery, if it is true, or if anything like it be true; and no event, however startling, which easily finds its appropriate niche in the structure of the physical sciences ought to exercise so much intellectual curiosity as this dull and at first sight commonplace phenomenon." (*Proceedings, S.P.R.*, vol. x. pp. 9-10.)

These were the words, not only of the Premier of England, but of an exceptionally well-balanced and learned man of science, from which it will be seen how extraordinary a thing this "thought-transference" or "telepathy" is to the scientific world; and how hard it is for the *savant* to accept it! Yet, as Mr. Balfour says, nearly every one at the present time believes in telepathy, and accepts it as the only explanation for certain facts, and as a more or less commonplace event. Why, then, is there so much mystery about it; *why* is it so extraordinary?

The reason for this lies in the fact that psychologists hold a certain view of the nature of the mind which is not shared or understood by the majority of persons. They believe that the mind, or consciousness, is bound up with the functionings of the brain; and that it is inseparable from them. Just as digestion is a function of the whole digestive apparatus, circulation of the circulatory apparatus, and respiration of the respiratory apparatus; just so, it is believed, is thinking a function of the thinking apparatus—the brain and nervous system. And one is no more detachable than the other; and one is no more "immortal" after the death of the body than the other. All these functions fall away and perish at once, at the moment of death. This is the position of positive, materialistic psychology—which is the psychology taught in our schools and colleges at the present day. Naturally, our professors do not believe in telepathy; were this theory true, it would be "impossible," just as impossible as it is for a solid object to be in two places at the same time. Consciousness cannot be both inside the brain and out of it; and as it is believed to reside inside, it cannot be outside! As it is a function of nervous tissue, how can it make itself manifest at a distance of 2000 miles—at the moment, too, when it is being annihilated. Obviously the thing is impossible!

But, alas for science (or rather for the dogmatic scientist), the experience of the past tells us that many things deemed impossible are nevertheless facts. Though they are jeered at when they are first brought to the attention of the scientific world, subsequent investigation has only served to confirm them.... It is on record that no physician over forty years of age at the time of his great discovery ever accepted Harvey's proof of the circulation of the blood—so great was the force of tradition and orthodoxy.... And today the facts of "psychical research" are laughed at, and its investigators held up to ridicule, because of this same spirit of prejudice and intolerance, and the desire to mock at what we do not understand. "But," as Professor James so well remarked *à propos* of this subject, "whenever a debate between the mystics and the scientists has been once for all decided, it is the mystics who have usually proved to be right about the *facts*, while the scientists had the better of it in respect to *theories*." But inasmuch as only the "facts" are now in dispute, and no one cares as yet what theory shall be adopted in order to explain them, is it not time at least to investigate them, and to see whether or not such facts exist—quite irrespective of whether they are explainable, when found?

The facts, then; are they true or are they not? It is a question quite open to discussion, one quite capable of being solved by scientific methods. It is useless to say beforehand whether or not such and such things are or are not possible; the question is: Do they exist? We must not question their utility either, even if true, for this never enters into any scientific question of fact. Like the celebrated French philosopher whose friend had proved to him the "impossibility" of a certain happening, he replied: "My dear sir, I never said it was *possible*; I said it was a *fact*!"

So, then, we come to the evidence for this wonderful power of telepathy or thought-transference. Here I must be very brief, indicating merely a fraction of the evidence which has been accumulated in proof of this startling scientific truth.

When the Society for Psychical Research was founded, in 1882, its main energies were directed toward the investigation of this faculty, and of the reality of thought-transference. The various Committees who were engaged in this investigation soon came to the conclusion that its reality was beyond doubt. Some of the most interesting and conclusive experiments were those conducted by Mr. Guthrie, a gentleman living in Liverpool, and two of his employés. The tests were so arranged that fraud was out of the question, even had it been attempted. All the subjects were in a normal state, blindfolded, and separated some distance. Strict silence was observed. In the presence of Messrs. Myers and Gurney, the following trials in transferring the sensation of taste were attempted. Various substances were provided the "agent" (the one who was to transfer the sensation) and he placed a small quantity of one of these in his mouth; while the "percipient" (receiver of the telepathically sent message) stated what his or her impressions were. To quote one set of trials:

SEPTEMBER 4

Substance Tested	Answers Given
Worcestershire sauce.	Worcestershire sauce.
"	Vinegar.
Port wine.	Between eau de Cologne and beer.
"	Raspberry vinegar.
Bitter aloes.	Horrible and bitter.
Alum.	A taste of ink—of iron—of vinegar. I feel it on my lips; as if I had been eating alum.
"	Do. distinct impression: bitter taste persisted.

Nutmeg.	Peppermint—no; what you put in puddings—nutmeg.
"	Nutmeg.
Sugar.	Nothing perceived.
"	"
Cayenne pepper.	Mustard.
"	Cayenne pepper.

The next series of experiments concerned the transference of bodily pains. The subjects still being blindfolded, and some distance apart, the agent was pricked in various parts of his body by a needle. Several physicians were present at these experiments:

Back of left ear pricked. Rightly located.

Lobe of left ear pricked. Rightly located.

Left wrist pricked. "It is the left hand."

Third finger of left hand tightly bound round with wire. A lower joint of that finger was guessed.

Left wrist scratched with pins. "Is it the left wrist? Like being scratched."

Left ankle pricked. Rightly located.

Now it would be foolish to attribute such results as these to chance. But let us proceed.

Dr. Blair Thaw tried a number of experiments in transferring colours. The following are samples:

COLOURS CHOSEN AT RANDOM

Chosen	1st Guess	2nd Guess
Bright red.	Bright red.	....
Bright green.	Light green.	....

Yellow.	Dark blue.	Yellow.
Bright yellow.	Bright yellow.	....
Dark red.	Blue.	Dark red.
Dark blue.	Orange.	Dark blue.
Orange.	Green.	Heliotrope.

In 1895 Mr. Henry G. Rawson published a paper on the subject, in which he narrated his success in transferring the diagrams of objects. Tracings of these are given herewith. (O = original and R = reproduction.) Further comment is hardly necessary.

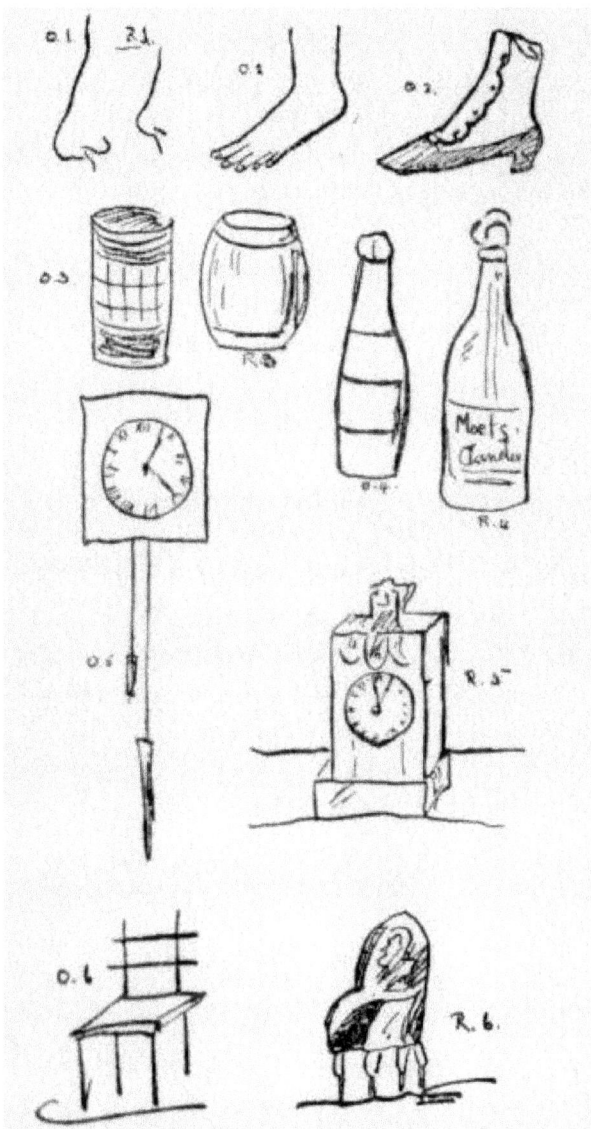

Diagram Illustrative of Thought-Transference.

He also tried a number of experiments in naming cards drawn at random from the pack (where the chance is always 51 to 1 of being correct, and the chance of being correct a number of times in succession is inconceivably great) and he attained the following results, among others:

Card Chosen	Card Guessed
5 of Hearts.	7 of Hearts, Ace of Diamonds.
8 of Hearts.	8 of Hearts.
10 of Clubs.	9 of Clubs, 10 of Clubs.
Jack of Diamonds.	Jack of Diamonds.
5 of Spades.	7 of Spades, 5 of Spades.
2 of Clubs.	2 of Diamonds, 2 of Clubs.
Queen of Hearts.	Queen of Hearts.
5 of Diamonds.	9 of Diamonds, 5 of Diamonds.
Ace of Diamonds.	Ace of Diamonds.
Ace of Hearts.	Ace of Hearts.
Ace of Clubs.	Ace of Clubs.
King of Spades.	King of Diamonds, King of Spades.

Again, it is useless to say that such results are attributable to chance. The good standing of the participants places their good faith beyond question; all normal means of communication were prevented. How are we to account for such facts—short of invoking some sort of mental interaction, through other than the ordinary channels of sense?

But these were experiments conducted in the normal state. Equally and even more interesting and conclusive results were obtained when the subject was placed under hypnotism. Of these, the most conclusive experiments were those conducted by Mrs. Sidgwick and Miss Alice Johnson. Put to the law of chance, it was shown that such coincidences were many hundreds, not to say thousands, of times more numerous than chance could account for. Then, again, we have the experiments at a great distance, in which Dr. Pierre Janet willed a patient of his to come through the streets, and she almost invariably came when he willed it. We have, too, a number of most interesting experiments in which *dreams* have been induced in others—by trying to influence the sleeping thoughts of the dreamer. Here is a fruitful field, as yet hardly touched, for an experimenter in this line of research.[40]

Among the most interesting and dramatic cases of the kind are those experiments in which one person has voluntarily caused a figure of himself to appear to another at a distance. Thus, A sits down and wills intently that he shall appear to B that night—in sleep or waking, as the case may be. The next morning A receives a letter from B, stating that he has seen an apparition of him, and asking him if he is well. The following is an example of a case of this character:

"One certain Sunday evening in November, 1881, having been reading of the great power which the human will is capable of exercising, I determined with the whole force of my being that I would be present in spirit in the front bedroom of the second floor of a house situated at 22 Hogarth Road, Kensington, in which room slept two young ladies of my acquaintance, viz. Miss L. S. V. and Miss E. C. V., aged respectively twenty-five and eleven years. I was living at this time at 23 Kildare Gardens, at a distance of about three miles from Hogarth Road, and I had not in any way mentioned my intention of trying this experiment to either of the above ladies, for the simple reason that it was only on retiring to rest upon this particular Sunday night that I made up my mind to do so. The time at which I determined to be there was one o'clock in the morning, and I also had a strong intention of making my presence perceptible.

"On the following Thursday I went to see the ladies in question, and in the course of conversation (without any allusion to the subject on my part) the elder one told me that on the previous Sunday night she had been much terrified by perceiving me standing by her bedside and that she screamed when the apparition advanced toward her, and awoke her little sister who saw me also...." (Corroborative evidence was obtained from the two ladies mentioned.)

Such a case is called a "telepathically induced hallucination" or an "experimental apparition," for the reason that the figure seen is doubtless hallucinatory in character and was induced by means of telepathy. Such cases (and there are plenty of them) are very striking proof of the direct action of mind on mind; and at the same time form a sort of bridge across the gulf which otherwise seems to exist between the experimental cases we have just quoted and the spontaneous cases to which we must now refer.

Soon after the Society began its work it was noticed that numbers of cases were sent in, in which apparitions were seen at the very moment of the death of the person symbolized by the apparition. In many such cases, no other experience such as this has happened to the percipient throughout his or her life; but on the very occasion when such a figure *was* seen, the individual was found to have died at that particular time! Can so many cases of so remarkable a character be attributed to chance?

The answer at first sight is: No. But here we must be cautious. In scientific research such as this, we must not be guided by impressions, but by facts and figures. Accordingly it was decided to put this matter to the test, and an "International Census of Hallucinations" was inaugurated, which extended throughout several countries (America being represented by Professor William James), and the taking of which lasted several years. As the result of this laborious undertaking, 30,000 answers were received—the percentage of coincidental apparitions being calculated. After making allowances for all possible sources of error, it was ascertained that the number of coincidences received were several hundred times too numerous to be attributed to chance; and the following statement was signed by Professor Sidgwick's Committee[41]:

"Between deaths and apparitions of the dying person a connection exists which is not due to chance alone. This we hold as a proved fact."

These are important words in many senses; and *donné à penser*. It shows us that, after all is said and done, this old theory of "ghosts" is not so far wrong, and that they, in a certain sense, *do* exist; it is only a matter of their interpretation: the "mystics" have as usual been right as to the existence of the facts, but the "scientists" may be right in their interpretation of them.

So we have the whole class of "spontaneous" telepathic phenomena, so called because they are not induced by direct experiment. In this class we have all those manifestations which take place at or about the moment of death; phantasms of the living, phantasms of the dying, and phantasms of the dead—according to whether the subject is yet living, is dying, or has recently died. In all such cases we may postulate a telepathic action at the moment of death, for in those cases when the apparition was seen but a few minutes or even a few hours after death, the impact might have been transmitted at the moment of death, and only have emerged into consciousness during the quietness and peace of the evening, or when night gave it a chance to do so. For we now know that subconscious ideas do tend to rise into consciousness when the latter is less occupied with the events of the day.

It is, of course, impossible to detail here the mass of evidence of all kinds which has been accumulated of late years in favour of the existence of telepathy, but enough has been quoted to indicate the method of approach and the character of the evidence adduced. Suffice it to say that, in the eyes of those who have inquired into the subject closely, telepathy is now held to be proved; it is now considered to be a scientific fact, though not as yet explained. Again I repeat, the question is not: Is it possible? but, Is it a fact?

Taking all that has been said into consideration, it may fairly be contended that the mere *fact* of telepathy may therefore be said to have been proved. This being so, the interesting question of its nature or character presents itself. How is such action to be explained? How account for the facts?

There are many theories which have been advanced from time to time to explain this remarkable phenomenon, and, if it be a fact in nature, its scientific explanation must some day be forthcoming. Once telepathy stands proved it will mean the remoulding and recasting of many of our scientific theories, and even a reconstruction of science—in so far, at least, as it refers to physiological psychology. Such being the case, and telepathy being proved, as many eminent men of science today believe, the question of its theoretical explanation becomes most important.

Now the first analogy which strikes one in the consideration of this question is that of wireless telegraphy—the subtle electric vibrations which journey to and fro with incredible swiftness through the universal ether. In short, telepathy is thought by many to be simply a species of physical vibration, proceeding from brain to brain, just as electric waves pass from the transmitter to the receiver in wireless telegraphy. This explanation is so common that many persons accept it without further ado, as being the correct explanation of the facts. But such a theory cannot be said to cover the facts in a satisfactory manner.

In the first place, there seems to be no definite or prescribed area in the brain adapted for such a purpose; no cell or centre has as yet been discovered which appears destined to send out waves of this character. Still, perhaps it will be some day, for the functions of certain portions of the brain—particularly the frontal lobes—are as yet very little understood. But there is the argument that, if such waves exist, they must be detected by means of our scientific instruments—instruments so delicate and subtle that they are able to measure the difference of the pull of gravity of an article when placed on the table or on the floor, or can register the heat of a candle at a distance of more than a mile (Langley's bolometer). Compared with such delicate instruments, our five senses are coarse indeed, and any vibrations which can affect these same senses must surely affect the more delicate and sensitive instruments just mentioned. Yet none of them have as yet been able to indicate the existence of any such vibrations, and this would seem to show that they cannot exist.[42]

But there is a reply to this argument. It may be said that, although the *senses* do not register any such vibrations, the *brain* might do so, in some direct manner; and the brain might be far more sensitive than any instrument so far devised. Indeed the definition of telepathy, "the ability of one mind to influence or be influenced by another mind otherwise than through the recognized channels of sense," would seem to indicate that in this process only the brain is involved, and not necessarily the physical senses at all. So far, then, so good; telepathy might still be vibratory in character.

But if so, how could such waves get through the skull to act upon the brain direct? This is a staggering thought to the ordinary materialist, and at first sight renders such an action unintelligible and hence "impossible"! But to reason thus would be very superficial. For we know that certain physical energies pass through solid substances—substances impervious to other physical energies. Thus we know that glass permits light to pass through it, but is a non-conductor of electricity; while steel is impervious to light, yet electricity can traverse miles of steel in the fraction of a second. "Gravity" seems the only energy which cannot be isolated by some means or other. No substance is opaque to gravity. It acts through all substances, at all times, continuously. In this respect telepathy may resemble gravitation.[43] If this were true, or anything like it were true, we could easily see why a solid substance, such as the human skull, might offer no appreciable resistance to the passage through it of undulations of a certain velocity—of a speed so great, perhaps, that they could not be detected by any of the instruments at the command of the physicist today.

But there are other and still more serious objections to the vibratory action of telepathy which have not as yet been mentioned. For if we try to push the analogy further, we shall find that it is by no means so clear as might be supposed. Thus in the case of wireless telegraphy the vibratory action of the ether is a purely mechanical process and does not carry emotion, thought, or intelligence with it—being vibration pure and simple. Now, in the case of a supposed telepathic message, thought flashed from one brain to another must be supposed to convey with it intelligence of some sort; for if it were a *purely* mechanical vibratory action, how is it that this would impress another brain in such an entirely different manner from all other vibrations as to create in that brain not only a thought, but the precise *kind* of thought—the *replica* of the thought—which originated in the brain of the agent? Granting that vibrations are but "symbols," and that they are interpreted by our brains *as* things, the difficulty remains that, in all other cases, such vibrations, no matter what their intensity, convey to the brain the idea of external objects, or qualities of those objects, and do not convey to it the idea of mind or intelligence. How is it, therefore, that one particular species of vibration, which, we must assume, would vary more or less with each individual, can convey with it the idea of thought, and that this vibration is associated with mind, and in fact is thought, while all other vibrations in the world are in nowise connected with intelligence and do not appear to us to be so connected? And further, how infinitely we should have to vary the degree and type of vibration to correspond to all shades of thought and feeling and emotion! Sir William Crookes some years ago urged the possibility of this vibratory action of telepathy; but Mr. Myers has pointed out its defects and stated that all we can at present say about telepathy is that "life has the power of manifesting to life"—a formula surely general enough, yet highly significant.

Again, the theory has been advanced that all minds are in touch in a sort of subterranean way—through their subliminal regions—just as all spokes of a wheel ultimately reach the hub, though each spoke is distinctive. In this way we could imagine an inter-connection taking place, of which we are quite unaware, under certain favourable conditions. To use an analogy somewhere employed by Professor James, our conscious minds are like the leaves of the trees which whisper together, but the roots of the trees are all embedded in the same soil and are interlaced inextricably. So our minds, though they appear to be so separate and apart, may really be at basis fundamentally *one*. There must be, it is said, some common ground of interaction; possibly a sort of universal fluid, in which all minds are bathed, and by means of which interaction of thought is effected. This is somewhat akin to the theory first propounded by Mesmer, and which has been revived, in somewhat altered form, more than a hundred years later. Mesmer held that thought was communicated from brain to brain "by the vibrations of a subtle fluid with which the nerve substance is in continuity." Truly, if any sort of physical action is employed, this seems a significant enough remark. We know that two tuning forks will resound in unison, if one of them be struck. Put in motion a magnetized needle; at a certain distance and without contact another magnetized needle will oscillate synchronously with the first. Set in vibration a violin string, or the string of a piano; and at a certain distance the string of another piano or violin will vibrate in unison with it. Such analogies make us wonder whether or not communication of this kind might not exist, and, certainly, in order to make telepathy intelligible at all, we must suppose some such action taking place. We all have a tendency to think in physical symbols, owing to our materialistic training.

For if we try to picture to ourselves the process of telepathy as taking place in some manner other than physical, how are we to conceive such action? Does one consciousness stretch out, as it were, and grasp the other passive mind? or does the agent project the thought from his brain and impress the mind of the percipient with it—just as a bullet might be shot from a rifle, or light waves radiate from some centre? The first of these theories would be somewhat akin to true mind-reading, the other to thought-projection or transference. But if the latter theory be correct, is all thought directed into one single channel—at a target as it were—or does it spread equally in all directions, like all other vibratory radiations? It may be conceived that telepathy is a combination of both the above processes—it being a kind of mutual action—a projection on the part of one, and a mental reception or grasping on the part of the other. If this be the case, we must conceive the thought as met, as it were, in space, and in some way joined or seized upon by the percipient thought; but how can we conceive such seizing or such perception?

It will be seen that the problems arising from a study of telepathy are numerous and remarkable. Let us briefly summarize the chief theories which have been advanced to date. These are:

1. *The Theory of Exalted Perception.*—This is, that the subject is in some manner enabled to see the thoughts of his "magnetizer" or hypnotist. This explanation applies only to those telepathic manifestations observed when the percipient is in a state of trance; and even here the theory cannot be said to explain, for it explains one mystery by propounding another.

2. *The Hypothesis of Brain Exaltation with Paralysis of the Senses.*—On this theory, a sort of sympathetic action and reaction or *rapport* is supposed to take place, but of the exact nature of this process its exponents can tell us nothing. Again, it only evades the direct issue and answers one problem by asking another.

3. *The Hypothesis of Direct Psychic Action.*—This is the view whose ablest exponent is Mr. Frederic Myers. It is supposed that such action takes place in its own world—its own sphere—just as distinct and just as real as the material world. If this were true we could never demonstrate the action of telepathy scientifically, since it would be beyond the reach of such demonstration. Others again believe that the action of telepathy is akin to the phenomena of *induction*; others that it is akin to *gravitation* or the *magnetic force*. While the details of these theories are lacking, there is here a valuable suggestion and a field for future research.

4. *The Hypothesis of Direct Physical Action.*—This supposes that the molecular changes in one brain, accompanying thought or emotion, set certain ether vibrations in motion, which are caught up by another brain, sensitive enough to receive them, or attuned to the proper degree. This theory is one which appeals to most persons, though it is open to the criticisms before raised. Nevertheless, it *may* be true; and if so, its law ought one day to be discovered. There is here also a field for legitimate scientific research.

5. *The Idea of a Universal Fluid.*—This is the theory held to by the majority of mystics and occultists. There is supposed to exist a sort of fluidic intermediary between mind and mind, which acts as the means for thought transmission, and it is upon this that all thought is impressed. It acts as a sort of mirror, which reflects the thoughts of all living persons, just as a material mirror might reflect material objects. In such a case, the thought is really *made objective* and is perceived by the subject in a sort of clairvoyant manner. I do not feel competent to pronounce upon this hypothesis in the present embryonic state of psychical science.

6. *The Theory of Spiritual Intermediaries.*—This is the theory that our thoughts are read by some purely "spiritual" process, by "spirits," who convey this thought to another individual and impress him in some psychical manner directly. They thus act as carrier-pigeons between mind and mind. To this theory it may be replied, as Professor Flournoy has replied in his *Spiritism and Psychology*, that it represents the grave methodological defect of multiplying causes without necessity; by postulating spirits and importing them into the problem when they are not wanted. It would be better to seek an explanation elsewhere.

7. *The Psycho-Physical Theory.*—This theory supposes that all thought is accompanied by nervous undulations, which are carried to the surface of the body, there setting the ether in vibration; and this, in turn, impinges upon the periphery of another person, particularly sensitive to receive them, and by him re-transformed into nervous currents—into thought! Such a theory completely fails to take into account those cases of long-distance telepathy, of which so many have now been collected; and in other ways is very defective.

8. Assuming all the above theories to be insufficient, we now come to:

The Elements of a Scientific Explanation

In studying this subject we must remember certain things:

(*a*) That telepathy is a highly complex phenomenon, and for that reason we must not expect to find its solution easily or state it in a single sentence.

(*b*) That we must consider it from the double standpoint, physical and mental; and

(*c*) That we must consider the conditions affecting the operator, the subject, and, if possible, the connection between them.

All scientific explanation consists in reducing the unknown to terms of the known. We can often *classify* a phenomenon without being able to *explain* its innermost nature. If we discover its laws, we have advanced to that extent.

Dr. J. Ochorowicz, who has made a prolonged and minute study of this question, writes as follows regarding the necessary conditions to be observed in the operator:

"On the side of the *operator* the conditions have been very little studied. But it is probable:

"1. That there are personal differences.

"2. That these differences may be due not only to the degree of thought intensity, but also to the nature of the thought itself, according as it is visual, auditive, or motor.

"3. That some account has to be taken of a sort of accord, of concordance between the two intelligences.

"4. That excessive will-power impairs the definiteness of the transmission without much enhancing its intensity.

"5. That strong, persistent, prolonged thinking of a thought repeated for a longer or shorter time constitutes a condition in the highest degree favourable.

"6. That any distraction which causes the thought to disappear for a moment, or that makes it cease to be isolated, seems eminently unfavourable to the mental action.

"7. That, nevertheless, thoughts that are not intense, and even thoughts that are at the moment unconscious (subconscious), may be transmitted involuntarily.

"8. That the muscular efforts which usually accompany an exertion of will are more or less indifferent; but that the muscle expression of the operator may be useful, subjectively, by reason of the habitude that connects thought with these expressional signs.

"It follows from these considerations that the operator should insist less upon the 'I will it' than upon the content of that willing; and hence it is probable that, properly speaking, it is not the 'strong will' that helps telepathy so much as clear thinking."

As to the subject or *percipient*, experience has taught us that the four following states are probably the most important for the recipience of a telepathic message:

1. In the state of profound *aideia* (complete lack of thought) transmission is never immediate, but it may sometimes be latent.

2. In the state of nascent *monoideism* (one idea) it may be immediate and perfect.

3. In the state of *passive polyideism* (many thoughts) it may be either immediate or may take place after an interval of greater or lesser length.

4. In the state of *active polyideism* the conditions are complex and subject to further subdivisions, for:

(*a*) Transmission may be direct if the subject helps by voluntary self-absorption in a concentration of mind more or less monoideic; he lends himself to the action; he listens mentally; he seeks, sometimes he finds!

(*b*) It may be indirect, i.e. latent; this time also with some concurrence on the part of the subject. This seems more frequent.

(*c*) Finally, it may in exceptional instances be either mediate (delayed) or immediate, even without the subject's being advised beforehand of the action.

Here, then, are the probable conditions; also the state of the agent and percipient. Now what about the *connecting links?*

Here we come to the heart of the problem. I shall be as brief as possible, since we cannot pretend that the problem is yet solved. I merely offer a few suggestions, some original, others advanced before by writers on these subjects.[44]

In order to obtain a specific action we must employ a specific instrument: a telephone for a telephone; a brain for a brain.

Every living thing is a dynamic focus.

A dynamic focus tends ever to propagate the motion which is proper to it.

Propagated motion becomes transformed according to the medium it traverses. A force may be transmitted or transformed.

In an identical medium there is only *transmission.*

In a different medium there is *transformation.*

A dynamic nucleus, in propagating its motion, sends it out in every direction; but this transmission becomes perceptible only on the lines of least resistance.

A process that is at once chemical, physical, and psychical goes on in the brain. A complex action of this kind is propagated through the grey matter, as waves are propagated in water.

Regarded physiologically, a thought is only a vibration, probably, which does not pass out of its appropriate medium. It is propagated, and it must be along the motor nerves, since science admits no other route. But the *thought itself* does not radiate; it remains "at home," just as the chemical action of a battery remains in the battery; it is represented abroad by its dynamic correlate, called, in the case of the battery, a *current*; and in the case of the brain, I know not what; but whatever its name may be, it is the *dynamic correlate of thought*. Thought, therefore, is dynamic. Thought is transformed; and may be re-transformed, in another organism which supplies the necessary conditions. Thought may be restored.

We have now reached, from a purely physiological standpoint, a position which I desired to reach before I advance the final part of the theory—which may at first sight appear somewhat fantastic. But telepathy itself is fantastic; and yet, being a fact, it must be accounted for somehow, or left altogether unexplained.

It has always been contended by a peculiarly-gifted group of individuals known as "clairvoyants," that we possess a "spiritual body"—just as we possess a physical body—of exactly the same shape and appearance; and that we inhabit this body at death. It is further contended that all our physical senses find their exact counterpart in this "etheric double"; there is a physical eye and a spiritual eye; a physical ear and a spiritual ear, etc. With the spiritual eye we see "clairvoyantly"; with the spiritual ear we hear "clairaudiently," and so forth. I shall not discuss the possibility of such a body, except to say that there is now a mass of evidence in its favour. Assuming it to exist—assuming it to be the exact counterpart of the physical body—then it too possesses a brain; and it too must pulsate and vibrate just as the physical brain does, when accompanying thought.

Now this inner body may be the *vehicle of thought*. It may possess "centres" whose normal office is to send and receive telepathic messages. One "etheric centre" may thus act upon another "etheric centre" directly—only indirectly upon the physical brain cells. The action would thus be dynamic, yet psychical; physical in a sense, yet not physical as we conceive it. Philosophy tells us that the table we see (the *phenomenon*) is not the "real" table (the *noumenon*)—the reality behind; but, if we knock the two tables together, the *noumena* touch, just as the phenomenal tables do; only we have no means of knowing or directly seeing it. Thus there is a sort of physical communication of a spiritual thing. Those who have entered rooms of a certain character have often sensed their "psychic atmosphere." This is a sort of duplicate or replica of the physical atmosphere, yet it is different from it. The whole subject is so subtle that one cannot follow it unless he has had some experience or some knowledge of these things. The process cannot be explained in clear-cut fashion—any more than mediums can tell the source of their thoughts and impressions. A little intuition is needed in order to grasp the problem and comprehend its difficulties.

Were I to try and state my theory briefly, then it would be somewhat as follows: Every thought necessitates a three-fold phenomenon—(1) the purely psychic activity; (2) the physiological correlate; and (3) the "dynamic correlate," which is as yet unrecognized by science. This "dynamic correlate" is the manifestation of the activity of the etheric double; which sets into motion certain vibratory activities which, though they are not physical vibrations, are their counterpart or *equivalent* on the plane above matter—the "astral" plane, if the term be allowable; which is parallel to, but not identical with, the material plane. Thus by a sort of "doctrine of correspondences" we arrive at the conclusion that telepathic action is physical, in a sense, yet is not sufficiently physical to be measured by our instruments in the laboratory. The activity is, as it were, the *noumenon*, of which the physical vibration would be the phenomenon; but no phenomenal aspect of this activity may ever be manifested to us; and hence never be capable of being registered by science, as it exists today.

I do not know whether or not I have made this theory very comprehensible, but it seems to me some such theory might explain the facts and at the same time do away with the difficulties. At all events no theory of telepathy which has been advanced to date can be said to be explanatory, when all the facts are taken into consideration; and if this first tentative groping serves to stimulate others to speculate, and above all to *experiment*, in this obscure field, I shall feel that a first onward step has been taken toward a correct understanding of the "Marvels of Telepathy."

FOOTNOTES:

[40] See Dr. G. B. Ermacora's paper in *Proceedings*, S.P.R., vol. xi. pp. 235-308.

[41] Professor Henry Sidgwick, as we know, was Professor of Moral Philosophy in Cambridge, and his works on *Ethics* and *Political Economy* are considered standard in all countries.

[42] This is the argument put forward by, e.g., Carl Snyder, in his *New Conceptions in Science*, pp. 306-7.

[43] See my article in *The Monist* (July-September 1913, pp. 445-58), "Earlier Theories of Gravity."—H. C.

[44] Especially Dr. Ochorowicz, in his excellent work, *Mental Suggestion*, to which I am indebted for several of the ideas which follow.

CHAPTER IX

THE USES AND ABUSES OF MIND-CURE

Within the past few years the country has been flooded by a host of books, pamphlets, and periodicals dealing with "psychotherapy" and mind-cure in general. In some ways it would be impossible to exaggerate the good which this has done. It has cheered-up many desponding souls; it has brightened many a life; it has stimulated activities and lines of thought which otherwise would have remained dormant; it has added real zest to life and made it worth living. Undoubtedly, too, real cures have been effected by means of these modern mental methods, and any one who denies this must surely be ignorant of the vast amount of steadily accumulating evidence in their favour. The many advantages of the system are doubtless pointed out with acuteness and insisted upon with vigour in the books which defend it, and need not be re-stated here. And yet, while I acknowledge all this; while I am forced to admit the many wonderful cures and much mental relief on account of these newer methods of healing, I still believe that a vast amount of harm is also brought about by the incautious application of the doctrines taught; by over-enthusiasm for the ideals which are ever before us, luring us on and on. In the present chapter, therefore, I propose to show in what these pitfalls consist; to illustrate some of the errors into which over-enthusiastic "mental-curists" are apt to fall.

First of all, however, a confession of faith! For a number of years I believed as implicitly as it was possible for any one to believe in the great power of mind to cure disease. I read nearly every book of importance that had been published on this theme—including Mrs. Eddy's books, all the standard works on hypnotism, mind-cure, faith-cure, new thought, etc. I was deeply imbued with the truths they contained. I became greatly opposed to the so-called "materialism" of medical science. The rationality and philosophical truth of the mind-cure systems appeared to me irrefutable.

The fundamentals of the system are indeed well laid. We know of the tremendous effects of the emotions upon the body—its functions, secretions, etc. Cheering faith and optimism are assuredly great incentives to health; more than that, they are actual physiological health-stimulators. We know that we can make ourselves ill by morbid and unwholesome thoughts; and, as Feuchtersleben says: "If the imagination can make man sick, can it not make him well?" By opening up the great "sluice-gates" of the organism we somehow allow a great influx of spiritual energy to pervade us, and the disease vanishes. It is a very fascinating doctrine, and, for many diseases, doubtless a true one.

In spite of all this, however, I believe the present tendency to treat all diseases—or next to all—by purely mental methods is a great mistake. It leaves many persons ill and crippled for life; it allows many hundreds of others to sink and fall into premature graves.

And the first objection I would make to mind and faith-curing, and all kindred systems, is this: that *they tend to suppress symptoms rather than remove causes.* This is a very grave objection indeed. If one suffers constantly from constipation or dyspepsia, the natural habit of the mind would be to worry about them more or less and take steps to prevent their continued progress. But the faith and mind-curists say: "No, it is not at all important; imagine yourself whole and well, and whole and well you will be!" Many persons have done this and their troubles have, apparently, lessened and disappeared. They may have and they may not. It is easy to ignore troubles of this kind; but this sort of ostrich-philosophy, which buries its head in the sand and refuses to look at what is before its eyes, is not natural or by any means the best for the bodily organism. Ignoring symptoms does not cure them. What such persons fail to take into account is this: that any unpleasant symptom which may have arisen must be due to *some cause*—sickness and disease do not arise *de novo* and without just cause. This is not the order of a good and kind nature. It must be due to *something*, and generally that "something" is the condition of the body at the time; and that condition depends, in turn, upon the previous habits and modes of life. These have engendered the diseased condition we see before us; and the only effective and rational way to stop the effects—the symptoms—is to stop the causes, to change the habits of life which have led to such results; and not to tinker with the effects. Even pain may be ignored to some extent; but pain is due to a certain pathological state which requires treatment. It is simply an indication of an existing bodily condition. What is the good of ignoring that state, when it exists? Symptoms may be ignored, but the causes of those symptoms run on in the body, nevertheless, and in the end work havoc and breed sickness and decay.

I am aware of the fact that the Christian Scientists, e.g., would reply to this that the bodily state (there is no body, according to them, but we let that pass, for the moment) *is* cured at the same time; that, by the mere affirmation that the body is whole, we thereby make it whole; we do not suppress symptoms, we remove causes as well. This I deny, at least in many cases. I have seen too many of such "cures" *and relapses* not to know whereof I speak. A patient goes to a "healer" and becomes "cured." A few weeks or months later his trouble returns; or, if not the same trouble, another and perhaps a worse one. This is "cured" in turn, and so on.

Now it is a well-known fact that a disease suppressed in one place or one direction has a tendency to break out in another. It has been gathering in force all the time within the body, and finally bursts forth again worse than before. "And the last state of that man was worse than the first." The *causes* have run on. Similar causes can produce opposite effects—just as opposite causes can produce similar effects. Although no tangible connection between the first and the second illness can be traced, it is there nevertheless; and both have been produced by a common cause. We cannot ignore causes; we must treat them; and if we do not, they will, in the majority of cases, repay us a thousandfold for our past neglect.

When a person is diseased the majority of mental-scientists would at least admit that certain unphysiological conditions were present and needed to be overcome. If this be so, I ask: Why should we allow the body to become diseased at all and thus necessitate its cure by mental or any other means? Would it not be much simpler to prevent such a diseased condition, in the first place, by proper physiological habits of life; and so render any cure by mental or other means unnecessary? It seems to me that, by thus allowing the body to become diseased, and then "curing" it by mental control (even granting that this is the case), we burn the candle at both ends—for the reason that we devitalize the body by allowing it to become diseased and then waste more energy in the mental effort to get well again! Would it not be more simple and more philosophical so to regulate the life that such diseased states and such cures are unnecessary?

The fundamentals of Mrs. Eddy's doctrine are well known. God is all in all; God is good; hence all is good. Sin and sickness are delusions of poor mortal mind. They do not really exist. And this, they say, may easily be proved—on the one hand by the cures which take place; and on the other by the doctrine of idealism, which philosophers and scientists alike are accepting more and more as a satisfactory interpretation of the universe. The whole system is very delightful—and very illusory!

In the first place, as to the cures. I must contend that because some remarkable cures have been effected, that, therefore, the *doctrines* of Christian Science are not thereby established. We know similar cures have been effected at Lourdes; over the bones of saints (which did not really exist under the sacred cloth); over (fraudulent) "chips of the Cross"; by means of hypnotism, and in a hundred ways. The whole root of the matter lies in auto-suggestion; in the patient's faith in himself, and in the degree of faith he places in the curing object or dogma. The dogma may be quite false, but the cures are effected just the same. Because cures are effected by Christian Science methods, therefore, it is no proof whatever that the Christian Science theology or philosophy is right. It may be one huge error, but the cures would be effected just the same—provided the faith, the emotions, the imagination and spirit of the patient be touched in an appropriate manner.

True it is that science and philosophy tend towards idealism; and the belief that there is, strictly speaking, "no matter." But this belief need not make us any the more believers in Christian Science and its methods. There is a subtle error here which is unperceived by the majority. When first the truth reaches the mind that there is "no matter" that matter cannot feel, etc., it bursts like a flood of light upon the unfettered mind and appears a fact so overwhelmingly great, so vast and so true, that to gainsay it would be to acknowledge ignorance of its teaching; to admit intellectual shortsightedness. (This is perhaps the reason for the supercilious superiority of many Christian Scientists; they imagine that no one perceives this truth but themselves.) And once grasped, is it not self-evident, and does not all else follow in consequence? At first sight it would indeed appear so!

The great error, however, lies here. Because this fact is *theoretically* true, it is not *practically* true also. We may admit the one; we cannot accept the other. The fallacy has been clearly pointed out by Sir Oliver Lodge (*Hibbert Journal*, January, 1905), and I cannot do better than to quote his words in this connection. He says:

"We cannot be permanently satisfied with dualism, but it is possible to be over-hasty and also too precisely insistent. There are those who seem to think that a monistic view of existence precludes the legitimacy of speaking of soul and body, or of God and spiritual things, or of guidance and management, at all; that is to say, they seem to think that because these things can be *ultimately* unified, therefore they are unified proximately and for practical purposes. We might as well urge that it is incorrect to speak of the chemical elements, or of the various materials with which, in daily life, we have to deal, or of the structures in which we live, or which we see and handle, as separate and real things, because in the last resort we believe that they may all be reduced to a segregation of corpuscles, or to some other mode of unity.... The language of dualism or of multiplism is not incorrect or inappropriable or superseded because we catch ideal glimpses of an ultimate unity; nor would it be any the less appropriable if the underlying unity could be more clearly or completely grasped. The material world may be an aspect of the spiritual world, or *vice versa* perhaps; or both may be aspects of something else; but both are realities, just the same, and there need be no hesitation in speaking of them clearly and distinctly as, for practical purposes, separate entities."

This, it seems to me, disposes of the argument for Christian Science drawn from idealism. No matter whether the material world exists or not, we always have to live *as if* it existed. If we close our eyes and walk across the room, we shall be rudely stopped by the brick wall at the opposite end when we come to it. No matter how strongly we believe that such a wall does not exist, it does, nevertheless, stop us; we have to live *as if* it existed. And, just so, it seems to me; no matter how strongly we may believe that the body does not exist, we always have to live and act *as if* it existed—so long, at least, as we live in and inhabit the body at all.

Christian Science says that hygiene, diet, etc., are unimportant factors in the cure of disease. They "do not count." Apart from the immediate, practical disproof which cases of blood-poisoning, etc., would offer to such a theory, it may also be disproved theoretically. For if it be unnecessary, e.g., to fast during illness—if food is a negligible quantity and can be left out of account—why do Christian Scientists ever eat at all? If food is unimportant in one case, it must be in the other case also. And if it be replied to this, as it is, that the only reason for food is because the Christian Scientists are not yet sufficiently "advanced" and have not yet sufficient "enlightenment" to do without it; then, I reply, by the same logic they are not as yet sufficiently advanced, and have not as yet sufficient knowledge to treat all cases of accident and disease, which, in point of fact, they do treat. If the limitation be acknowledged in one direction, it must be acknowledged in the other direction also. Christian Scientists cannot yet live without food because they have not yet sufficiently "perfected" themselves. So, in like manner, they should not treat many cases of disease they do treat because they have not yet sufficiently "perfected" themselves.

I might advance arguments such as the above to fill many pages. But I do not think it necessary. As a cure for certain functional diseases, for nervous disorders, and for many of the affections of the mind, mental methods of treatment must be acknowledged to be a great and a most important factor. But when an organic lesion is present, in grave states demanding immediate attention, I think it little short of criminal that such states should meet with almost total neglect because of the perverted ideas of physiology and a sickly sentimentalism illogically extended from the philosophical doctrine of idealism. As a metaphysical doctrine, it may be correct; as a basis for medical practice, it is certainly incorrect. Let us once more set our feet to earth and determine to live a good and a useful life in the material world of which we undoubtedly form a part. We are *in* a material world, and I believe we should be *of* it. I, for one, raise my voice in protest against the tide of intellectual asceticism which is inclined to accept without question the modern doctrine and methods of "psychotherapy" and mind-cure in place of the more rational and certain measures of hygiene and medicine. The further a pendulum swings in one direction, the further will it swing in the other, when released. And I believe that the modern extreme acceptance of faith and mind-cure in all its forms is but the moral and intellectual and spiritual reaction against the materialism of the past generation. Hail the day when it again swings back to its mid-position; and when mental methods of cure and bodily hygiene shall together march hand in hand to the joint attack against disease! They each have their mission to fulfil, their cases to cure. Tolerance, tolerance! Let them each recognize the rights of the other!

CHAPTER X

THE PSYCHOLOGY OF THE OUIJA BOARD[45]

Before we proceed to discuss the intelligence lying behind the Ouija Board, I must offer a few remarks upon the subject of automatic writing in general, passing in very brief review the various theories that have been advanced from time to time by way of explanation of the action of this extraordinary little device.

One of the sanest and most rational popular accounts of this instrument and its workings that I have so far come across (all things considered) is a little pamphlet entitled *The Planchette Mystery*, very little known, from which I shall quote in writing this review. Epes Sargent's book, *Planchette: the Despair of Science*, contains in reality very little on the planchette board, and the title is somewhat deceptive. Mr. Myers's articles on the subject (particularly in *Proceedings of S.P.R.*, vol. ii. pp. 217-37; vol. iii. pp. 1-63; and vol. ix. pp. 26-128) are, of course, classical, but are involved and inaccessible for the general reader, even had he the time to read them carefully; so that perhaps the following résumé may not be unnecessary or out of place.

It is to be presumed that every reader of this book knows what a Ouija Board is, and, roughly, what it does. *How* it does it is a more difficult question to answer; in fact, it may be said that no definite answer has even yet been forthcoming. All that has been done, or that we can do, is to examine the facts, and to advance an explanatory theory that is really explanatory and in accord, as nearly as possible, with accepted theories and teaching.

First, let us consider the movement of the board. There can be little doubt that the same force which propels the planchette board propels the ouija board also; and this is still further demonstrated by the fact that, in many experiments, the planchette board is used as a ouija, and points to the letters, which are written out on a large piece of paper, and the pencil point indicates the letter in the same manner as does the ouija. It certainly appears far easier for the board to point to letters than to write—and this is most suggestive and interesting when we consider it. It would seem to indicate that the controlling intelligence found it easier to convey its thoughts when the letters were before it, in plain sight—a very suggestive fact, taken in conjunction with certain mediumistic phenomena.[46] Of course there is the alternative explanation of this fact—that a straight push-and-pull action is easier to accomplish than the more detailed and complicated action of forming words and letters. But that would not make plain to us why it is that no *attempt* at writing should be made, very often, until the letter-pointing system is adopted.

Presuming, then, that the movement or impelling force is the same in each instance, the question is: What is this force? In the great bulk of cases there can only be one answer to this question: unconscious muscular action. Whenever muscular contact is allowed, this may safely be assumed to be the explanation of the movements of the board—even if it shows an apparently independent will and movement of its own, and apparently drags the hands of the sitters with it. I have discussed this at some length in my *Physical Phenomena of Spiritualism*, pp. 66-72, and it is unnecessary to go into the question again here. Unconscious muscular action will account for so much that, even if it were not the true explanation of the facts, in reality, we should have to assume that it was.

It will be observed that I have said "in the great bulk of cases." Some of my readers may object to this limitation, and say that it is the true and sufficient explanation of *all* the cases, without exception. Personally I doubt that fact. There are numerous cases on record when the board has continued to write after the hands of all the sitters have been removed from it. Now, if there be operative a force which has been in some way generated during the sitting, it is quite possible, of course, that this same force may be operative in those cases where contact is allowed, only it is difficult to prove that fact.[47] Personally I have no difficulty in conceiving such a force or power, at least theoretically. This force may be the first glimmerings of the force whose more powerful manifestations we see in the movements of tables (witness Gasparin's experiments, e.g.), and ultimately in telekinetic phenomena, as, for example, in the Palladino case. This would seem to indicate that such forces and powers are possessed by every one in a limited degree, but that it is only in certain individuals that it becomes so marked and extraordinary that it produces the phenomena spoken of above.

Granting, then, for the sake of argument, that the board is moved by the sitter, either consciously or unconsciously; by unconscious muscular action or by some "fluid" emanating from his fingers (and we must remember that even were a spirit using the writer's organism to manifest through, it must use the muscular and motor system), the great and vital question still remains: What is the intelligence behind the board that directs the phenomena? Who does the writing? What is the source of the information so often given?

Let us first consider the theory held by a very large number of persons— that the board is moved by some kind of "electricity." We must suppose that the generally recognized electricity is meant, because, if not, the motive force would be electricity *plus something*, and the "something" would be the explanation. And yet, if the force moving the board be "electricity," how comes it that this "electricity" can answer back, and possess an individuality so independent from that of the writer; capable, too, of giving a vast mass of information to the sitters, on occasion, of which they knew nothing? Then, again, it must be remembered that a ouija or planchette is almost universally made of *wood*—not metal or any well-known good conductor of electricity, but of wood—which is generally recognized to be an exceedingly bad conductor. Obviously the theory is absurd. And when we come to remember those cases in which the board gave information previously unknown to the writer having his hands on the board at the time, the theory sinks into its proper place—oblivion.

Then there is the theory of a floating, ambient mentality. This theory is held by many, and it is contended by them that this mentality is clothed, by some mysterious process, with a force similar to that which it possessed in the living organism; and that, in its expression of the combined intelligence of the circle, it generally follows the strongest mind, or the mind that is best qualified or conditioned to give correctly the thought. This theory found its champion in the person of Dr. Joseph Maxwell (see his *Metapsychical Phenomena*), and must be taken into account seriously. But an objection, and to my mind a fatal objection, to this theory is the fact that the intelligence seems to possess, not a collective but a decidedly personal character—one which is sufficiently stable and individual to argue back and to maintain its own opinions and beliefs in the face of great opposition from all the members of the circle. Is there anything in all this that suggests a floating, compound mentality; or does it not rather bear the marks of being a theory made up for the occasion, in order to evade some alternative explanation, objectionable, perhaps, to the sitters or critics?

All that has been said above also applies to the theory of a *spiritus mundi*, or spirit of the universe, which formed so large a part in the cosmological theories of many ancient philosophers. It is supposed to be a sort of all-pervading nervous principle, having, however, a mind of its own, when occasion demands—for otherwise how are the results to be accounted for? I think this and the preceding theory can best be met, perhaps, by asking its supporters to produce one iota of evidence in its behalf. When this has been forthcoming it will be time enough to consider it seriously.

Then there is the theory that the unconscious muscular action of the sitters is the cause of the movement and writing. This has been considered before, and it was pointed out that, even granting for the sake of argument that the board was actually moved by this means, the question still remains: How are we to account for the mentality behind the movement—especially when facts are given unknown to all the members of the circle? (For an example of this see *Proceedings, S.P.R.*, vol. ix. pp. 93-8.)

The question thus arises: *What* did the writing? The theory of unconscious muscular action has been considered, and found not to explain all the facts. Many might contend that the board was moved by a principle or force as yet unknown, and think the question settled in that way. Of course this is a mere begging of the question, for all practical purposes, because, if the explanation were known, there would be no mystery and no argument about it. But the mere statement that the board is operated by a force as yet unknown merely restates the problem, without in any way attempting to solve it, and hence leaves us precisely where we were. Certainly this theory will not do!

Undoubtedly, the simplest explanation—and the correct one—for the majority of the facts is that the subconscious mind is alone responsible for them. Thoughts, images, reflections, imaginations, tend to externalize or express themselves in this manner,—in motor avenues,—through the movement of the board. The vast majority of ouija board "communications" are to be accounted for in this way. But what of those other (relatively rare) cases in which supernormal information, unknown to the sitter, is obtained? Any theory which is advanced must explain these cases also, as well as the movement of the board, and pure subconscious activity does not. We should still have to account for this knowledge, unknown to the writer; so that we shall have to seek further yet, in order to discover the true cause of the intelligence doing the writing.

We seem to be driven, then, into one of two alternatives: (1) that unconscious muscular action pushed the board, and that the supernormal information given was obtained by telepathy, clairvoyance, etc.; or (2) that spirits did the writing. Let us examine each of these hypotheses in turn a little more carefully. It seems to me that the first theory is practically unable to account in any satisfactory way for many communications that have been received. On the other hand, it would be perfectly absurd to invoke the agency of "spirits" for every one of the messages that have been written out—I mean supernormal messages. On the contrary, there are many experiments that point to clairvoyance or telepathy as the true explanation. It is highly probable, it seems to me, that the same agency is not involved on every occasion, but that there may be spirits (granting such to exist) on some occasions; telepathy and clairvoyance on other occasions; and purely unconscious muscular action on most occasions, when no supernormal is involved. It is only the prevailing tendency to cover all facts by a single explanation that has led to the difficulty. If we were willing to admit that there may be operative many different influences and causes, on different occasions, it seems to me that much of the difficulty would vanish.

There can be no doubt as to the fact that the ouija board is a far more mysterious little instrument than the majority of persons suppose—or rather, the forces and the mentalities behind the movement of the board are exceedingly complex, and but little understood. As the author of *The Planchette Mystery* said: "A wonderful jumble of mental and moral possibilities is this little piece of dead matter, now giving utterance to childish drivel, now bandying jokes and badinage, now stirring the conscience by unexceptionable Christian admonitions, and now uttering the baldest infidelity or the most shocking profanity; and often discoursing gravely on science, philosophy, or theology." Any theory that is advanced to explain the facts must take all this into consideration, and much more. Let us turn for a few minutes to consider the automatic script, as frequently obtained.

There are, very frequently, answers to mental questions—questions, too, the answer to which none of those having their hands on the board could possibly know. Often, again, remarks are volunteered conveying information not possessed by any one of the writers. The distinct characterization of a personality is frequently seen,—and a personality of a very detestable sort. The language employed, frequently, is quite unprintable. The "ouija" lies as coolly and confidently as it tells the truth; in fact, it is dogmatically positive that its statements are correct in every case, even when they are glaringly incorrect at the very time they are written. This spirit of dogmatism is shown in many passages, and suggests to us the attempt at domineering on the part of an intelligence unused to such a position, and rejoicing in its supremacy.

I wish to insist primarily upon the action of the board itself, and its apparently *human* characteristics—quite apart from any information which it volunteers; and this will be of the greater interest, I fancy, for the reason that such observations have, to the best of my knowledge, rarely been made. I can perhaps best illustrate my point by giving a few concrete examples.

There can be no question that the board has *moods*. It gets angry on occasion, for example, and at such times will tear round the table like a living thing, pointing first to one letter and then to another, and accentuating its meaning or calling attention to certain letters that are important, or that have been omitted in the rapid spelling, by rapping impatiently on the latter with the point—the point being lifted off the board at such times half an inch or so, and the board remaining planted on its two hind legs. I have seen the front leg of the board rap a dozen or so times on a letter that had been omitted; and sometimes the board would get so violent that it had to be quieted—just as the hand in automatic writing has to be quieted. Then, again, the board gets a certain "technique" of its own, acting in certain ways on certain occasions, and in other ways on other occasions; and frequently assuming a perfectly definite *form* of movement with certain persons—a certain sweep or an erratic manner of pointing to letters which it maintains uniformly so long as that person has his or her hands on the board. Occasionally the ouija will assume a different personality, according to the communicating intelligence, and not according to the person having his hands on the board. Just as raps or tables assume distinct personalities (see Dr. Maxwell's book for examples of this), so the ouija board assumes a perfectly definite personality, on occasion, and moves and writes according to that personality's idiosyncrasies. And this becomes all the more marked when we take into account certain peculiarities of the board—for example, its unwillingness to give names and dates, or to furnish any definite information about itself. I have observed over and over again that, whenever the intelligence doing the writing is closely questioned about itself, it will become angry, and refuse to give this information—either sulking or swearing at the writers. On the other hand, the board has some good points. It refused to disclose secrets about other persons, and got angry in the same way when pressed. Another exceedingly interesting and suggestive thing is that the intelligence operating the board occasionally gets tired. "Give me a rest now" is an expression frequently observed, and would seem to indicate that the "intelligence" gets confused and fatigued by the very process of communicating its thoughts—just as the "controls" do in the Piper case.

The very movements of the board frequently showed great skill and intelligence also; for instance, if the ouija encountered a rough or uneven place in the paper on one occasion it would always avoid crossing that spot in the future, and would go carefully round it, so as to avoid catching its legs in the hole or rough place in the paper. Still more striking was the manner in which the board pointed to certain letters on occasion. Many times the board was unable to point to a certain letter because the point of the ouija was in an awkward position, or on the edge of the table, or for some other reason. On such occasions the board backed one of its hind legs around until one of these legs pointed to the desired letter! Those having their hands on the board had many a hearty laugh over these antics, and particularly this one, which always reminded them of a horse backing itself round in this ludicrous way. It was always entirely unexpected, and was the source of great amusement. But what was the intelligence guiding the board when the only person having her hands upon it was not looking at its antics, or paying attention to what it was spelling out? Was it a spirit? If so, how did it manage to move the board? Did it act directly upon the matter of the board, and push it with its hands, as a material being would push it, or did it act in some more mysterious manner? Granting, for the sake of argument, that a spirit of some sort was involved in the production of the writing, how are we to assume its interaction with the matter of the board and its movements?

Two theories will at once present themselves to the reader: (1) that the spirit acts directly upon the matter of the ouija board, and pushes it as any mortal would push it; and (2) that the spirit acts only through the brain and nervous and muscular system of the person or persons having their hands on the board. I leave these for the present, because they have been discussed so often before. The following is *the ouija board's own theory* of such action—so we can at least listen to it with interest. In the course of some writing obtained, the following explanation of the action of the board was given by the "spirits" controlling it. I quote from the record:

"... Two spirits can always, when it is in divine order, readily communicate with each other, because they can always bring themselves into direct *rapport* at some one or more points. Though matter is widely discreted from spirit, in that the one is dead and the other is alive, yet there is a certain correspondence between the two, and between the degrees of the one and the degrees of the other; and according to this correspondence, relation, or *rapport*, spirit may act upon matter. Thus your spirit, in all its degrees and faculties, is in the closest *rapport* with all the degrees of matter composing your body, and for this reason alone is able to move it as it does, which it will no longer be able to do when that *rapport* is destroyed by what you call death. Through your body it is *en rapport* with and is able to act upon surrounding matter. If, then, you are in a susceptible condition, a spirit can not only get into *rapport* with your spirit, and through it with your body, and control its motions, or even suspend your own proper action and external consciousness by entrancement; but if you are at the same time *en rapport* with this little board it can, through contact of your hands, get into *rapport* with *that*, and move it without any conscious or volitional agency on your part. Furthermore, under certain favourable conditions, a spirit may, through your sphere and body combined, come into *rapport* even with the spheres of the ultimate particles of material bodies near you, and thence with the particles and the whole bodies themselves—and may thus, even without contact of your hands, move them or make sounds upon them as has often been witnessed. Its action, as before said, ceases where the *rapport* ceases; and if communications from really intelligent spirits have sometimes been defective as to the quality of the intelligence manifested, it is because there has been found nothing in the medium which could be brought into *rapport* or correspondence with the more elevated ideas of the spirit. The spirit, too, in frequent instances, is unable to prevent its energizing influences from being diverted by the reactive power of the medium into the channels of the imperfect types of thought and expression that are established in his mind, and it is for this simple reason that the communication is as you say often tinctured with the peculiarities of the medium, and even sometimes is nothing more than a reproduction of the mental states of the latter—perhaps greatly intensified."

Such is the theory originated by "ouija" itself—ingenious enough, if not very scientific. The majority of my readers will probably prefer to believe, either that some external intelligence moved the board directly; or that the sitter himself did so—from purely subconscious motives, or because he was thereby externalizing or acting as the channel for the expression of ideas imparted to him from without. In view of the reality of physical phenomena, I should be inclined to leave the question open as to which of these two interpretations is correct in any specific case. But there can be no doubt that, in most instances at least, the board is moved by the subconscious muscular activity of the sitter; and this is the most sane and rational view to take until definite proof to the contrary be forthcoming.

FOOTNOTES:

[45] More properly, "the psychology of ouija board *writing*" or "of writing obtained by means of the Ouija Board." This general title is shorter, however, for a chapter heading.

[46] I have in mind especially one remarkable (but hitherto unpublished) experiment with Mrs. Piper. A certain lady of my acquaintance—an old Piper sitter—has tried to convey a certain word to "Rector" telepathically—to be given by automatic writing through the trance. Several attempts failed. Finally, one day, the lady in question wrote out the word on a blackboard, and sat looking at it for about half an hour. The word was given the next day through Mrs. Piper. The blackboard was in the lady's own house, distant some 800 miles from Mrs. Piper, in Boston. This certainly seems to show that there is a peculiar "magic" in thoughts or things that are objectified in this manner. It serves to explain why it is that many clairvoyants cannot read thoughts and questions—e.g., until written out on paper—as in the case of Bert Reese, whom I have frequently seen.

[47] Dr. W. J. Crawford's experiments have since confirmed this.

CHAPTER XI

WITCHCRAFT: ITS FACTS AND FOLLIES

It has frequently been pointed out that, "where there is so much smoke there must be some fire"; also that there is, probably, and almost necessarily, some grain of truth in any popular superstition, no matter how absurd it may appear at first sight. This is not less true of witchcraft—though it would be difficult to convince the average person, in all probability, that there was anything connected with it but the grossest and most repulsive superstition. Taken all in all, it most assuredly is that, and very little else; and, before proceeding to examine the *residuum* of truth that probably exists in connection with this subject, it will be well for us briefly to examine the other and darker side of this curious relic of mediaeval superstition, and to see it in its most sombre hues. A belief for which more than nine million persons were either burned or hanged since it sprang into being; in whose cause five hundred persons were executed in three months in 1515 in Geneva alone, is not to be put aside as unworthy of a moment's consideration; but should, on the contrary, be considered as a most extraordinary and lasting delusion—helping to colour the times in which it occurred and influence the whole course of a nation's history.

The first trial for sorcery in England was in King John's reign; the last within the past two hundred years. In England, America, Germany, France, Italy, Spain, Russia—every country without exception—witches have lived, flourished, and been burned at the stake. Laws were enacted against witches, and they were condemned on the most trivial and even ridiculous evidence imaginable. If an old woman were seen to enter a house by the front door, and a black cat was seen to leave the house by the back door, it was deemed sufficient evidence that the old woman was a witch, without further evidence or investigation—and indeed much of the evidence was not nearly so good and circumstantial as this! When a witch was caught, she was questioned and generally tortured; but it was soon ascertained that torture was a very unfair and unsafe method of extracting the truth (here as elsewhere), for the reason that a weak soul, even if innocent, might confess, and a strong and stubborn one would hold out and contend for her innocence to the last, whether guilty or not. For these reasons, it was finally given up before the burning was abolished.

Witches were supposed to be possessed of the most extraordinary powers for evil; they could bewitch a man, woman or child—even the cows and flocks—by casting an "evil eye" upon them, by uttering an imprecation, or in other ways casting a spell upon them. This power was derived directly from the devil himself, with whom witches were supposed to be in direct compact; consequently their influence was all for evil. These deeds were practised daily throughout the year; but every year there was a grand meeting of the demons and witches—a "Sabbath," as it was called—and here were recounted all the evil deeds of the past year, and here the witches saw and conversed with the devil himself, and received their instructions from him. It would be almost impossible to conceive a more grotesque and gruesome picture than some of these Sabbaths were supposed to be: every impossible and inconceivable thing that man's mind could invent was apparently attributed to these meetings. In order to form some faint idea of men's beliefs in those days, I quote the following, supposedly from a more or less contemporary account, of what actually transpired at these Sabbaths:

"A witch should be an old woman with a wrinkled face, a furred brow, a hairy lip, a gobber tooth, a squint eye, a squeaky voice, a scolding tongue, having a ragged coat on her back, a skull cap on her head, a spindle in her hand, a dog or cat by her side. There are three classes or divisions of devils—black, grey, and white. The first are omnipotent for evil, but powerless for good. The white have power to help, but not to hurt. The grey are efficient for both good and evil.... The modes of bewitching are: by casting an evil eye (fascinating); by making representations of a person to be acted upon in wax or clay, roasting this image before a fire; by mixing magical ointments, or other compositions or ingredients; or sometimes merely by uttering an imprecation.... Witches can ride in sieves on the sea, on brooms, or spits, magically prepared. The meeting of the witches is held every Friday night—between Friday and Saturday.... They steal children from the grave, boil them with lime till all the flesh is loosed from the bones, and is reduced to one mass. They make of the firm part an ointment, and fill a bottle with the fluid; and whosoever drinks this with due ceremony belongs to the league, and is capable of bewitching.... Every year a grand Sabbath is held or ordered for celebration on the Blocksberg Mountains, for the night before the 1st of May. Witches congregate from all parts, and meet at a place where four roads meet, in a rugged mountain range, or in the neighbourhood of a secluded lake or some dark forest; these are the spots selected for the meeting....

"When orders have been issued for the meeting of the Sabbath, all the wizards and witches who fail to attend it are lashed by demons with a rod made of serpents and scorpions. In France and England the witches ride upon broomsticks; but in Italy and Spain the Devil himself, in the shape of a goat, supports them on his back, which lengthens or shortens according to the number of witches he is desirous of accommodating. No witch, when proceeding to the Sabbath, can go out by a door or window, were she to try ever so much. Their general mode of ingress is by a keyhole and of egress by the chimney, up which they fly, broom and all, with the greatest ease. To prevent the absence of the witches being noticed by their neighbours, some inferior demon is commanded to assume their shapes and lie in their beds, feigning illness, until the Sabbath is over. When all the wizards and witches arrive at the place of rendezvous, the infernal ceremonies begin. Satan, having assumed his favourite shape of a large he-goat, with a face in front and another in his haunches, takes a seat upon the throne; and all present in succession pay their respects to him and kiss him on his face behind. This done, he appoints a master of the ceremonies, in company with whom he makes a personal examination of all the witches to see whether they have the secret mark upon them by which they are stamped as the Devil's own. The mark is always insensible to pain. Those who have not yet been marked receive the mark from the master of ceremonies—the Devil, at the same time, bestowing nicknames upon them. This done, they all begin to sing and dance in a most furious manner, until some one arrives who is anxious to be admitted into the society. They are then silent for a while until the newcomer has denied his salvation, kissed the Devil, spat upon the Bible, and sworn obedience to him in all things. They then begin dancing with all their might, and singing.... In the course of an hour or two they generally become wearied of this violent exercise, and then they all sit down and recount all their evil deeds since last meeting. Those who have not been malicious and mischievous enough towards their fellow-creatures receive personal chastisement from Satan himself, who flogs them with thorns and scorpions until they are covered with blood and unable to sit or stand. When this ceremony is concluded, they are all amused by a dance of toads. Thousands of these creatures spring out of the earth, and, standing upon their hind legs, dance while the Devil plays the bagpipes or the trumpet. These toads are all endowed with the faculty of speech, and entreat the witches there to reward them with the flesh of unbaptized infants for their exertions to give them pleasure. The witches promise compliance. The Devil bids them remember to keep their word, and then, stamping his foot, causes all the toads to sink into the earth in an instant. The place being thus cleared, preparations are made for the banquet, where all manner of disgusting things are served and greedily devoured by the demons and witches—although the latter are sometimes regaled with choice meats and expensive wines from golden plates and crystal goblets; but they are never thus favoured unless they have done an extraordinary number of evil deeds since the last period of meeting. After the feast they begin dancing, but such as have no relish for any more exercise in that way amuse themselves by mocking the holy sacrament of baptism. For this purpose the toads are again called and sprinkled with filthy water, the Devil making the sign of the cross, and the witches calling out [oath omitted]. When the Devil wishes to be particularly amused, he makes the witches strip off their clothes and dance before him, each with a cat tied round her neck and another dangling from her body in the form of a tail. When the cock crows they all disappear, and the Sabbath is ended...."

There, reader, is a very fair idea of the monstrous form of belief held during the Middle Ages. Scarcely anything that was fanciful and diabolical was not conjured up to the mind and said to happen at these Sabbaths. There was also a certain amount of ingenious theorizing afoot in order to account for certain facts, as, for instance, the cloven hoof, which it was said must always appear, no matter how concealed—it being due to the fact that the devil took the form of a goat so often that he finally acquired the hoof. Sir Thomas Browne explains it to us thus:

"The ground of this opinion at first might be his frequent appearing in the shape of a goat, which answers this description. This was the opinion of the Ancient Christians concerning the apparitions of the ancient panites, fauns, and satyrs; and of this form we read of one that appeared to Anthony in the wilderness. The same is also confirmed from exposition of Holy Scripture. For whereas it is said, 'Thou shalt not offer unto devils,' the original word is *Seghuirim*, i.e., 'rough and hairy goats,' because in that shape the Devil most often appeared, as is expounded by the rabbis, as *Tremellius* hath also explained; and as the word *Ascimah*, the God of Emath, is by some explained."

It will be noted that the word "Devil" is invariably capitalized by the mediaeval writers, and to them he must have been a very real personage, and these curious beliefs terrible truths. Indeed, if true, what could be more terrible? Even so learned a man as Bacon, we are told—whose soul was promised to the devil, no matter "whether he died in or out of the church"—endeavoured to cheat the devil out of his due, and had his body buried in the *wall* of the church—thus being neither in nor out of it—and so he hoped to cheat the devil of his due!

With the coming of Reginald Scott there arose a certain scepticism throughout Europe, which was later echoed in America. Scott wrote a monumental work entitled *The Discoverie of Witchcraft*, in which he bitterly attacked the credulity of the people, and showed himself entirely incredulous of any of the alleged phenomena. Some years before, had he published such a book, it was likely that he would have been burned himself; but the times were probably ripe for just such a publication; there was already much unrest and uneasiness afoot, and his book appeared in the nick of time. Scott attempted to account for the phenomena of witchcraft on a rational basis, and showed himself completely sceptical of the reality of most of the manifestations. He even went so far as to attack many of the older "miracles," which apparently supported the newer, even taking the very bold course (in that day) of attacking some of the Biblical miracles. Thus we read:

"The Pythoness (speaking of the Witch of Endor) being *ventriloqua*, that is, speaking as it were from the bottom of her belly, did cast herself into a trance, and so abused Saul in Samuel's name in her counterfeit hollow voice."

Indeed, something was necessary to check the rank credulity of the times. If an old woman scolded a carter, and later on in the day his cart got stuck in the mud or overturned, it was positive evidence that he and his cart and horse had been "bewitched"! If an old woman kept a black cat or a pet toad, it was most assuredly her "familiar," and she was branded as a witch forthwith. If cows sickened and died, it was because a "spell" had been cast over them; and so on and so on. The superstitions of witchcraft were as innumerable as they were extraordinary. Are there any facts, amid all this superstition and ignorance, tending to show that genuine supernormal phenomena ever occurred at all? And if so, what are they?

It must be remembered that, in the days of witchcraft, virtually nothing was known of hysteria, epilepsy, the varied forms of insanity, hallucination, hypnotism, or of the possibilities of mal-observation and lapse of memory: while such a matter as first-hand circumstantial evidence seems to have been lost to sight entirely. If any mental or extraordinary physical disturbance took place, if the witch went into a trance and described things that were not, this was held to be proof positive that she was bewitched and under the influence of the devil. But we now know that most of these facts really indicated disease—mental and bodily—or the results of hysteria or trance, spontaneous or induced. Possibly there were also traces of hypnotism and telepathic influence, upon occasion. Of course, fraud pure and simple would account for many of the phenomena—the vomiting of pins and needles, for instance. But there remain certain facts which cannot be accounted for on any of these theories. Let us see, briefly, what these are.

First there are the "witches' marks." These were anaesthetic patches or zones on the body that were quite insensible to pain. They were searched for with the aid of sharp needles, and often found! It was thought that these were the spots which the devil had touched; this was his "trade-mark," so to speak, by which all witches were known. Now we know that just such anaesthetic patches occur in hysterical patients, and are not due to supernatural causes at all, but to pathological states.

Then, again, there is the possible occurrence of hallucinations. Edmund Gurney pointed this out in *Phantasms of the Living*, vol. i. p. 117, where he said:

"We know now that subjective hallucinations may possess the very fullest sensory character, and may be as real to the percipient as any object he ever beheld. I have myself heard an epileptic subject, who was perfectly sane and rational in his general conduct, describe a series of interviews that he had had with the devil with a precision and an absolute belief in the evidence of his senses equal to anything that I ever read in the records of the witches' compacts. And further, we know now that there is a condition, capable often of being induced in uneducated and simple persons with extreme ease, in which any idea that is suggested may at once take sensory form, and may be projected as an actual hallucination. To those who have seen robust young men, in an early stage of hypnotic trance, staring with horror at a figure which appears to them to be walking on the ceiling, or giving way to strange convulsions under the impression that they have been changed into birds or snakes, there will be nothing very surprising in the belief of hysterical girls that they were possessed by some alien influence, or that their distinct persecutor was actually present to their senses. It is true that in hypnotic experiments there is commonly some preliminary process by which the peculiar condition is induced, and that the idea which originates the delusion has then to be suggested *ab extra*. But with sensitive 'subjects' who have been much under any particular influence, a mere word will produce the effect; nor is there any feature in the evidence for witchcraft that more constantly recurs than the *touching* of the victim by the witch. Moreover, no hard and fast lines exist between the delusions of induced hypnotism and those of spontaneous trance, or of the grave hystero-epileptic crises which mere terror is now known to develop."

Unquestionably, hypnotism and hallucination played their part; also perhaps telepathy; and, as Gurney points out elsewhere, "The imagination which may be unable to produce, even in feeble-minded persons, the belief that they *see* things that are not there, may be quite able to produce the belief that they *have seen* them, which is all, of course, that their testimony implies" (p. 118).

Doubtless a large part of witchcraft, particularly that portion of it which relates to the Sabbath and the scenes said to be enacted there, can be explained as being due to the morbid workings of the mind while in a trance state. It is asserted on good authority that salves and ointments were rubbed into the pores of the skin all over the body; and that soon after this the witch would feel drowsy and lie down, and frequently remain in a semitrance state for several hours. During that time she would visit the

Sabbath,—so it was said; but her body remained on the bed meanwhile, clearly showing that *it* had not been there.[48]

One of the most curious beliefs prevalent at the time was the belief in *lycanthropy*, that is, that certain individuals can, under certain conditions, change their bodily shape, and appear *as animals* to persons at a distance! Frequently this animal would be injured, in which case the person whom the animal represented would be found to be injured in the same way, and in exactly the same place. The witch in such cases would frequently be lying at home in bed in a trance state, while her "fluidic double," in the shape of the animal, would be roaming about "seeking whom he might devour." The following is a typical case, which I quote from Adolphe D'Assier's *Posthumous Humanity*, p. 261:

"A miller, named Bigot, had some reputation for sorcery. One day, when his wife rose very early to go and wash some linen not very far from the house, he tried to dissuade her, repeating to her several times, 'Do not go there; you will be frightened.' 'Why should I be frightened?' answered she. 'I tell you you will be frightened.' She made nothing of these threats, and departed. Hardly had she taken her place at the wash-tub before she saw an animal moving here and there about her. As it was not yet daylight she could not clearly make out its form, but she thought it was a kind of dog. Annoyed by these goings and comings, and not being able to scare it away, she threw at it her wooden clothes-beater, which struck it in the eye. The animal immediately disappeared. At the same moment the children of Bigot heard the latter utter a cry of pain from the bed, and add: 'Ah! the wretch! she has destroyed my eye.' From that day, in fact, he became one-eyed. Several persons told me this fact, and I have heard it from Bigot's children themselves."

How does our author attempt to account for such a fact as this? He says:

"It was certainly the double of the miller which projected itself while he was in bed and wandered about under an animal form. The wound which the animal received at once repercussed upon the eye of Bigot, just as we have seen the same thing happen in analogous cases of the projection of the double by sorcerers."

Without endorsing such a view of the case, it may be said that recent experiments have shown it to be less incredible than might at first appear. Thus: We read further:

"Innumerable facts, observed from antiquity to our own day, demonstrate in our being the existence of an internal reality—the internal man. Analysis of these different manifestations has permitted us to penetrate its nature. Externally it is the exact image of the person of whom it is the complement. Internally it reproduces the mould of all the organs which constitute the framework of the human body. We see it, in short, move, speak, take nourishment; perform, in a word, all the great functions of animal life. The extreme tenuity of these constituent molecules, which represent the last term of inorganic matter, allows it to pass through the walls and partitions of apartments. Hence the name of phantom, by which it is generally designated. Nevertheless, as it is united with the body from which it emanates by an invisible vascular plexus, it can, at will, draw to itself, by a sort of aspiration, the greater part of the living forces which animate the latter. One sees, then, by a singular inversion, life withdrawn from the body, which then exhibits a cadaverous rigidity, and transfers itself entirely to the phantom, which acquires consistency—sometimes even to the point of struggling with persons before whom it materializes. It is but exceptionally that it shows itself in connection with a living person. But as soon as death has snapped the bonds which attach it to our organism, it definitely separates itself from the human body and constitutes the posthumous phantom."

This interpretation of the facts, it will be seen, forms a sort of connecting link between apparitions, ghosts, materializations, vampirism, and witchcraft; it is also in accord with the statements of the theosophists as to the astral body, conforms with certain statements made through Mrs. Piper and others as to the fluidic or ethereal body, and accounts for many of the phenomena of "collective hallucination" and haunted houses. I am far from saying that I think such a theory proved, but it is at least consistent and plausible; it is also in accord with many facts, and explains them as no other theory can or does.

Colonel A. de Rochas, in his article on "Regression of Memory" (*Annals of Psychical Science*, July 1905), claimed that he had experimentally produced one of these doubles in a mesmerised subject. After several séances, and while the subject was in a deep trance, the following occurred:

"The astral body is now complete. M. de R. tries to make it rise, to send it into another room. The body is stopped in its journey by the ceiling and the walls. M. de R. tells Mayo to stretch towards him the astral right hand, and he pinches it; Mayo feels the pinch."

Experiments such as these could be multiplied *ad infinitum*. There are cases on record in which the astral form has been pricked with needles, while the "sensitive" felt the prick, and so on. These experiments are suggestive, and if they should prove an etheric body, or anything corresponding to it, that would be at least one great step in advance in psychic research. It would also enable us to understand many of the phenomena of witchcraft, which are at present looked upon as mere superstitions.

A word, finally, as to the phenomena of "exteriorization of sensibility," to which reference was made in the last paragraph. Many French observers have, apparently, obtained these phenomena; but there seems to be much scepticism regarding them in England and America, where they are generally considered to be due entirely to "suggestion." For my own part— while I do not uphold past experiments in this direction as being particularly convincing—I must confess that I see no inherent improbability in the facts themselves. If we have an etheric body, this is doubtless more or less detachable, at times—indeed, the ingenious author of *The Maniac* suggests that the premature loosening of this body is the cause of much insanity. (See also my own remarks along the same general lines in the *Annals of Psychical Science*, October-December 1909, pp. 657-67; "Concerning Abnormal Mental Life.") This etheric body is doubtless highly sensitive to external forces and energies acting upon it, and would also feel physical pressure, etc., when applied. If this were true, we should have a ready explanation for these cases of exteriorized sensibility.

But it would not even be necessary for us to assume this! If the phenomena of exteriorization of *motivity* be true (the phenomena produced by Eusapia Palladino, for example) then we have here nervous energy or "fluid" existing beyond the periphery of the body—that is, in space, detached from the nerves. And if a motor current can exist and travel in this manner, why not a sensory current? It would only have to travel in the opposite direction. For these reasons, therefore, I am disposed to regard the phenomena of exteriorized sensibility as highly probable, if not actually proved.

FOOTNOTES:

[48] See the article on "Witches' Unguents" in the *Occult Review*, April 1912, pp. 275-77.

CHAPTER XII

SCIENTIFIC TRUTHS CONTAINED IN FAIRY STORIES

How many of us, re-reading the fairy stories of our childhood have for a moment believed that many of these tales might be based upon scientific truths? Of course it is probable that most of these stories have *no* basis of fact behind them, but that they are merely the product of the story-teller's imagination—just as similar stories today are produced in this manner. But, on the other hand, it is quite conceivable that many of the seemingly fabulous accounts are in truth based upon realities; and that genuine occurrences may have happened, giving birth to these tales. We all know the general character of many of the legends. I may mention, as typical of the marvellous things done: becoming visible and invisible, as did "Jack the Giant Killer"; the existence of giants and dwarfs, as in *Little Tom Thumb*; incredibly rapid growth of vegetation, as in *Jack and the Beanstalk*; being suddenly transported without effort through immense distances and seeing at the other end of such a journey scenes and events actually transpiring at the time—as occurred in many of the *Arabian Nights* stories; cases in which plates and dishes washed themselves, and many other household feats were performed, as in *Prince Hildebrand and Princess Ida*; cases of long sleep, such as the *Sleeping Beauty*; cases in which human beings have been transformed into animals, and vice versa, as in *Beauty and the Beast*; cases in which palaces have sprung up over night, existing on the desert plain, only to vanish the next night and leave it as barren as before—as so often happened in the *Arabian Nights*.

Let us first of all consider the cases in which persons have caused themselves to vanish and reappear at will. This power of becoming visible and invisible to others is not limited to mythical times, but may be reproduced today by artificial means. If a sensitive subject be hypnotized (and there is some analogy to the hypnotic pass in the fact that the fairy invariably waved her wand before the eyes of the onlooker), hallucinations of various types may be induced. Thus, our subject may be persuaded to see, for instance, a dog walking across the carpet, whereas there is no dog there. He may be persuaded that there is a stream in front of him flowing through the drawing-room, and that it is necessary for him, in order to prevent his feet from becoming wet, to take off his shoes and socks, and turn up his trousers. Hypnotic suggestion will perform this, and it may be said that suggestion alone, even when the subject is not in the hypnotic state, may be employed to produce many of these hallucinatory pictures. On the contrary, it is possible to suggest to our subject that such and such an object is gradually diminishing in size, and finally that it disappears altogether. He sees and describes this diminution, and finally looks in vain for the object which, he asserts, has vanished, but which, as a matter of fact, is perfectly visible to all others not under the influence of the suggestion. We frequently suffer from these "negative hallucinations," as they are called, in our ordinary daily life. We cannot find an object which is perfectly visible—resting in the very centre of the area over which we are searching diligently. Suddenly we discover it; it seems incredible to us that we have not seen it before; it seems to have sprung into being as though placed there by some invisible hand. Nevertheless it had remained throughout in the one position, and the only remarkable factor was our inability to see it. Such cases are well known to psychologists (the power of suggestion in inducing both positive and negative hallucinations), and this—both in the normal and the hypnotic state—is well recognized.

Now it is only necessary for us to extend our conception somewhat in order to see the scientific truths contained in many fairy stories, in which one of the characters—hero, fairy, or what not—becomes visible and invisible at will. It is only necessary for us to conceive that some degree of mental influence had been brought to bear upon the minds of the onlookers, and that suggestion had been skilfully employed, in order to account for many of these stories. I know of a case in which the operator made his subject, who remained practically in a normal state throughout, see him floating about the room—whisking over chairs and tables, as though the law of gravity had no further influence upon him!

We might, perhaps, also account for "invisibility" in one or two other ways. Thus, the magician or fairy might possess the power of interposing some veil or screen between himself and the seer—etheric or physical—by some act of will. Or we could suppose that some chemical might be applied to the body, rendering its structure and tissues transparent. (One is here reminded of H. G. Wells' *Invisible Man.*) Or, we might assume that the magician possessed the power of neutralizing light-waves, reflected from his body, by some method of "interference"—thus rendering himself invisible. This might be due either to a greater understanding of the laws of physics—i.e., the ability to manipulate light-energy in this manner, or to some purely psychic power—volitional, etc. Precise instructions for doing this have indeed been published (*Equinox*, vol. iii.). Of course, all such speculations as these are purely fantastic, until some proof of their possibility be forthcoming.

It may be thought that this knowledge was not possessed by the ancients to the requisite extent; but there is abundant evidence to show that "mesmerism" has been practised from very ancient times. It is probable that the passage in Exodus vii, 10, 11, 12, refers to this, when it says:

"Aaron cast down his rod before Pharaoh and before his servants, and it became a serpent. Then Pharaoh also called for the wise men and the sorcerers: and they also, the magicians of Egypt, did in like manner with their enchantments. For they cast down every man his rod, and they became serpents; but Aaron's rod swallowed up their rods." It is interesting to note that Professor S. S. Baldwin, otherwise known as "The White Mahatma," recently saw a very similar feat performed in Egypt, and gives an account of it in his book, *The Secrets of Mahatma Land Explained.* Doubtless the effects in both cases were produced by suggestion, and a species of hypnotic influence. That the ancients were well versed in magic, and the power of suggestion and personal influence, is best illustrated by an old Egyptian papyrus at present in the British Museum, which contains an account of a magical séance given by a certain Tchatcha-em-ankh before King Khufu, 3766 B. C. In this manuscript it is stated of the magician: "He knoweth how to bind on a head which hath been cut off; he knoweth how to make a lion follow him, as if led by a rope; and he knoweth the number of the stars of the house (constellation) of Thoth." The decapitation trick is thus no new thing, while the experiment performed with the lion, possibly a hypnotic feat, shows hypnotism to be old.

In the *Arabian Nights,* and in various other fairy tales, we also read of the sudden appearance and disappearance of palaces, castles, and other buildings of monumental character. This strange phenomenon has frequently been paralleled in recent times. It is a species of hallucination, induced by auto-suggestion or hetero-suggestion—that is, suggestion given to oneself, or suggestion from outsiders. Madame Blavatsky, in her *Nightmare Tales,* relates an interesting experience of this character:

"A curious optical effect then occurred. The room, which had been previously partially lighted by the sunbeam, grew darker and darker as the star increased in radiance, until we found ourselves in an Egyptian gloom. The star twinkled, trembled, and turned, at first with a slow, gyratory motion, then faster and faster, increasing its circumference at every rotation until it formed a brilliant disk, and we no longer saw the dwarf, who seemed absorbed in its light.... All being now ready, the dervish, without uttering a word, or removing his gaze from the disk, stretched out a hand, and taking hold of mine he drew me to his side, and pointed to the luminous shield. Looking at the place indicated, we saw large patches appear, like those of the moon. These gradually formed themselves into figures, that began moving themselves about in higher relief than their natural colours. They neither appeared like a photograph nor an engraving, still less like the reflection of images on a mirror, but as if the disk were a cameo, and they were raised above its surface—then endowed with life and motion. To my astonishment and my friend's consternation, we recognized the bridge leading from Galata to Stamboul spanning the Golden Horn from the new to the old city. There were the people hurrying to and fro, steamers and caiques gliding on the blue Bosphorus, the many-coloured buildings, villas, palaces reflected in the water; and the whole picture illuminated by the noonday sun. It passed like a panorama, but so vivid was the impression that we could not tell whether it or ourselves were in motion. All was bustle and life, but not a sound broke the oppressive stillness. It was noiseless as a dream. It was a phantom picture.... The scene faded away, and Miss H—— placed herself in turn by the side of the dervish."

We thus see that expectancy and suggestion alone may induce sufficiently abnormal mental states to ensure the occurrence of such images—especially in a mind previously wrought by imagination, superstition, love, or any emotion tending to bring about its temporary lack of balance. The visions induced would, of course, be mental, and not physical, in their character; they would nevertheless appear just as real to the onlooker.

Closely akin to these visions are those in which, it is reported, journeys have been made through space on a magic carpet—as in the *Arabian Nights*—or merely at the wish or command of some fairy or magician. Frequently, in such cases, it is reported that a vision is seen at the other end of the journey, coinciding with reality. It may be that the princess is, at that moment, being captured by a hideous giant; or that her lover is in great danger of losing his life. These visions have stirred the recipient into action, the result being that he or she arrives in the nick of time to prevent some fearful catastrophe. Such visions, too, have foundation in fact. There are many cases in which distant scenes have been visited in sleep, and places accurately remembered—the seer never having visited that locality in his life. Very much the same has happened in hypnotic trance, and even occasionally in the waking state, spontaneously. This is a species of clairvoyant vision; operative either during sleep, hypnotic trance, or daydream; and while it accurately represents scenes transpiring at a distance, here too, it will be noted, there is no corporeal transition—only mental adjustment from one scene of activity to another. Yet the subject remains under the distinct impression that he has been there in person, and actually visited the spot indicated.

The Sleeping Beauty is an example of a story, typical of many, which illustrates the tradition that on certain occasions persons have passed into a sleep-state in which they have remained for long periods of time without apparent injury. While we must assume that the periods over which this sleep-state extended have been greatly overdrawn, the reported cases of hypnotic trance, and of voluntary interment, among the Hindus and elsewhere, lend probability to these stories, because of the fact that long periods of trance have been undergone by various individuals—who awakened from these states in apparently perfect health, and none the worse for their remarkable experience. Several spontaneous cases have been reported quite recently, in which the subject has passed several months, or even a year or more, in a sleep-state—awaking every few days or weeks, speaking a few words, taking perhaps a little nourishment, and then lapsing into oblivion! The older cases of extended sleep thus find a close parallel in the newer cases.

One of the chief constituents of every fairy story is the giant or dwarf, who occupies a central position. That giants and dwarfs exist today there can be no doubt. They are frequently to be seen in the side-shows, and even in public life. But it is now known that giants and dwarfs suffer from a certain disease, which renders them particularly short-lived; and they are, generally speaking, muscularly weak for their size. They are not the stalwart, fierce race of beings imagined in the fairy stories, and which popular belief still pictures them. For the fairy tale, the giant is always enormous and powerful, and generally cannibalistic in his habits! Have giants of this character existed? Could such a race have existed? To this question it is almost certain that we must answer "No." M. Dastre, of the Sorbonne, Paris, has gone into this question at great length, and has given us the result of his researches in his essay on *The Stature of Man at Various Epochs.* Here he says:

"It is incontestable that beings of gigantic size do appear from time to time.... Giants are men whose development, instead of pursuing a normal course, has undergone a morbid deviation, and whose nutrition has become perverted. They are dystrophic. Their great stature shows that one part has gained at the loss of another. It is a symptom of their inferiority in the struggle for existence. Their condition is not only a variation from the ordinary conditions of development—that is to say, they are 'congenital monsters,' the study of which belongs to the science of teratology—but it is a variation also from a state of health, physically and normally sound. In other words, they are diseased, and fall within the domain of the pathologist. Here then, as Brissaud says, you have your giants despoiled of their ancient and favourite prestige. Mythology yields the place to pathology."

The *causes* of gigantism and of dwarfs are now well known. In the brain there is a tiny gland known as the pituitary gland, weighing little more than half a gram, and divided into two portions—the "anterior" and the "posterior" lobes. Hypertrophy of the *anterior* lobe causes gigantism. The bones grow to an exaggerated length; the hands, feet, and bones of the face grow enormous. When, on the contrary, the secretions of the anterior lobe are insufficient, the body remains small, undergrown and delicate. The secretions of the *posterior* lobe, on the other hand, insure the undue accumulation of fat, and disturb the functional activities. Other ductless glands in the body also affect the mental and physiological functions of the whole organism.

Nevertheless it is realized that beings have existed from time to time far larger and more powerful in every way than the ordinary human being, and the mythopoeic tendency of the human mind has doubtless supplied the rest, and accredited to them marvellous powers which they did not in reality possess.

In not a few fairy tales we read that the plates and dishes, which were upon the fairy's table, ran of their own accord to the kitchen, washed themselves, and came back to the table; that a cake was cut by a knife held by no visible hand; a decanter of water, of its own accord, moved about from place to place on the table, refilling the glasses of the guests; and in various other ways duties were performed which we are accustomed to consider as necessarily performed by ourselves. All this was accomplished by the objects without any external assistance, and of their own accord. Incredible as such accounts may appear, they are, nevertheless, not so extraordinary, viewed in the light of some newer researches—which in fact, if proved to be true, render phenomena of this sort quite credible. During séances held with Eusapia Palladino, objects were moved from place to place in the room without visible contact, and apparently of their own accord. They were also lifted from place to place and floated about in the air without visible support. These phenomena have been observed for a number of years by scientific men on the Continent, and they are unanimous in asserting that manifestations of this character do in fact take place, and that they are not due to any force or forces known to physical science. On one occasion, for example, a glass decanter was seen to be moved from the sideboard on which it stood on to the séance table, and thence rise and float around the room, no one touching it—there being no possibility of any connection between it and any object in the room. Finally, the glass bottle held itself, or was held by invisible hands, to Eusapia's mouth, and she thereupon drank some of the water it contained. The same thing happened to an investigator, another member of the circle. The glass decanter was then transported back to the sideboard, and a pile of dishes and other objects were moved on to the table.[49] Similar phenomena are said to have occurred in the presence, or through the mediumship, of D.D. Home. Sir William Crookes informs us that on several occasions a bunch of flowers was carried from one end of the table to the other, and then held to the noses of various investigators in turn, for them to smell. Some of those present at the séance saw a white hand, visible as far as the wrist, carrying the bouquet. Others saw merely a whitish cloud-like mass connected with the bunch of flowers. Still others saw nothing—save that the flowers themselves were transported through space without visible means of support.

Here, then, we have phenomena, attested by scientific men, all happening within the past few years, rivalling any of a like nature that are reported to have occurred in fairy stories! If *invisible beings*, possessing intelligence, constantly move about us, and are capable, at times, of affecting the material world, surely there should be no objection to many of these fairy stories, since the difference in the facts is one merely of *degree* and not of *kind*; and this would be true even were the phenomena proved to be due only to the action of some force or forces (under more or less intelligent control) within ourselves, producing the phenomena.

Other extraordinary narratives will doubtless occur to the mind. The bean-stalk which grew overnight, might be referred to; and it is possible to compare this with cases of electrically or artificially forced vegetation. But, of course, the majority of the wonders reported in fairy stories find their probable interpretation in those tricks of the imagination which have now been duplicated by artificial means, and which science is beginning to understand and interpret according to well-known psychological laws. Fairy stories may thus present (in many instances) the germ of a truth, which it has taken many centuries to elaborate and comprehend in detail.

FOOTNOTES:

[49] *Journal S.P.R.*, vol. vi. p. 356. All this was observed by Sir Oliver Lodge, Prof. Ch. Richet, Mr. Myers, and Dr. Ochorowicz.

Milton Keynes UK
Ingram Content Group UK Ltd.
UKHW030623061024
449204UK00004B/358

9 789362 518095